D1602323

U R B A N F O R M S THE DEATH AND LIFE OF THE URBAN BLOCK

PHILIPPE PANERAI
JEAN CASTEX & JEAN-CHARLES DEPAULE
ENGLISH EDITION AND ADDITIONAL MATERIAL BY IVOR SAMUELS

URBAN FORMS

THE DEATH AND LIFE OF THE URBAN BLOCK

Translated by Olga Vitale Samuels

ARCHITECTURAL PRESS

OXFORD   AUCKLAND   BOSTON   JOHANNESBURG   MELBOURNE   NEW DELHI

Architectural Press
An imprint of Butterworth-Heinemann
Linacre House, Jordan Hill, Oxford OX2 8DP
225 Wildwood Avenue, Woburn, MA 01801-2041
A Division of Reed Educational and Professional Publishing Ltd

$\mathcal{R}$ A member of the Reed Elsevier plc group

First published 2004

Chapter 9 and additional text © Ivor Samuels and Philippe Panerai 2004
Translation © Elsevier Ltd 2004
Translated from the original French by Olga Vitale Samuels
Original Title: *Formes urbaines, de l'Îlot à la barre*
ISBN 2-86364-6028 © editions Parenthèses, Marseilles
1997, 2001

British Library Cataloguing in Publication Data
A catalogue record for this book is available from the British Library

Library of Congress Cataloging-in-Publication Data
    Panerai, Philippe,
      [Formes urbaines. English]
      Urban forms : the death and life of the urban block / Philippe Panerai, Jean Castex,
    and Jean-Charles Depaule ; English edition and additional material by Ivor Samuels.
        p. cm.
    Includes bibliographical references and index.
    ISBN 0-7506-5607-7 (alk. paper)
      1. City planning—Europe—History—19th century. 2. City planning—Europe—History—20th century. I. Castex,
Jean. II. Depaule, Jean-Charles. III. Samuels, Ivor. IV. Title.

NA9183.P35 2004
711'.4'09409034—dc22   2003063574

ISBN 0 7506 5607 7

Printed and bound in Great Britain by, WWW.BIDDLES.CO.UK

CONTENTS

INTRODUCTION TO THE FIRST ENGLISH-LANGUAGE EDITION OF *URBAN FORMS: THE DEATH AND LIFE OF THE URBAN BLOCK*

It has taken more than 25 years to publish an English version of *Formes urbaines: de l'îlot a la barre*, yet the story it tells – of the erosion and disappearance of the urban block – is as relevant today as ever. The book has been translated into Italian, Spanish, Dutch, German and Serbo-Croat and the tardiness of this present translation is a rebuke to our Anglo-Saxon culture. We seem willing to venture abroad in search of the latest fashions in dress or design but are reluctant to make available to an English-speaking audience works of a more enduring relevance. This is surprising when we consider that the potential audience is much larger than only those countries where English is the mother tongue.

The first French edition was published in 1977 by a team from the School of Architecture at Versailles, which was supported by a grant from the Direction d'Architecture of the Ministère d' Équipments. Versailles was one of the newly created schools of architecture that were established after 1968 and this research group had close links with the Italian Typomorphological School of urban analysis. (Darin, 1998).

I bought a copy in 1978 and very much regretted not having this work available in English, because this was just the time when urban design was emerging as a separate activity among the environmental professions in the Anglo-Saxon countries. It should be noted that, in these countries, unlike much of Continental Europe, where town planners are still struggling for a separate professional identity, there have been two professions responsible for the built environment ever since the early years of the last century. By the late 1960s, the reaction against modernism had led to the claim that the poor quality of the public realm, which was one of the main targets of this critique, was largely due to this division of responsibility between the two professions. That this was a simplification is borne out by the equally poor quality of the public realm in those parts of the world where there was no such schism.

Hence it was in the 1970s in the UK that the notion of urban design began to emerge as a discipline to fill the gap between the two professions of architecture and planning. It was suggested that architecture was too concerned with individual special buildings, while planning at that time, particularly in academic circles, had become preoccupied with process and management, economics and social welfare, and any concern with physical form was perceived as being academically frivolous. The public realm was a sort of no-man's-land between the two – and it was the public realm of postwar development that was the target of so much popular discontent. Urban design as a separate activity with its own pressure groups and (later) journals was invented to fill the gap. The first postgraduate training courses were also being set up at this time and this book would have made an ideal basic text for these courses for a number of reasons, which are still relevant today.

First, *Formes urbaines* acknowledged the importance of the detailed physical design of our environment in the enabling of populations. This was at a time when the social-science preoccupations of planning implied that, if we got the economic and social policies right, it did not matter about the design of physical form. It used scaled plans and sections of urban tissues, not diagrams. It is important in elevating the detailed discussion of urban form beyond the functional level of Neufert or *The Architect's Handbook*, but it also points out the importance of economic processes and social and cultural determinants to the use of space in different contexts.

Secondly, it is truly a work of urban design in the way that it focuses on the connection between the form of cities and their architecture – especially with respect to ordinary buildings. Our towns and cities are made from these ordinary buildings and most of them are houses in some form or other – 'thematic buildings'. The urban tissue is only infrequently punctuated by special buildings – art galleries, churches, even schools. This is self-evident, yet a quick look through architectural journals and, even more, the curricula of our architecture schools will indicate how little importance is given to these ordinary buildings by the profession or those that train them. Dunham Jones has pointed out that in the US – where, unlike in many European countries, there is no need for architects to 'sign' every project – 75 per cent of all new construction occurs in the suburbs and 'is shunned by most architectural designers' (2000, p. 5). It is this book's great virtue that it is exclusively concerned with these ordinary buildings and their designers.

Thirdly, it is important because it brings a genuinely Europe-wide vision to the topic. We all know how much the Hausmannien urban surgery, the *percée* (a new route cut through the existing urban fabric) was emulated in other countries. But it also tracks the remarkable interchange between Berlage, Unwin and May and how they were all linked by a common experience, which included working in one another's office. It also acknowledges and discusses the importance of the transmission of ideas through meetings, conferences and publications. The chapter added to this English-language edition extends these interchanges across the Atlantic: from Clarence Stein – who knew and was influenced by both Howard and Unwin and visited Hampstead Garden Suburb, Letchworth and Welwyn and later worked as a consultant to Stevenage, the first of the post-World War Two British New Towns programme – through Jacobs and Lynch to Krier's influence on the Congress for the New Urbanism.

As a study whose methods are based on the techniques of urban morphology, it also links to a wider cultural basis, which crosses both countries and disciplines. The authors connect to Italian and German traditions of morphological study, which owe as much to historians and geographers as to architects and town planners. Again, at the time of publication of this book, the study of urban morphology was little known in Britain outside a limited circle of geographers, and even less known in the United States.

With respect to the position of the book in its French context, Manuel de Solá-Morales has summed this up in his Foreword to the Spanish edition of 1986 (reprinted in the latest French edition) and we can do no better than quote him:

> Until then [the publication of *Formes urbaines*] modern French town planning was seen by any external observer as associated to the crude sketches of master plans, general lay-outs and growth corridors, always succeeding in deviating the treatment of all spatial projects towards an abstract and imprecise dimension, where the claim of being synthetic was often translated in a simplistic way with felt tips and great gestures, rendered more with the arm than with the hand, carried out more on the boards of municipal meetings than on the drawing tables of professional designers. [M. Solá-Morales in Panerai, Castex and Depaule, 1998.]

The final reason for translating this work so long after it was first published is that the last decade has seen a revived use of the street and block by designers in the Anglo-Saxon countries (the French lump Britain and the US together under this term, so we think it is particularly appropriate for us to do so in this work). In the United States the work of the New Urbanists and the Charter for the New Urbanism has returned to the street and block as basic elements of the urban tissue, whether in urban renewal projects or urban extensions. In the UK the Urban Villages Movement, the building of Poundbury and the renewal projects at Hulme, Manchester, and Crown Street, Glasgow, demonstrate a similar return to traditional forms.

These facts on the ground are the justification for a new chapter 'An Anglo-Saxon postscript'. The story, so passionately told by the three original authors, has thus come full circle, which is closed or, better, continued by this chapter. This edition, then, becomes a celebration of the urban qualities set out in the earlier parts of this book and a salute to the prescience of those who first wrote it.

Ivor Samuels
Oxford 2003

INTRODUCTION TO THE SECOND FRENCH EDITION

INTENTION

If one were to define this book in one word, that word would be 'agony'. The agony of a well-defined spatial organization: the urban block, typical of the classical European city that the nineteenth century transforms and the twentieth does away with altogether. Behind the block there is thus a notion of the city whose evolution we are trying to outline.

In 1975 we started the introduction to this study in this way. At the time the issue seemed original, indeed ludicrous. Interest in the form of the city had not yet become a common concern. In France, architects as a whole had taken to methodological-structuralist games (we did that, too), and the town planners still believed in the magic power of planning on a grand scale. Some politically involved groups, infiltrated by the sociologists, were addressing the city inhabitants and rightly denounced the bulldozer-type renovations and the consequences they brought. Renovation = deportation.

The large housing schemes had already been discredited, but one believed that 'bending' the blocks or introducing some facilities on the ground floor could correct their excessive harshness. The examples of Toulouse Le Mirail or the Arlequin of Grenoble carried everyone's hopes for the future. Criticism of recent urbanization did not yet dare to attack the dogmas of modern town planning or, if it did at all, only from a political point of view, for analysing the form of the built reality was still something unusual.

The issue, though, of 'capturing the formal qualities of space' had already been vigorously raised by Henri Lefebvre, even though not everyone agreed on what he meant to say. Our study, in any case, drew on his proposals for its legitimacy: space and formal qualities were here taken literally, while borrowing, without too many ideological precautions, some of his tools from the Italians.

The interest in 'the physical dimension of the city' and the attempt to penetrate the mysteries of the 'urban tissue' seem to us, looking back, a relevant pursuit, and in attempting to understand how buildings had, little by little, distanced themselves from the city, and exploring, through some revealing examples, the painful history that we have inherited, can be called, after the elegant formula of Frédéric Edelman, 'a discreet and useful indicator of the disconcerting ways of architecture'.[*] It is still necessary in presenting this new edition, to remove some misunderstandings.

[*] *Le Monde*, 1977.

The relative autonomy of urban form, which we have tried here to highlight, is not an absolute autonomy. It does not exclude either the economic or cultural determinants, which have their significance in the production of the city and of architecture, nor the pressure of social conditions on the life of the city's inhabitants. In stating this notion, we wanted to confirm the legitimacy of a reasoned approach to the models or references on which depend the work of the thinkers (the idea of developing and transmitting architectural models).

We are tempted today to go even further, following Henri Raymonde in the reversal of the point of view that he suggests,[*] i.e. to state that the understanding of architectural and urban forms is as legitimate and effective a means of understanding a society as any other. The reality of the built environment sometimes brutally informs us of the operating ideologies, the economic conditions and the social relations. This is not the case in the discourse. The reality of the built environment also allows us to capture the discrepancy between talking about and acting on the reality. Which architect's, planner's or politician's text does not declare its extreme sensitivity to the wellbeing of the city's inhabitants, but in practice . . .?

The issue of the block has also been a source of confusion. In raising it we were initially indicating a scale – the scale of the local organization of urban tissues. We were not thinking of the city of grand layouts or great monuments, nor of domestic details, but of a long-ignored, in-between realm.

And, at the same time, how could one not be affected by the emblematic character of the block and of its slow disintegration so expressively shown in Ernst May's scheme?

Nevertheless the fact of having brought the block to the foreground has had some perverse effects. It has brought the careless reader or the hurried designer to transform the issue into a caricature: city = block or modernity = single building. The new neighbourhoods of the new towns or modest urban renovations were thus filled with pseudo-blocks, which are but the urbanistic rendering of a valueless postmodern formalism. This has brought us to develop the initial conclusion insisting on the importance of the subdivision of plots and of the status of spaces and of developing a reflective attitude towards the projects.

The choice of examples (the definition of the corpus) finally requires some commentary. The chosen period – from Haussmann to Le Corbusier – strongly indicates a succession of changes without precedent in urban history. In order to capture these changes, the proposed itinerary implies a degree of arbitrary choice, due to our interests and to the material we had at our disposal at that time. Other itineraries could possibly have said the same things – the breaking up of the urban tissue – but we insisted on choosing some realized examples, in order to be able to reflect not only

[*]Homage to Friedman.

on projects or intentions, but to confront the projects, to see the theories that supported the built and inhabited reality.

Even if this study deals with historical facts – how could one have an interest in the city and not play about a little with history? – this piece of work is not the product of a historian. It does not have either the pretences or the methods. It mixes architectural knowledge, awareness of context and direct observation in order to bring about some reflection (which, then, of course, takes you back to history) while raising questions over our capacity today to design the city. Questions, that, even if the context has changed in twenty years, are still current today.

CHAPTER 1
HAUSSMANNIEN PARIS: 1853–82

The transformation of Paris under Haussmann is of interest not only due to the fact that it gave the city the aspect that it still has today. Paris became a haussmannien city (with the help of the Third Republic), but it also became the 'bourgeois city' par excellence. With Haussmann, 'the city becomes the institutional place of the modern bourgeois society'[1] and, evidently, it is here where the essential interest of the Haussmannien interventions reside. They created a certain type of city, a space devised from the logic of the bourgeoisie, now the predominant class; they imposed a specific spatial model, which remains after Haussmann and the fall of the Empire and conditioned town planning at the beginning of the Third Republic.

THE BOURGEOIS CITY: THE GRAND PROJECTS OF PARIS

Haussmann took the oath as prefect of the Seine on 29 June 1853. His nomination to Paris[2] had as its explicit aim the implementation of the large plans required by Napoléon III; the discussions following the oath taking dealt with this topic and on the means needed to achieve it. He immediately had to change the attitude of the Municipal Council, which was considered to be recalcitrant, even though it had been nominated by the government, and created an unofficial committee, which would have control of the large state plans and would function as a sort of private municipal council.[3] This committee, which Haussmann considered unnecessary, did not meet more than once. Nevertheless, it is important, because it shows the type of relationship between the various authorities, government, municipality and administrations and it

---

1 M. Tafuri, 'Lo spazio e le cose', in *Lo Spazio visivo della città* (Capelli), 1969.
2 George Eugene Haussmann was born on 27 March 1809 into a Lutheran family stemming from the Electorate of Cologne, which, from 1703, first settled in Alsace, then in Versailles and then in Paris. He attended the Lycée Henry IV, where he had as a fellow student the Duke of Chartres, eldest son of the future Louis-Philippe. In spring 1831 he obtained his doctorate in law and on 22 May of the same year he became general secretary of the Préfecture of the departement of the Vienne. He then became *sous-préfet* of Yssingeaux (on 15 June 1832); *sous-prefét* of Nérac (October 1832), where he obtained the collaboration of the bridge engineer Alphand and established the road system of the canton; then *sous-prefét* of Saint-Girons (1 March 1840) and took an interest in the lunatic asylum of Saint-Lizier; then *sous-prefét* of Blaye (23 November 1840), where he took charge of roads and schools and where he entertained steady relationships with the bourgeoisie of Bordeaux. In 1848 he became adviser to the prefecture of Bordeaux and in the autumn of 1848 Haussmann supported Bonaparte in his candidature for the presidency of the Republic. In January 1849 he was nominated *prefét* of the Var, where he took on a political role: to redo the elections; he organized the plot subdivision of Cannes. From May 1850 he was prefét of the Yonne; he 'reorganized' the Municipal Councils; he supported the countryside in favour of the re- establishment of the Empire; and he obtained the collaboration of the Bridge engineer Belgrand in the water distribution works of Auxerre. As *prefét* of the Gironde (26 November 1851) he took on the mission to engage the 'support of Bordeaux' in the *coup d'état* of 2 December 1851; he collaborated with Alphand in the organization of official receptions, like the one of 7 October 1852, in which Louis Napoléon proclaimed the keynote speech of the Empire. On 21 June 1853 he eventually became the *prefét* of the Seine.
3 We owe many clarifications to H. Malet, *Le Baron Haussmann et la renovation de Paris*, (Paris: Editions municipales), 1973. Haussmann even proposed himself later as 'minister for Paris' and wrote a letter to Napoléon III, which even included the text of the decree of nomination (December 1860). Napoléon III only gave him the right to be present at the council of ministers and then gave the name of Haussmann (by the decree of 2 March 1864) to one of the principal axes of the new Paris, which was round the corner from the house of his birth in the Roule quarter).

clearly defines the Bonapartiste political regime. The prefect had a privileged status and was classified as being in the private domain. It was executed with the minimum of publicity and through special channels in order to allow maximum efficiency.

From the time of his taking on this role, Haussmann took the opposite view to the administration of the previous prefect, Berger – whose hesitation with regard to action plans resembled those of Rambuteau, the prefect of Louis-Philippe. It was no more the case of administering the city 'as a good father', respecting the rules of prudence and with due care shown to private interventions. Haussmann's methods, like those of his predecessors, had the same relationship as the one between the new and aggressive capitalism of the merchant bank and the consummate capitalism of the first half of the century, the capitalism of the grand Parisian bank. They no more corresponded to 'a period of moderate, but constant growth in production and income, 1815–1852', a growth that still rested on an archaic structure, where wealth was built on agriculture and commerce, but not yet industry. On the contrary, at the heart of the 'prosperity regime' of the Empire, Haussmann's methods were there to stimulate growth. They were part of the new enterprising fervour, which promised 'a perspective of rapid profits and an unlimited future for the banks'.[4] This coincided with an unprecedented accumulation of capital (especially between 1852 and 1857 with some still good periods until 1866).

Haussmann developed, as a management method, the theory of productive expenditure. The point of departure was the traditional Parisian budget surplus, which is difficult to assess, but which, on 55 million francs in receipts, fell to 10 million, once the debts are deducted, if one can believe in Haussmann's analysis presented to a badly disposed, if not hostile, council. This was pushed up to 18 million francs in the budgetary projections for 1853 and which he found to be near to 24 million at the end of the exercise.[5] The theory of productive expenditure recommends the use of the surplus, all or in parts, not for some direct short-term interventions, but to finance the interest on a considerable and long-term loan.[6] But the municipal finances can face this discounting of a rapid and constant growth of resources only if it is based on a growth in economic activity, business and population.

The wealth of the taxpayers was the city's wealth. The best way to increase the budget was to make the taxpayers richer, and the very large projects were at the same time the instrument and the product of this strategy. The city was managed like a capitalist business. In fifteen years, the surplus borrowed against the 'productive expenditure' increased from 20 million to 200 million francs.[7]

4 R. Cameron, *La France et le développement économique de l'Europe 1800–1914* (Paris: Le Seuil), 1971.
5 H. Malet, op. cit.
6 In 1867 the city had issued savings certificates (which are in fact a disguised way of borrowing money), almost 400 million francs in the Land Credit, refundable in ten years; and the project of debt liquidation envisaged a loan for sixty years at an interest of 5.4 per cent (H. Malet, op. cit.).
7 H. Malet, op. cit.

But one cannot stress too highly the stimulative function of Paris's great projects vis-à-vis the development and improvement of the capitalist system after 1852. We know that the projects of the first network (1854–8) were carried out partly under public control by the city, which was its own developer, even though it had not yet sufficient technical and controlling expertise and was risking longer delays in their execution. This happened because the developers were not able to cope with the organization of very large building sites, being short of capital and without sufficient financial means. It was, in fact, necessary to deliver to the city some entirely completed and paved large arteries with laid-out and planted pavements. Haussmann's programme was, thus, a call for the intervention of large financial firms, which, following the Saint-Simonian principle of marrying banks with industries, gave rise to large projects and undertakings.

The Crédit foncier of the Péreire Brothers (founded in 1852), four-fifths of whose lending went to the property market, was Haussmann's chosen tool for financing the planning of Paris. The Crédit mobilier (Pereire, Morny and Fould, 1852), while being the bank of the industry, also financed some large estate companies such as: the Société de l'Hotel et des Immeubles de la rue de Rivoli (1854), which became the Compagnie Immobilière de Paris in 1858. Shortly after 1863, it failed as the Société Immobilière de France, in a Marseille speculation, which expected too much from the opening of the Suez Canal (this did not happen until 1869).

The similarity of methods and aims between those large banking firms and Haussmann's productive spending was striking: he wanted to activate credit and drain vast markets by using large organizations capable of lending for the long term (this was a new technique in 1852). It was intended to direct the economy by founding large enterprises (this is again the Saint-Simonian idea). Haussmann could adopt these objectives as his own, since he had perfectly understood the methods and possibilities of investment banks and these were the methods that he applied in the management of Paris.

Obviously it was not presented in this way. Rather, Haussmann promoted a 'cult of the Beautiful and the Good, with the beauty of nature as inspiration for great art'.[8]

The economic mechanism was concealed under the technical arguments, which in turn were hidden under aesthetic pretexts. Classical culture was used as reference, at least on the surface, and without being embarrassed by eclectic contaminations. In the city a rhetoric of axes, of squares marked by monuments, a network of monuments, whose returns were from now on visible, claimed to reproduce the forms codified in the classical system. We can observe that, whatever our judgements on aesthetic matters, the image of the capital city that Haussmann gave Paris entirely pleased the new bourgeoisie. The infatuation was complete. Zola says of the key characters of *The Quarry* that 'the lovers felt the love of the new Paris'. Foreign tourists

---

8 Baron Haussmann, 'Confession d'un lion devenu vieux', quoted by W. Benjamin, 'Paris, capitale du XIXe siècle', in *L'Homme, le langage et la culture* (Paris: Denoël), 1971.

Figure 1
Paris and Haussmann.
a. The rue des Moineaux in 1860 (cliché Marville) before the opening of the avenue de l'Opéra.

and visitors from the provinces, attracted by the exhibitions, returned to their homes amazed and conquered.

If there was any criticism of the work of Haussmann, it was mainly political: it recognized in Haussmann 'the typical Bonapartist civil servant';[9] it attacked, directly

9 A. Dansette, *Du 2 décembre au 4 décembre* (Paris: Hachette), 1972.

b. The avenue de l'Opéra today.
By making the administrative circumscription coincide with the defensive walls built in 1843, Haussmann defined the framework into which the evolution of Paris would take place up to today. Simultaneously, the interventions that took place in the historical centre led to the disappearance of popular areas, with the intention of giving a 'modern' image, appropriate to a commercial and cosmopolitan city.

or indirectly, the unconditional bond that tied him to Napoléon III and to the political/financial system of the Empire. The 'bourgeois' republicans would only need the change of government in 1870 to turn over their criticism and leave to the Third Republic the task of completing what had been started. The criticism of the Orleanistes coincided with that of the old banking system, which was annoyed by the unorthodox audacity of the new commercial banks. Their spokesman, Thiers, came to pour out his criticism from his home in the place Saint-Georges, in the centre of the Dosne housing development of 1824 (Thiers was Dosne's son-in-law) – that is to say in the centre of one of those speculative operations of the Restoration, whose methods had been overtaken by Haussmann. With regard to the criticism of the Radicals, it was the Commune that managed the project and it was no more mentioned than it was implemented.

The technical challenge was that of modernization and sanitation and, more importantly, the improvement of living conditions, transport and infrastructure. Haussmann's city experienced the most profound structural change to become a planned city. The notion of route was transformed, thus allowing the diversification and multiplication of distributive functions in a complex context with an efficient distribution of people, food, water and gas, and the removal of waste. Facilities, in the contemporary meaning, suddenly appeared everywhere: town halls, offices, ministries, schools, post offices, markets, abattoirs, hospitals, prisons, barracks, chambers of commerce, stations and so forth. The challenge was to distribute these facilities in the urban structure and to allow them to develop and expand.[10] To the functional specialization, which in itself implied the notion of facility, was related a goal of systematization and control, of which they became a tool in their relationship to the urban structure. The identification of a hierarchy was established by the road network and by the facilities that it distributed. The setting up of these complex mechanisms emphasized the differences that were supported an ideology of separation, the practice of zoning.

This strategy of control and separation, which is the ultimate result of Haussmannization, becomes clearer when one discovers that, between 1835 and 1848, 'Paris had become the biggest industrial city in the world'[11] with more than 400,000 workers employed in industry out of a total population of 1 million inhabitants in 1846. The embellishments of the Paris of Napoléon III are, first, a result of a problem of quantity: in absolute terms, since the city had already more than a million inhabitants in 1846; then in terms of growth, because, with the same boundaries, those of the Thiers enclosure, the population practically doubled, going from 1,200,000 inhabitants in 1846 to 1,970,000 in 1870, according to the last estimate of Haussmann.[12] But, beyond quantity – from then onwards, Paris must be treated as a very big city – there was the problem of the relationship of the social actors who made up these numbers. In the light of such a large number of workers and after the many ups and downs of the Second Republic, complacently exaggerated as 'great fears' by the bourgeoisie, the relationship between the domineering and the dominated classes was sharply defined. And the bourgeoisie, which took the initiative and

---

10 One can see that the problem concerning facilities was widely solved after the Revolution and during the Empire, by expropriating properties belonging to the nobility and to the Church. In any case, Paris in 1848 was a city with a small infrastructure and was very congested. Facilities and *percées* went hand in hand in Haussmann's vision for Paris.
11 R. Cameron, op. cit.
12 D. H. Pinkney, *Napoléon the Third and the Rebuilding of Paris* (Princeton: Princeton University Press), 1958.

was at the zenith of its power, set out all its tools of control. A new type of space took shape, not totally dissociated from the old space, but capable of reinterpreting it, to reproduce or to deviate its forming mechanisms, to develop them into a more and more ample and coherent project. The aim of our study is, first, to describe Haussmann's spatial models, not from an exhaustive analysis of the urban whole, but starting from one urban element that is at the same time characteristic and essential: the block. The block dominates our perspective; but it is necessary to ask how it was produced and how it was organized in the structure of the haussmannien city.

MODES OF INTERVENTION IN THE CITY

THE NETWORK OF *PERCÉES*

The existence of a plan, drawn by the very hand of Napoléon III, as many witnesses attest,[13] would lead us to expect a global and coherent scheme for Paris. Several critics[14] have insisted on Haussmann's ability to control the whole city, something that is quite in contrast with previous practice, which fell short of wide-ranging actions and was quite incapable of conceiving a plan at the level of the urban whole.[15] The setting up of a developed administrative and technical tool, the Direction des Travaux de la Seine, could be interpreted as the clearest proof of the global dimension of Haussmann's concerns.

However, one must not think that the control over the city by Haussmann happened everywhere, nor that it was felt at all levels and affected all authorities. Haussmann was far from having to create a city with all its components: he worked in an already largely structured environment. He did not deal with the whole city but, using a limited range of modes of intervention, was concerned only with certain selected elements. In this way, as can be seen even in the plan designed by Napoléon III, his intervention happened at first at a level he favoured to the point of becoming sometimes exclusive: the global level. At this level is the network of *percées*, which both pierce the city and connect the large monumental establishments such as squares, stations and important public buildings. For example, the boulevards of Strasbourg and Sebastopol, which were created in sections from 1852 to 1858, established a perspective

13 D. H. Pinkney, op. cit. tells us of the adventures of this famous plan 'in colour', of which one copy was given to William of Prussia and where the original drawings were lost in the fire of the Tuileries. Napoléon III is said to have redrawn by memory one copy after the fall of the Empire, to be of help to the memoirs of Merruau, the former secretary of the Prefecture. The content of this plan remains very hypothetical, with Haussmann's consummate shrewdness having always conjured to put into it afterwards all sorts of innovations and transformations.

14 Notably P. Lavedan, *L'oeuvre du Baron Haussmann* (Paris: PUF), 1954, and L. Hautecoeur, *Histoire de l'architecture classique en France* (Paris: Picard), 1957.

15 The dissociation of Paris and Versailles explains in the greater part the unsuitability of the urban structure of Paris. The new plans addressed the territorial dimension, especially in the west, reusing the parks and gardens of the seventeenth century. The plan of the artists, laid out by the Convention, beside the idea of an east–west axis, which would be taken up by all later regimes, was still a catalogue of fragmentary interventions, standing curiously between late baroque and the Enlightenment. The First Empire did not have the means or the understanding of a global intervention: it only showed, by a complex contradictory architectural way of thinking, a semantic value alien to the structure of the old city, which was therefore globally condemned. The palace of the king of Rome by Percier and Fontaine, in its anti-urban isolation on the slope of Chaillot, plays this role, a little like, in Milan, the more consistent project of the Forum of Antolini of 1807 (M. Tafuri, op. cit.). The 'urban fragment' was favoured, and this preference continued all through the Restoration and the July Monarchy.

of 2.3 km between the Gare de l'Est and the dome of the Chamber of Commerce and distributed this complex of open spaces, created in crossing Paris by the square Saint-Jacques and the place du Châtelet, with its two theatres symmetrically aligned.

This double network of *percées* and monumental buildings had a triple aim:[16] to enhance the monuments by isolating them and making visual connections between them, and to do away with unhealthy and degrading living conditions and establish modernity everywhere: space and light and easy connections between stations and districts.

He carried out, in fact, a correction at the global level of the urban structure. This level represents the new totality (the very large city, the capital), that ensures connections at the scale of the ensemble, the level that understands the characteristic institutions of this global order. By the forms used and the way they were implemented, the creation in Paris of an overall order places these projects firmly within the tradition of the classical city. In fact, the manifestation of a global level in the city was characteristic of the baroque city:[17] it coincided with a stage in the urban growth that made a structural readjustment necessary and called for new structuring elements: boulevards and avenues. These were devised from a culture that was anchored in the visual and was largely dependent on representational issues in a delicate moment of history, where there was a coming and going between the city and the regional territory (from the city to the villa, from the villa to the park and the region). The above-mentioned elements express themselves in the visual, which can be read best in spread-out areas, i.e. in contrast with the concentrated city with its closeness and overlapping.[18] These avenues, planted with trees, were the basis of Haussmann's formal vocabulary. With Haussmann, only certain agreed values were made readable. They functioned like masks, hiding differences in social status, in districts, in activities. The haussmannien *percées* are of a rigorous, almost monotonous, formal conformity: they overshadow the identity of the districts (the centre, the working-class east, the residential west) to the benefit of the global signifier of Paris, the capital city. We can observe here the social implications of a mechanism that cannot be understood in terms of formal structure: we will call this uniform mask, projected onto the city and its history, the space of the nineteenth century bourgeoisie.

In practice, the haussmannien *percées* were divided into three networks, not hierarchical, but based on financial considerations. The first network (1854–8) comprises some essential work, financed by the state, that paid half or two-thirds of the costs (for the clearing of the Louvre, for example). The crossing of Paris was an important compo-

---

16 Morini, *Atlante storico dell'urbanistica* (Milan: Hoepli), 1963. The drawing up of the plan by Haussmann added a fourth aim, that of safety (military), in which we did not want to get involved.

17 The term of classical culture sends us back, even beyond the French classicism of the seventeenth and eighteenth centuries, to the formal language and the operating methods in architecture and in the city that was set up at the time of the Renaissance. The Baroque is a critical readjustment to this culture after the crisis of the sixteenth century. M. Tafuri, *Architecture et Humanisme* (1969) (Paris: Dunod), 1980. G. C. Argan, *L'Europe des Capitales*, Paris, Skira, 1964.

18 M. Tafuri, 'Lo spazio e le cose', op. cit.

nent of this network. The rue de Rivoli was extended from west to east, while the north–south axis was formed by the boulevards de Sebastopol and Saint-Michel, the sequence of the central spaces was greatly energized from Châtelet to the Hotel de Ville, with extension to the future Halles and towards the Cité. The avenue de l'Impératrice became an access route for parades, 140 metres wide in the replanned bois de Boulogne.

The second network (1858–68 and beyond) was defined by a convention between the city and the state, decided, not without problems, by the Legislative Body in April 1858 and known as the 'treaty of the 180 million'. The state and the city shared the expenses roughly one-third to two-thirds – 50 million francs to 130 million. This network established the *percées* of Paris, formed by routes radiating from important nodes such as the place du Château d'Eau (de la République), the Etoile of the Arc de Triomphe and the place du Trocadéro. Some rectilinear connections were also created, which catalysed the remodelling of several districts: the boulevard Malesherbes between the districts of the gare de l'Ouest (gare Saint-Lazare) and Monceau; the boulevards Saint-Marcel and des Gobelins, which gave access to the rear of the hill of Sainte-Geneviève; the avenue Daumesnil in the direction of the bois de Vincennes. The clearing of the Cité was also part of this programme.

The third network, the decision for which was rushed through because of the annexation on 1 January 1860 of the peripheral communes, was in reality the remainder of the operations that had been left out of the second network. But these operations were taken on board by the city alone, whose revenue office received some credit facilities, such as the right to create the Office of Public Works in 1858 (in this way 100 million francs in short-loan credit was given to developers), or the authorization to borrow 270 million francs in 1860. However, this form of financing would be insufficient and Haussmann resorted to more or less orthodox expedients, such as paying firms with delegation-of-debt vouchers, a private form of legal tender. The third network achieved the completion of the star-shaped squares of the place du Château d'Eau and of the place du Trône. It made proposals for the Halles and the Opéra with its connections with the stations through the rue Lafayette, on the left bank with the boulevard Saint-Germain and the rue de Rennes and with the relatively isolated parks of Montsouri and Buttes Chaumont.

THE UNITY OF THE INTERVENTIONS

This network of axes made its mark on urban growth. The Haussmann intervention presupposed a particular form of growth and we will try to find the consequences at the level of urban tissues, in the organization of districts and blocks. On the plan of Paris it is easy to identify, besides the *percées* or rectified arteries, some districts that bear the hallmark of Haussmann: the Plaine Monceau, Chaillot, the back of the Mont Sainte-Geneviève, the Buttes Chaumont, even if they are only sketched out and like Clignancourt, still very incomplete. We have to ask ourselves to which growth process these districts owe their appearance and, for this, we are going to proceed by comparing other modes of growth, whether earlier or foreign.

The Paris of the Restoration – in fact, in the absence of global networks other than the incomplete boulevards and the barrier of the Fermiers Généraux, which by substitution would itself become a boulevard – shows a fragmentary growth. Each period tends to leave discrete and finite elements within that growth, which can be extended only by adding other elements. The connection of the fragments was a simple juxtaposition. The city was a collage of dispersed or adjoining fragments. This was an eighteenth-century idea, represented by Laugier's theories of the city or by Piranesi's settings, which reduced urban space to a collection of pieces of architecture in a game of different forms devoid of connecting logic. Georgian Bath, Edinburgh and London are cities of fragments par excellence.

In Paris, the fragments became entangled among the spontaneous growth that followed the axes. But they are recognisable as developments often of rationalized forms. The kingdom of Charles X had a real wealth of speculative enterprises:

- In 1824, the development of the village of Beaugrenelle, a chequerboard with squares; the subdivisions behind the Madeleine, of the old Beaujon folly and the Saint-Georges district above Notre-Dame de Lorette;
- In 1825, the subdivisions of the Plaine of Passy through the creation of wide radiating routes converging on existing (Etoile, Maillot) or on new *rond-points*; the development in a rectangular grid of Batignolles, which, later, in 1845, would extend over the Cardinet estates;
- In 1826, the development of the Europe district, a very ambitious project with 26 streets, many of which were in a star layout;
- In 1827, the development of the Saint-Lazare property, which comprised thirteen streets in a rather closed plan, which extended around the church of Saint-Vincent-de-Paul.

If each of these developments thus constituted a perceivable unitary 'fragment' within the plan, in general construction continued to take place through autonomous and dispersed elements, without any more control over the building envelope than the current spontaneous developments, i.e. without more regularity than the one that, at a given time, generally defined a type of building. In the pre-established layout of plots a certain relationship can be observed between the form of the buildings and the whole form of the development. But this relationship remains implicit; there is no intermediate unit of intervention like the block or a grouping of the buildings. On the contrary, the situation was completely different in Georgian England. First, a range of types existed that were completely standardized by means of codes of construction which regulated, in great detail, dimensions and the quality of the material of each portion of the building. Secondly, they had 'units of intervention' connected with each other, which were entities capable of dealing with issues of project planning, financing or site supervision: the house (by class), the row, the group of rows, the estate.[19]

The method employed by Haussmann was very different and did not attempt in any case to form autonomous fragments as in previous periods or in the English city. The objective of the structural adjustment imposed by the global network went precisely against the city conceived by fragments; and, even in the free zones, where a continuous and logical planning was still possible, one did not see the setting up of a rational and coordinated *percée*, but rather a division carried out in successive waves. The district of Wagram, for example, was constructed in fragments, in 1858, in 1862, in 1866 and into 1884–99, and it is but the result of a succession of plans conceived at the global level, which cut through the area. The haussmannien city did not intend to add fragments, like London, but it superimposed hierarchical grids, of which each element belonged to a star-shaped network; it hierarchically redivided areas. This practice did not leave us a sample of intervention units as in England. At one end there was a central authority, which called on large financial groups, which would deliver some completed large arteries. But this process does not set any unit of intervention with the exception of the road works. At the other end of the spectrum, the plot continued to be recognized as the unit of intervention suitable for the erection of blocks of flats. The same owner could have a certain number of flats, but scattered around and not part of a whole or a physical unity of intervention. In *La curée*, Saccard 'had six houses on the boulevards. He had four completely finished, two on the rue de Marignan and on the boulevard Haussmann; the remaining four, on the boulevard Malesherbes were still being built.'

The relationship between these two levels of intervention, spaced out at each end of the hierarchy, is not clarified – far from it – by an implementation process, which would link the project, site and financing.

The *percées*, in the more general cases and excluding the more modest connecting blocks, produce edges. The expropriation law, modified by the Second Republic, authorized the acquisition of all plots left by the line of the *percée* once the route was set up, and there remained here and there a fringe to be divided up following a new

19 Summerson, 'Georgian London', London 1945 and 1962. There were four types of taxation that dealt with the extent of the area and the price of construction. Within these limits, a small number of solutions were possible and it was easy for them to be established in the form of models by some architects, such as George Dance, who established, with Robert Taylor, those of the Building Act of 1774. Each building, identified in relation to its type, was defined by its associative properties to form the *rangée* (row or terrace). The grouping of the building in the row had its own rules, which were a little freer. The operations of punctuation, of blocking (at the end) of the row were commonly understood, including the subtle modifications of the public–private axis at the ends of the block, when the private space stopped being totally hidden. The row was a finite and regular fragment of an inferior level and one could go from the row to the fragment of a superior level, the plot subdivision, the estate, through a certain number of forms, themselves also codified: the crescent, the square, the association, back to back or at a corner of two or more rows, formed a more or less open block. This method was strictly additive from end to end. Those who took part in this operation went from 'the modest mason or carpenter who, holding their peaked hat in their hands, apply for some plots at the price of five shillings per foot in a back street to the rich gentlemen, who are quite ready to deal with one side or more of a square paying around 15 shillings or one pound'. And, in spite of the efforts of the controlling public authority to prevent 'each speculator [from taking] on more than a moderate portion of the land', vast monopolies were formed, which gathered in one global unity all these hierarchical units of intervention.

a

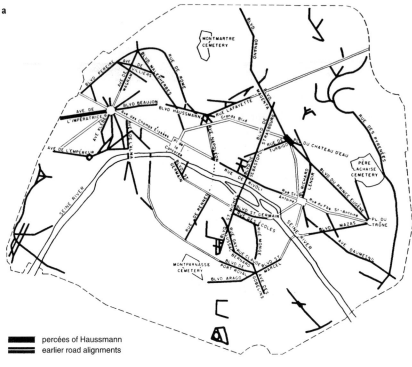

■■■ percées of Haussmann
≡≡≡ earlier road alignments

b

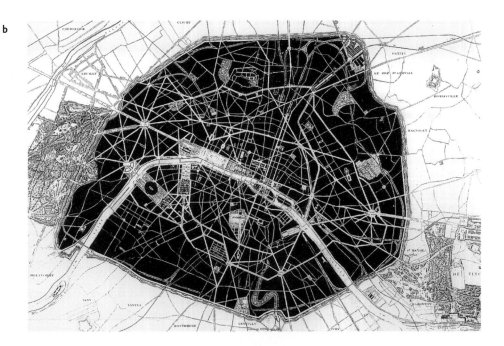

Figure 2
Paris's transformations.
a. Plan showing the new roads cut into Paris between 1850 and 1870.
b. Haussmann's Paris, by Alphand.

plot subdivision. The relationship here was direct between the intervention at the global level, the *percée* and the interventions on the plots. The block was not taken into account in defining an intermediary unit of implementation. If the relationship was mediated by the type of building, we would find ourselves faced with a subordinate type, which was often adapted in a rather improvised manner. The organization of the *percée* dominated the plan; each building façade was nothing more than the results of this cut, a small separate unit, and was incapable of being separated from the global organization, with its specific rules. What we might

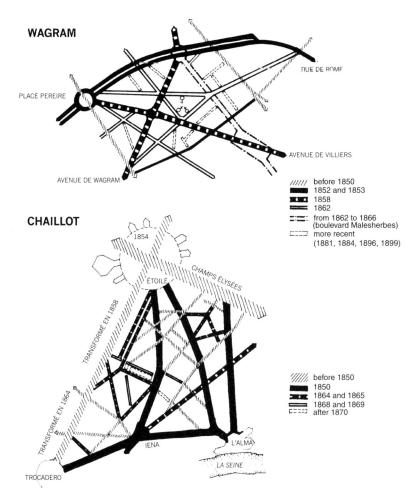

Figure 3
Percées in the Wagram district.

call the punctuation, such as corners and rotundas, related to the monumental axes and only contributed in a minor way to the definition of the façades of the individual blocks.

The more extensive developments produced both edges and blocks. The process of construction of these blocks was often laborious and it was not uncommon for them to be subdivided later. This was what happened in the Wagram district in 1882 and again in 1899. Certainly, in a very classical manner, the corners and the more valuable edges had been built first, leaving free the heart of the block and some backs, which then lent themselves to future subdivision. The block did function as the traditional structure but it was an implicit unit. This did not stop it from suffering the indirect consequence of the *percées* at the global level, followed by the capitalist requirements of densification, apparent both in the type of building and in the plot subdivision. But this type of block was not an unchanging unit of intervention.

Finally, there were some concentrated operations that directly produced a small number of blocks in a more rigorous form. Some of these are in the form of St Andrew's crosses while others are rectangles cut on the diagonal, like the crossing of the rue Perdonnet, the rue Louis-Blanc and rue Cail (1866), between the rue du Faubourg Saint-Denis, the boulevard de la Chapelle and the rue Philippe-de-Girard; or, later, the junction of the rue Eugène-Sue and the rue Simart, between the rue Orderer and the rue Mercadet (1882–5). Rarer are the forms derived from the monumental vocabulary, such as the trident that is situated in the Sainte-Pérrine de Chaillot convent, developed in 1865 (rue Bassans, rue Euler, rue Magellan). Here in a relatively modest way, which was out of the influence of the large networks, the intervention unit is explicitly the block. A precise method of coordination was set up, in which we can recognize a model to which the less organized and more complex interventions can be linked. It is, thus, as a model that we clearly see the new appearance of a haussmannien block.

If Paris, unlike London a century earlier, did not succeed in regularising the units of intervention in an organized sequence – i.e. the clarification of a precise relationship between the property, the financial organization and the working of the *percées* within the urban structure – this can be ascribed to two causes. The first is related to the degree of development of the banks and enterprises, to the status of property and to the role of the bourgeoisie, in spite of the parallels that one would wish to establish between the two periods of construction of industrial capitalism. There was not yet a lasting organization or a stable concentration of finance in France. The second cause derives from the city itself or, rather, from the relationship between the new interventions and the existing city. On the one hand there is a free association of fragments and, on the other hand, a project of global reinterpretation which attempts a degree of overall control.

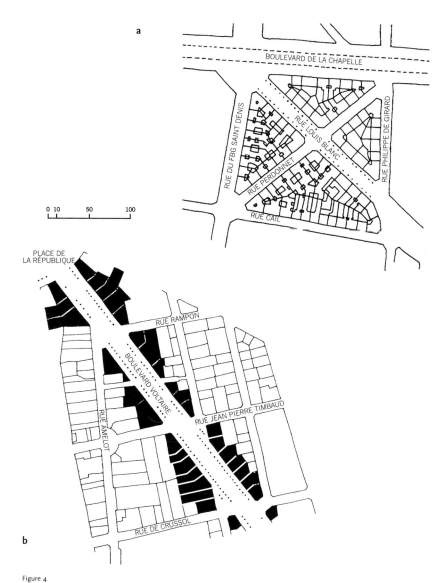

Figure 4

The haussmannien tissue.

a. The intersection of Saint-André between the rue Perdonnet and the rue Louis-Blanc in the 10th arrondisse-
ment. In 1866 four homogeneous blocks resulted from the cutting on the diagonal of an older quadrangular
grid between the rue du Faubourg Saint-Denis, the rue Phlippe de Girard and the boulevard de la Chapelle.
b. *Percée* of the boulevard Voltaire starting from the place de la République. The diagonal of the boulevard
disturbs the tissue of the plot subdivision. From both sides of the cut arbitrary shaped left over plots appear,
which, when compared with the old subdivisions, look even more irrational. But the junction between old and
new is perfectly accomplished: the continuity of the built-up area is scrupulously observed.

THE RELATIONSHIP WITH THE EXISTING CITY: INSERTION AND EXCLUSION

The block is an implicit given which was inherited from the traditional city, but the network of the great *percées* had as its objective to correct the structure of an imperfect whole by supplying it with a new type of space. As mentioned earlier, behind these interventions was the bourgeois strategy. This, the relationship of Haussmann's interventions in the old city is at the same time one of conformity and correction, continuation and destruction, acceptance and violence.

We have shown already how the project of providing Paris with a global network could be read through reference to classical culture. It is this reference that we would like to identify and enlarge upon, because for us the relationship with the existing city is completely mediated by the relationship with the classical culture. It is easy to identify in Haussmann's plan some elements or some forms from the classical language. For example, from the plan of Rome of Sixtus V, the haussmannien networks take on a functional role of connecting some distant poles of the urban space. In one the Roman basilicas, in the other the stations and some important strategic nodes. The extension of routes is the same, and each of these is focussed on a building or monumental site which are seen as landmarks at one end, with no relationship between architecture and the intervening space. The vocabulary of tridents and stars derives its origins again from Rome and Versailles and from the plans of Le Nôtre. One can even recognize a relationship between St Augustine, embraced by two boulevards (of which one has remained on paper) and the way in which Christopher Wren had thought of placing St Paul's in his plan for the complete reconstruction of London.

It seems to us, however, that we have to go beyond those instrumental references. In fact, most plans available for comparison are those created on a *tabula rasa* or are extensions, while Haussmann worked within an existing structured space, making *percées* through it, which produced a very different result. His intervention, in fact, recalls the ways of working in cities in the early Renaissance and, more precisely, those ways whose objective was 'the revision of the plan of the old city, by opening new streets and spacious and regular squares'.[20] This revision did not use the existing growth structures, nor did it develop existing elements, but, as if history had been interrupted, it was intended to install inside the city and regardless of the existing tissues an entirely new system, 'to transmit a new code of behaviour, a new rationality, complex and, at the same time, dialectic, in the laying out of the space of human activities'.[21] This revision, thus, was underlined by a principle of exclusion – exclusion of history, of social issues, of spatial elements – and, at least at the beginning, it was 'in substance unacceptable by contemporary critics'.[22]

20 G. C. Argan, *The Renaissance City* (New York: Braziller), 1969.
21 M. Tafuri, op. cit.
22 M. Tafuri, ibid., applies this judgement to the first manifestations of the new urban order devised by Brunelleschi. The idea of an inorganic space, isomorphic, established outside any possibility of growth, where buildings did not have any more associative properties and were purposely isolated in squares was, at first, unacceptable. The Renaissance shows a wealth of examples of 'resistance' of the old tissues to this new morphology.

The process aimed at confiscating a certain number of sites in the city to the advantage of the new aristocracy in power, to set up there its residence and to show the ideology on which rested its power. To confiscate these sites (generally in the centre) meant confronting the space of the authority which conceived the plan with the space of the acting classes (the periphery). Later on, this cutting of the city by exclusion would find bigger applications as the modes of intervention were improved into a better-organized classical culture. Some districts in the periphery – where everything was new, the orientation, the pronounced opening up of the city towards a man made landscape, in which it was establishing itself, the structure of property ownership and the built types – had become in the seventeenth and eighteenth centuries the exclusive sites of the ruling classes. In Rome, these were the hills of the Quirinale and of the Trinitá dei Monti, in Amsterdam the three canals, and in Paris the faubourg Saint-Germain, which faced the Tuileries and the large landscaped areas opening up towards the west, along the Seine (Cours la Reine, Champs Elysées, etc.).

Haussmann understood this process of exclusion very well when he took from the classical culture these types of intervention and especially so in developing into a system of effective control. Not only did he confiscate the centre (the Cité, the sequence Châtelet-Hôtel de Ville), and open up some bourgeois peripheries (the Plaine Monceau, Chaillot, even the Buttes-Chaumont), but he also inserted in the old tissue a continuous network whose grid provided a context for future development. The exclusion relationship, instead of being confined to the centre and some other areas, was finally dispersed wherever the new bourgeois space contrasted with the interior of the districts it tried to hide. As a result, there was a disconcerting visual clash between the two types of space, because this exclusion, carried out in a violent way by demolition[23] moving people about, does not always supress the old tissue, which it tends to conserve in a relationship of domination.

In concrete terms this confrontation happened by a layering process. The Haussmannien edges were fused to the existing tissue, so that nothing could be seen and there was the possibility of misunderstanding the plot subdivisions and their relationships. The plot subdivision demonstrates the compatibility between the new edges and the old blocks, through some skillful sutures. Haussmann was tolerant of the archaic elements and he left, on the contrary, the new to insinuate itself further into the old. One only needs to follow the boulevard Haussmann from end to end to recognize this ability, which the smallest observation of this Grand Boulevard in its old part (from the rue de Richelieu to the Porte de Saint-Denis) does not demonstrate. He did not have to solve the problem of inclusion: the tissue all around was perfectly homogeneous and the rules of the subdivisions of the plots were the same everywhere, in the boulevard and in the neighbouring blocks. Along the hauss-

---

23 L. Hautecoeur, op. cit., tells us that 27,488 houses were demolished from 1852 and 1870 in order to build 102,487.

mannien *percée*, the easily followed rules of inclusion have a meaning: it was the other face of the exclusion–conservation relationship that we describe. It is also the mark of an act of violence.

It is within this exclusion–insertion relationship that the structuring role of the haussmannien block must be understood. A large majority of blocks were modified by Haussmann; these were cut in half and belonged to an ensemble that the underlying strategy of the division of space threatened its functional, structural and, in the long run, physical unity. Essentially it is a reductive reinterpretation of the block, which started in this way, but which we find completed in the typically haussmannien blocks, which we have already noted as models for a whole series of operations. The haussmannien block totally conforms to the urban composition, but it went through a series of modifications, which ended up by altering and deforming the nature of this conformity. It is the idea of the city, which, in the end, was changed.

THE HAUSSMANNIEN BLOCK

THE MORPHOLOGY

The block produced by the cutting of the star plan grids of the haussmannien networks was almost inevitably a triangular slice across the traditional Paris block, which usually was rectangular. But there were also some rectangular haussmannien blocks and we will make reference to some of them.

The dimensions of the triangular block, which is the most common, vary a great deal and seem to exclude the definition of an optimal building envelope, which could have been more or less valid everywhere. Nevertheless, it seems that either the very large blocks were excluded, like those which the previous periods favoured (the convent of the Filles-Dieu, between the faubourg Saint-Denis and the faubourg Poissonière had been divided between 1772 and 1792 into blocks of between 30,000 and 50,000 square metres), or the block was now compact and tended, because of its triangular shape, to a reduced depth. This is the case around the college Chaptal and in the northern portion of the Europe district, which had been restructured by Haussmann (between 1867 and 1881), where the greatest depths of the block is about 60 or 65 metres, rarely reaching 90 metres, for a total area of 3,400, 6,300 and up to 20,000 square metres.

The rectangular block was often a residual block linked to a *percée* that did not touch the original grid of arteries. It had the possibility of being very long for its width: in a relationship of 1 to 7 along the boulevard Sébastopol and of 1 to 4 along the boulevard Péreire, with widths of 16 metres in one case and 36 metres in the other. These very compact rectangular blocks are not far from becoming single building blocks surrounded by the streets.

THE SUBDIVISION OF THE BLOCKS INTO PLOTS

The subdivision of the blocks into plots followed rules dictated by the form of the triangular blocks.

- Each plot is carefully laid out so that it is perpendicular to the street.
- The central dividing line in the interior of the block is the bisector of the acute angle formed by the streets (in the case of corners of the triangular blocks), a median line that accommodates the geometrical irregularities.
- If we exclude the deep plots such as those aligned along the street, each plot is of around the same proportion.

It seems, thus, that the haussmannien block derived from an overall organization, a clear rationalization and a certain regularity. But these first conclusions must, after all, be seen as largely relative. If the management of the whole was carried out by a developer, then its realization, which depended on private owners and on small companies, hardly ever happened all at once. The block was built in plots, one by one, although these were sometimes grouped so as to form fewer units. A single intervention is rare only for the small operations we have already mentioned and in those cases there is a clear regularity of the block. The block between the rue de Moscou and the rue de Berne is symmetrical in two halves about the bisecting line and, on the rue de Berne, it faces nineteen double buildings, perfectly identical over the length of 250 metres, in one single row, backing onto the chemin de fer de l'Ouest.[24] But, in general, the progressive development of the buildings followed a set of rules, although in some cases the division of plots did not happen on the bisecting line and there were some arrangements where the form of some plots was anormal.[25]

Rationalization and its corollary, regularity, have to be correctly interpreted. The triangular outline obviously produced inequalities. There were undoubtedly some acute angles that were difficult to deal with, especially for the layouts of flats. Thus, whatever one tried to do, the plots were all different. The aim was thus not to achieve a beautiful uniformity in the English manner. In many cases (but it is not absolutely so) one can find some large plots in the corners and in the centre of the block. One can find some traverse plots in the best portion, then, when they approach a depth of perhaps 30 metres, some single-orientation plots were inserted. These plots have varied, even unusual, shapes, which range from triangles, which are sometimes very acute, to a V and trapezoidal forms and, through combinations of these, sometimes resulting in complicated polygons.

More than their form, it is the plot area that varies so as to offer a range of sizes. In the Moscou-Clapeyron block of the Europe district, they range from 200 to 1,100

24 The rue de Berne, which was listed in 1881, was opened by a landowner, Monsieur Monnier, in a part of the Europe district, which had been disturbed by the cutting of the chemin de fer de l'Ouest in 1837. The block, situated between the rue de Berne and the rue de Moscou, was not entirely dealt with in one operation after all, because its façade on the rue de Léningrad existed already.
25 The conserved remains in the ground were sometimes taken into consideration, but these cases remain exceptional in the small homogeneous blocks we are dealing with.

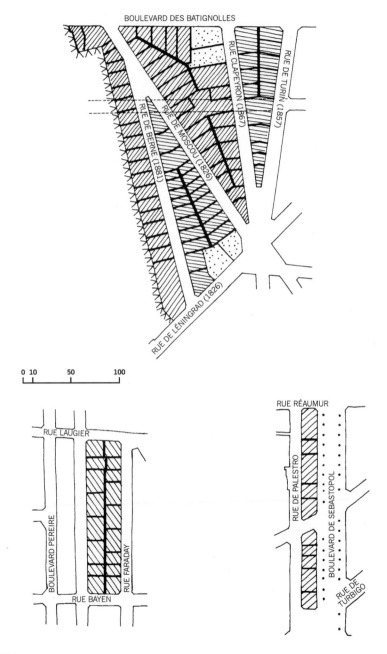

Figure 5
Haussmannien blocks, *percées*.

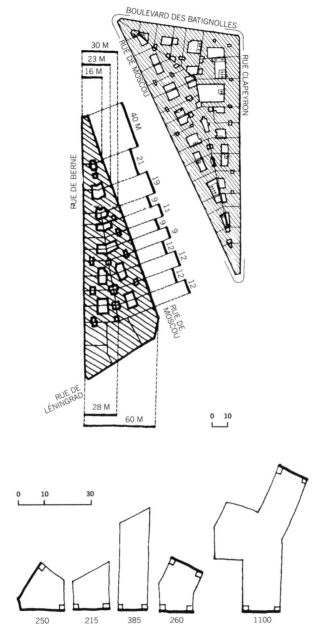

Figure 6
Haussmannien blocks, dimensions.

square metres; in the Moscou-Berne block, from 135, which is particularly small, to 360 square metres. The depth of the plots varies because of the triangular shape of the block, but the street façade width of the plots varies also. In the Moscou-Berne block one can find plots of 9, 11, 12, 19, 21, 28 and 40 metres frontage (these last ones at the most acute corner); elsewhere (near the college Chaptal) they are 8, 10, 11, 12, 15, 19, 20 and 23 metres wide. The rectangular blocks show a similar range. Along the boulevard Péreire, the Laugier-Faraday-Bayen block, connected to the Ternes market, which was inaugurated in February 1867, contains six small plots of 115 square metres each and eleven large ones of 300, 400 and up to 460 square metres. The layout of the whole is exceptionally orderly, in spite of the fact that boulevard Péreire and the rue Faraday are not parallel. The corner plots have an area of 300 square metres for a frontage of 18 metres; with a strip only 12 metres wide inserted, which allowed two small plots to be accommodated back to back. The central part is in staggered rows, with 24 metres of façade for each plot, with the exception of two leftovers of 12 metres on the back street (rue Faraday). The whole is almost symmetrical. This organization demonstrates a single authority, which makes the subdivisions at the same time as it shows the variety of developers, who are offered a range of plots from the single to the quadruple.

THE ARRANGEMENT OF THE BUILT FORM

The coordinated plan of the Péreire-Laugier-Faraday-Bayen block, which we have just studied, went hand in hand with careful location of the buildings. One can even say that the subdivision of the plots was *determined* by the future configuration of the built-up areas and not vice versa. For seventeen plots there were only six main courtyards of an identical size and of a simple square shape. These courtyards were common to three or four plots. Some ventilation wells were used in the interior of the buildings and these were connected in pairs, overlapping on the edge of the plots. In this respect one could say that the block was a single building, a unit in which courtyards had been carved out. But, in reality, this unit resulted from the association of identical elements (identical in so far as it was possible, because of the absence of two parallel streets). The basic element was an L-shaped building, which was used even for the small plots. Two Ls form a U or a T, which was suitable for the large plots. In the corners a slight adaptation of the L took into account, because of the extra thickness of one of its sides, the more open orientation. Everything then started from this L-shaped element, combined in such a way – in L, T or U shapes – that the courtyards would always be associated four by four. From here stemmed the particularities of the plot subdivision – the narrow 12 metre strips and the intermediate staggered rows.

In less rigorously organized blocks, one can again see this common use of ventilation wells and courtyards. The plot was thus no more just an autonomous unit, and a sort of structuring system was put in place that was halfway between the block and the plot. It is because of the very heavy densification to maximise the profitability of the ground that the plots became so diminutive in relation to the building types and

a

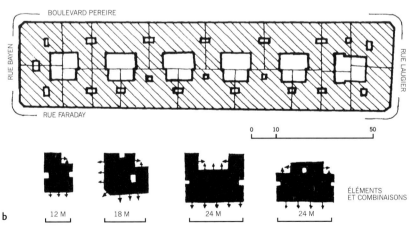

ÉLÉMENTS
ET COMBINAISONS

b

Figure 7

Layout of the rectangular block of Bayen-Faraday-Laugier, along the boulevard Pereire.

a. Façade composition on the boulevard Pereire.

b. Starting from an L-shaped element, which is to be found in the four smallest plots, some U-shaped combinations (on the boulevard Pereire) and T-shaped ones (on the rue Faraday) are carried out as well as a corner solution, which gives the block its particularly orderly aspect, due to the grouping in three or four of the courtyards.

could no longer be regarded as an equal number of single units. The collective space of the courtyard no more coincided with the unit of the plot: it achieved a hybrid status, neither relating to the single plot, nor to the whole block. Above all, this floating collective space had lost its capacity to identify with a single plot because, at the same time, its usefulness as a private space had disappeared. On the ground floor a wall, often of a forbidding aspect, continued to separate the buildings, but, at the upper level, the volume of the courtyard was common: i.e. overlooked by others with whom it had no direct relationship, because they had no access from this side of the courtyard. This is tolerable only when 'the others' can be considered 'the same' in an anonymous confusion of status. One can see that this solution presupposed a flattening of the social spectrum, a convenience that functioned as a mask in order to hide differences. Since then, there were no more private social relationships in the courtyard and no more hidden or barely tolerated activities. There was no other place in the plot where these activities were tolerated, either: the plot had lost its depth and the succession of spaces towards the interior had been truncated. The imperative of densification subjugated the interior space of the courtyard to two of the character-istics where the public space of the street was governed by the clarity of a rule: custom and sterility. The courtyard was carefully looked after, and could not become a dumping ground for objects and vehicles and to any activities, which reduced its quality. If there were alterations such as well-designed penthouses or verandas or glazed roofs, this was the owner's business. The pretext was functional (an office, for instance). In any case, it was an improvement that had to be agreed and approved by all.

The sequence of internal spaces had been truncated, but a minimal hierarchy of places remained. A second courtyard sometimes followed the first one and this was accessible only from one of the ground-floor flats or by a service entrance. In any case, apart from people passing through, it was a quiet space. The morphology of the block showed a continuous perimeter of a constant thickness and an interior that, at first sight, appeared less orderly. Rigour and perfection belonged to the perimeter: the more regularly laid-out flats or the planned parts of flats faced the street and were directly accessible from the vestibule, without having to cross the courtyard, which was an ambiguous place too visibly accessible from a number of buildings. The end of the plot, sacrificed to the geometry of the triangle and trapezoid, permitted less well laid-out flats, often without a double orientation. One can read into these differences evidence of a social hierarchy under the subtle mask of a uniformity of rules.

THE CAPACITY FOR ACCOMMODATING A RANGE OF FUNCTIONS

The subdivision of the block as it appears to us now must be compared with the traditional Parisian block in order to better measure the effects of the reduction that had been carried out.

It is not the case to categorise the pre-haussmannien blocks into one type only, but it is possible to make a few general observations on the subject. The block, in its entirety, was divided into an edge and an interior. The dense edge was directly connected with the street, understood as the place for exchange and as the presentation space controlled by rules. The interior of the block, on the other hand, was a zone at a distance from the street, cut off from it, which had the characteristics of a space that was not necessarily seen, i.e. hidden. It no more had the functions of public representation. It was malleable, transformable, marked by some loose rules, which contrasted with the strict rules on the public front. It was offered to private appropriation.

The opposition within the block between perimeter and interior should be understood as a system of differences, which allowed for an organization of the complexity of the tissue. It was a model for integrating activities and established the possibility of distributing some multiple functions. It worked as an efficient system, which did not have to designate changing and relative functions, but rather the association and exclusion relationships between functions and places. It was then subject to the application of rules of integration, conceived in such a way that the functions were defined in substitution terms (one function could be substituted for another), over time, which took into account historical change, modification, 'do-it-yourself' (i.e. the recuperation of an empty and available structure), even the diversion of access ways.

It was often the case that at the edge, which was directly connected with the street, the ground was more carefully subdivided, so that a densification took place, which allowed the interior of the block to be the place for larger land use and a less tight plot subdivision. There was often some space in the heart of the block where one could find heavy workshops or industrial establishments, garages, sheds or depots, gardens, the park of a private hotel, a public facility, which could be extensive (formerly a convent with its cloisters or a college, nowadays a primary school, a high school or an administrative building). All these elements would not appear together, but they occupied the same position in the structure of the block. Therefore, in the same block were found mixed together living quarters, exchange and work places and, very frequently, collective facilities.

The block was then capable of an internal complexity that, without being codified in an explicit manner, could be explored[26] and tested, especially through processes of adaptation and correction, which was subject to certain constraints. The hierarchy towards the interior of the block often happened in a sequential order (first courtyard, interruption, second courtyard, interruption etc.) and the interlocking of places resulted in a subtle juxtaposition of uses. A vertical hierarchy, more or less extensive and recurring in different parts of the block complicated the horizontal hierarchy. Finally, this complex wholly depended on the status of the streets that surrounded it, on their position in the hierarchy of the city or the district, which gave a particular meaning to each front. The block strongly reacted to any hierarchical imbalances. In

---

26 See our previous studies, especially *Analyse du tissu du Nord-Est parisien*, study contract APUR, 1971; 'Marcillac, autopsie d'un village', in *L'Architecture d'Aujourd'hui* (Paris), October–November 1972.

Figure 8
Blocks in the quartier de l'Europe.
a. Façades.   **b.** Courtyards.

a district where the middle class was little or not at all represented, the block compensated for this anomaly by enlarging its internal hierarchy – it was subdivided into passages, by interior streets and by multiple courtyards.

In the haussmannien city the block had only a reduced multifunctionality left. In a very characteristic manner César Daly, who describes private living conditions, emphasises that 'commerce and industry are equally needs one has to take into account: in that portion of the city where high-class commerce, luxury commerce, predominates with the luxurious shops its needs will necessarily differ from the small shops... which need... the retailing of objects of pure necessity'.[27] Through this quotation we can observe how functional integration enters the space of the architect. It seems better to translate the word 'organization' by the phrase 'fitting out'. In spite of his repetitiveness, Daly's collection shows this. The fitting out of the space more often than not has to overcome the difficulties of extremely restrictive building types, constructed with small resources for which the architect has in each case to compensate with his skill. One could measure how many layouts proved to be unuseable and to what extent the logic of the type has had to be modified. It would then be interesting to ask to what extent the type retains its content in these difficult cases and eventually to note at which point the type becomes impoverished by not being able to accommodate spatial changes, so that the functions are accommodated in an organic way. In this space, glass roofs, steel walls, cast-iron columns and metal beams, and

27 C. Daly, *L'architecture privée au XIXe siècle sous Napoléon III: Nouvelles maisons de Paris et de ses environs* (Paris: A. Morel and CIE), 1864.

ceramic facing represent the intrusion of positive elements which transform the haussmannien building.

Multifunctionality is hardly mentioned (commerce and industry) and is altered by social convention so that industry is brought closer to commerce and immediately diverted towards the sphere of the luxurious. Industry was used only in this way and it was not used to recall the world of work and production. One did not 'combine' (in the architectural meaning) in the same building, the living space of the bourgeoisie, even if it was a bourgeoisie deriving its wealth from industry, and the place of manufacturing. This rule is absolute for the best environments; after all, mines and large production establishments had their own space, which had been away from the city since the beginning of the Industrial Revolution. Some modest workshops and some offices existed for which rules had been devised by the architects for their inclusion. All the ground-floor area was used and it had to be lit by windows located at the edges of courtyards. But, here again, convention prevailed: the real function remained masked as much as possible.

Multifunctionality cannot be considered at the level of the block, which is not a recognized unit of intervention; it is hardly so at the level of the building type and it is even rejected at the level of the city. In the haussmannien city the workplace was excluded from the private residential block. On the other hand, one can detect the specialization of some districts. Some residential areas appeared free from any connection to production, and were in contrast to districts that one can generally define as working-class and where the principle of separation between workplace and living quarters was not yet applied. Paris remained the city where industry was undertaken in small workshops, which kept alive the old grid structure where it had not been affected by Haussmann. The old space (the subdivided substituted space) was opposed to the new space (the functionally separated space). In this space the functional possibilities were those that were valid only in the periphery of the old block, which was its most public part (living, commerce, offices and professional activities). One can say that the haussmannien block, when compared with the old block, no more functioned as a thickened-up perimeter. Its form was to have this consequence, because what the triangle could offer most generously was a perimeter open to the streets to the detriment of the protected and hidden interior, which was of lesser importance. What began to disappear with the haussmannien block was the interior of the block with its functional properties and the richness of its articulation.

THE BLOCK IN THE URBAN COMBINATION

The haussmannien block continued to function as the indispensable element for the structuring of the city. Like the old block, it was a unit that could be assembled with others and the city was seen as a combination of blocks. The haussmannien and the pre-haussmannien blocks were compatible in spite of their differences, and the first outcome of this compatibility was the maintenance of a rigorous continuity of the urban landscape. If the image of the city was identified with this continuity, following the uninterrupted rows of façades on both sides of the streets, then the haussmannien block can be said to contribute to an eminently urban image. This image, exaggerated into a caricature of itself and simplified, is often but a reduction of the image rich in meaning, which was typical of the old urban landscape. It does not matter: there was no interruption and no gap. The subdivided blocks were quickly closed up without leaving any gaps. The public space was rigorously enclosed by the line of façades and it was carefully contained by a well-defined walled enclosure. Under Haussmann there was even a tendency to overvalue the public to the detriment of the private (we refer of course, to external spaces and not to private living areas). All the public space became monumental and this included the ordinary streets. Many of these residential streets had an overblown appearance, with a heavy respectability that gave the façades an accumulation of cultural references. But, above all, their monumentality came from their impassiveness. Businesses were driven out of them (with the occasional exception of the two ends of the block); the street was free of the daily bustle; its space was surprisingly abstract, and had the same form everywhere, divorced from time and defined in its form and use: it did not know any variation. It was a caricature-like metamorphosis, in a continuous attempt to recapture the quality of classic space. The consequence of this is important. Internally, the Haussmannian block could no more articulate differences in use, but also externally the block was located in relationship to the roads so as to erase all differences. It was the whole urban space that was homogenized in a long-term project that went beyond the apparent monumentality to which it was subjected under Haussmann. The space, which was established as dominant in this subdivision of the city, which rejected everything else, was in fact this weakly articulated space or, at least, it was weak at this stage of its implementation. It is a space that interacts minimally with the inherited pattern and had to be this way to enable it to be inserted into the city.

Since the haussmannien block was not capable internally of incorporating a variety of functions, one can observe that some single-function blocks appeared. These were principally for facilities and monuments. The monument block, which was not far removed from the single-building block, which succeeded it after the definitive devaluation of the monument, was common. It is not necessary to go back to the clearance policy advocated by Haussmann, of which the île de la Cité is an example, with monument blocks like the courts, the police headquarters, the Hôtel-Dieu and Notre-Dame, which were practically laid out in the same way in their respective isolation and the empty neutrality of their relationships to the spatial system of streets and squares such as the square of Notre-Dame and the Flower Market. Empty of any significant order, this monumental system lost all its meaning. With the churches isolated, first 'the college Chaptal' (1867), then the department store of Bon Marché (Boileau 1879) also became a block. The Printemps department store, by Sédille (1882), took up two blocks, while the Hôtel des Postes, by Gaudet, (1880) detached itself, through a small service lane, from the buildings that bordered it on the south and no longer had any direct connection with them. The block containing public facilities had a tendency to become an isolated building.

It is not in Paris, where the tissue had a great resistance, that we will be able to observe the pursuit and the conclusion of this process of classification, separation and specialization, which affected at the same time both the arrangement of the block and its combination as the basic physical unit of urban subdivision. The block entered a critical phase, even a crisis, but Paris's poor economic condition during the forty years of deflation that followed the Empire masked the acute aspects of a crisis that was to reappear in a more serious way in the urban failure that would show itself in the incapacity to plan the suburbs.

Bibliographical note to Chapter One.
In the French editions, apart from the references in the footnotes, no separate bibliography is given for Chapter One, We have therefore added the following general references in English.
Michel Carmona, (2002), Haussmann: his life and times and the making of modern Paris (Chicago: I R Dee)
D.J. Olsen, (1981), The city as a work of art, London, Paris, Vienna (New Haven; London: Yale University Press)
Anthony Sutcliffe, (1993), Paris: an architectural history (New Haven; London: Yale University Press)
Anthony Sutcliffe, (1970), The autumn of central Paris: the defeat of town planning 1850-1970 (London: Arnold)

CHAPTER 2
LONDON: THE GARDEN CITIES, 1905–25

'The day on which I will be the head of a kingdom, my ambition will be to own a cottage.'

WHY WELWYN AND HAMPSTEAD?

The satellite garden city, as an urbanization process, was invented and tested in England at the beginning of the twentieth century. Whatever the genesis and the context of its production, this process of urbanization first appeared theoretically in 1898 with the publication by Ebenezer Howard of *Tomorrow: A Peaceful Path to Real Reform*. From this date onward, it is easy to set out the history of the evolution of this process according to some specific dates:

1904: Letchworth, the first garden city built according to the economic development model of Howard and the first important realization by Raymond Unwin and Barry Parker;
1909: Hampstead, the first garden suburb built according to the design ideas of Unwin;
1919: Welwyn, the first garden city that combined in the same project the theories of Howard and the practical methods of Unwin;

If we have not chosen to discuss Letchworth, it is because Welwyn showed the same means of production while profiting from the experiences of its older sister.

Hampstead was the experimental city, the attempt to codify an urban design concept. It was an experiment, which would benefit Welwyn, where the tools first used were systematically applied.

THE CONDITIONS OF TOWN PLANNING IN LONDON AT THE END OF THE NINETEENTH CENTURY

From 1840 to 1901, London's population doubled while that of Greater London tripled.[28] This growth demonstrated the vitality of some of the capital's industries,

---

28 Greater London until 1963 is only an administrative census definition. For the period taken into consideration one can note the following figures:

	London	Suburbs	Greater London
1840	2,250,000		
1891	4,227,000	1,405,000	5,632,000
1901	4,536,000	2,045,000	6,581,000
1939	4,000,000		8,650,000

especially clothing and leather. At the same time the City had become the financial centre of nineteenth-century capitalism while port traffic had grown. All of this attracted the rural population to the city so that London's growth up to 1870 was essentially the outcome of provincial or foreign immigration of a population that could not find work in the countryside or had been driven out by famine, like the Irish between 1820 and 1850. From 1870, immigration continued, but the increase in population was also due to factors of natural growth.

During the same period, the growth of financial and commercial activities had shifted the resident population of the City to the periphery. Thus, the suburbs became the place of residence of a large population – in 1901, there were 6,581,000 inhabitants in Greater London, of whom 2,045,000 lived in the suburbs. From the middle of the century, the establishment of high-capacity suburban transport networks facilitated the spread of these suburbs. The railways were developed and the underground rapidly evolved beyond a simple interurban service and became the reason for the rapid growth of Hampstead, Golders Green and other suburbs.

In this way, between 1820 and 1914, the radius of the urbanized space of London increased from 5 to 15 km. This growth was partly made possible by the construction of estates, groups of houses built as a single scheme by speculative builders, following a mode of operation already established during the Georgian period.[29] This construction was undertaken systematically, with row housing of a defined and codified typology, which facilitated the urbanization of large areas. The open and airy estates of the rich suburbs contrasted with the gloomy estates of the popular districts. The London suburbs grew inexorably, systematically and disastrously.

It was only in 1888 with the setting up the London County Council that London succeeded in intervening more effectively in this process by superimposing a municipal structure over the diverse private, speculative and philanthropic initiatives.[30]

This administration with a socialist majority threw itself into the construction of large estates. However, in spite of its efforts the LCC could not control the urbanization of the suburbs. Since the beginning of the nineteenth century, a passionate debate had taken place in intellectual circles about the problems of large cities in general and London in particular. It also ran through popular literature with Dickens's dramatic descriptions and led to the exaltation of the characteristics and the beauty of the medieval city and drove the efforts of William Morris and the Arts and Crafts

---

29 'The prototype (of the estates) dates from 1661 with Lord Southampton's Bloomsbury estate.' C. Chaline, *Londres* (Paris: Arman Colin) 1968.
30 Since 1851 a series of laws facilitated municipal intervention. First, due to the Common Lodging House Act, there was the possibility that the municipality would control the sanitary state of old or new housing. Then, the Labouring Class Lodging Houses Act facilitated the financing of housing for the more disadvantaged sections of the population. In 1859 the Metropolitan Board of Works was created, which initiated slum improvements and the construction of social housing. In this way, up to 1890, 30,000 people were displaced and rehoused and 30,000 new homes were built. A parallel agency, the Metropolitan Association, during the same period built 70,000 homes and several charitable and private associations built another 150,000 homes.

Figure 9
The city as a garden: Welwyn Garden City.
a. The main axis.
The reference to the French garden is present in the theories of the garden city.

Movement towards cottage industry and the reform of industrial work. This ruralist movement derived from a hundred-year-old architectural culture because rural architecture and especially its manifestation through the cottage had been a source of inspiration for architects since around 1780.[31] The working-class home had benefited from this infatuation with the cottage whose forms had already been codified and while individual examples had been built, including some employers' homes, they still needed to be included as part of a larger-scale urbanization project.

In this way, the idea of the garden city as a solution to the London problem had a

b. Advertisement published in *Punch* in 1920.

31 See the article by G. Teyssot, 'Cottages et pittoresque: les origins du logement ouvrier en Angleterre 1781–1818', in *Architecture Mouvement Continuité* (Paris), No. 34, 1970.

firm base. This context gave Ebenezer Howard the opportunity to publish *To-morrow*,[32] a theoretical and personal work, which proposes a particular mode of growth: the satellite city. Howard's proposals are essentially economic in their pre-occupations. He examined the problem of municipal management and of financing the construction of cities, and presented the garden city as the most economical and the soundest solution for the growth of a large city.

Howard, convinced of the soundness of his theories, threw himself into the creation of a garden city. With no pretensions of being a town planner, he turned to two young architects, Raymond Unwin and Barry Parker, and, in 1904, the works for the setting up of Letchworth began, financed by a joint stock company. Howard's hope to see his example spread was frustrated, but the young architect Unwin used the experience to devise a theory for the planning of cities that he was try out in Hampstead and that would provide the tools for English town planning up to World War Two.

In 1906 the Town Planning Act,[33] which codified the density of plot subdivisions and the standards of housing construction, was passed. This Act was revised on 1909 in order to give municipalities more power over town planning matters. This was the occasion for Unwin to publish *Town Planning in Practice*.[34]

Because of all this activity, the garden city and the idea of satellite cities was at the heart of the debate of British town planners at the beginning of the century. In addition, there was a climate of research and experimentation. In 1910, there was an international exhibition of city planning in London as well as in Berlin and Düsseldorf. This exhibition with all the meetings associated with it shows the perti-nence of Unwin's theories and the topicality of the problems he was dealing with. It also explains the rapidity of the diffusion of these ideas.

Town planning thus had the legislative and conceptual tools for better controlling London's growth. But it was necessary to wait until the end of World War One to see them systematically carried out.

The interwar period was the determining period for suburban growth. The extensive London suburbs, which had to accommodate the massive migration provoked by the economic crisis, were well placed to become convenient and sought-after living areas, which developed their own poles of attraction. During this time the role of the financial and commercial City continued to evolve and London's plans had to take into account this growth as well.

32 In 1899 E. Howard's first version was published, *To-morrow: A Peaceful Path to Real Reform*; this book was re-edited in 1902 under the title *Garden Cities of To-morrow*.
33 'The "Town Planning Act" made compulsory the control of all plot subdivision projects proposed, either by a city or by a private individual, once they had obtained the approval of the Local Government Board.' G. Benoit-Levy, *La cité jardin*, Vol. 2 (Paris: Editions des cités-jardins de France), 1911.
34 *Town Planning in Practice. An introduction to the art of designing cities and suburbs* (London: Unwin) 1909.

The transport system again played an important role. First there was the underground, where the extension of some lines far into the suburbs gave rise around each station to a number of growth poles. The origin of these poles in some cases was promoted by the railway company, which even went as far as creating plot subdivisions, which were sold at reduced prices to future residents – this became London's Metroland.

There was a process of cutting through wide arterial roads, which created a linear pattern of growth, which connected old towns and gave the suburbs their characteristic profile of a succession of centres separated by less dense residential zones.

This growth depended on two modes of finance: on the one hand, private capital through such intermediaries as building societies and speculative builders; on the other, public investment through the municipal housing estates.[35] The existence of precise rules for construction and the reduction of the houses to a limited range of types give these suburbs a reassuring unity. But beyond these suburbs the idea of satellite cities and of a garden city had not been abandoned.

From 1919 onwards Howard was trying desperately to implement a second garden city. This was to be the conception and realization of Welwyn Garden City.

Welwyn is part of a group of new towns that were eventually to surround London and support its growth. Although they were well connected to the capital by railway, these towns were originally intended to have a degree of economic autonomy.

The interest of Welwyn resides in the fact that in it were superimposed the idea of the satellite city and the principles of Howard's garden city (autonomous management, relationship with the countryside), which were realized through Unwin's ideas about town planning. As was Unwin's intention, this realization was to be undertaken systematically by other architects. In reality, his ideas were only partially carried out because neither the attitudes nor the techniques prevailing at the time were yet ready for them. The 25 garden cities built around London by private enterprise or by municipalities all carry more or less the mark of this compromise. Nevertheless, this experience was to emerge after 1945 in the form of policies for new towns and green belts.

HAMPSTEAD GARDEN SUBURB

Caught up by the growth of neighbouring suburbs, Hampstead has now become an integral part of London and it is difficult to isolate the Unwin and Parker experimental core from the nearby tissue. However, arriving from central London along Finchley Road after the succession of high-density and commercial centres and resi-

---

35 The housing estates were of two types: the garden city of single family houses in the suburbs and the collective housing blocks in the renovation of central districts (slum clearance).

dential areas, one easily recognizes the gate that marks the entrance into Hampstead Garden Suburb. Two symmetrical buildings, looking like a picturesque reconstruction of medieval structures, refer to both the image of a town hall and that of a fortified gate.[36]

The origins of this garden suburb lie in the work of Henrietta Barnett, who was the rich heiress of a beauty-products company. Married to Canon Barnett, she spent thirty years of her life among the poor in Whitechapel, where her husband set up several charities.

In 1896 the Barnetts came to hear about the extension project of the underground as far as Golders Green and of the location of a station immediately to the north of Hampstead Heath, in the immediate vicinity of their country estate. At the beginning of 1905 Henrietta Barnett bought from Eton College a piece of land (80 acres) to donate to the LCC to be developed as a public green space. Her years spent with her charities had given her the idea that any community should be based on good neighbourliness and on the mixing of all social classes. She dreamed of an ideal community.

Having read several articles by Raymond Unwin, she went to Letchworth in order to discuss her project for a community with him and asked him for some sketches (the plan of February 1905). She then bought two additional pieces of land from Eton College so that it would be possible to build the garden suburb. On 6 March 1906 she set up the Hampstead Garden Suburb Trust with the following rules:

1 People from all classes of society and of all levels of income should be able to live together and handicapped people would be welcomed.
2 Cottages and houses should be built at an average density of eight dwellings per acre (20 dwellings per hectare).
3 Streets should be 40 feet (13.2 metres) wide and the façades of houses should be at least 50 feet (16.5 metres) from each other, with gardens in between.
4 Plots should not be separated by walls, but with hedges or trees or fences.
5 All streets should be lined with trees whose colours should harmonise with those of the hedges.
6 Woods and public gardens should be free for all residents independently of the amount of rent they paid.
7 Noise should be avoided, even that of church and chapel bells.
8 There should be low rents in order to allow weekly paid workers to live in the suburb.
9 Houses should be designed in such a way that they should not spoil each other's view or beauty.

36 '... we must forget the gateway and the importance of marking in some way the entrances of our towns, our suburbs, and our districts ... it would be fitting to mark the points where main roads cross over boundaries and enter towns, or new districts within the towns.' R. Unwin, op. cit. (p. 171).

a

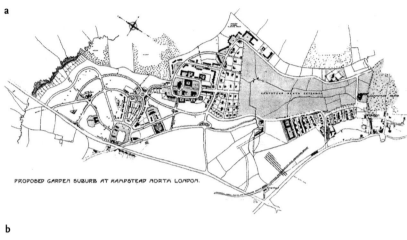

b

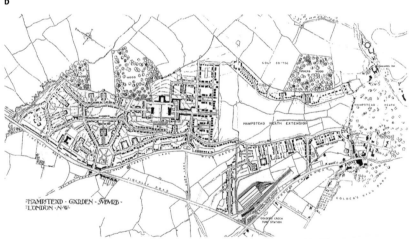

Figure 10
R. Unwin, B. Parker, Hampstead Garden Suburb.
a. Plan of 1905.
b. Plan of 1911.
The intervention of Lutyens in the design of churches organizes the square and its relationships with the park.

Henrietta Barnett appointed Raymond Unwin and Barry Parker as chief architects, with Edwin Lutyens as a consultant.

With Hampstead only eight kilometres from central London, its realization as a garden city was extremely compromised by the then current legislation concerning suburbs. Unwin's previously built projects, such as Letchworth and, previously, New Earswick for the Rowntree family, built in the open countryside, had not encountered any administrative constraints. Bournville, on the contrary, built for the Cadbury family in the suburbs of Birmingham, had encountered many difficulties. In 1906 Henry Vivian presented to Parliament in the name of the Hampstead Garden Suburb Trust a proposal for a law that would have allowed some amendments to the legislation. This project was adopted and voted for under the name of the 'Hampstead Garden Suburb Act'. With the participation of Unwin, these principles were later adopted as the basis of the 'Housing and Town Planning Act' of 1909.

Raymond Unwin's sketch of February 1906 took into account the wish expressed by Henrietta Barnett that from everywhere in the suburb one should be able to obtain panoramas or views of the neighbouring countryside. Most of the houses are thus grouped around a park and sited so as to be able to see Hampstead Heath.[37] Unwin concentrated the major facilities in a dense centre and created some smaller local district centres. But the sketch remained at the planning stage because of contradictions between Unwin's theories and the wishes of his client.

THE PLAN OF 1909

After various vicissitudes, a new plan was agreed. The whole development was much more structured and Unwin's great themes made their appearance. The overall structure, a dense centre and diversified residential areas, the hierarchy of spaces, the notion of limits: Hampstead Heath, the wall between the park and the city, the marking of entrances. Besides this overall structure, the treatment of details makes more concessions to the picturesque, so that Hampstead resembles a catalogue of picturesque treatments. But the diversity of these treatments and the diversity of the architects who designed them bear witness to Unwin's strong idea: only through a reading at different levels can the urban reality be understood. Starting with an analysis of several European cities, he lays down some precise rules: a clear overall organization, consisting of dense and easily legible centres, some morphologically differentiated districts, a limit and barrier to the city's growth, an axis, a landmark (special building, entrance etc.), then more picturesque local buildings, picking up at this level the ideas of Camillo Sitte.

The plan of 1909 has been carried out in its entirety. But financing problems transformed this social city into a residential city.[38] If this shift is not visible from a simple

37 In Letchworth and, more precisely, on the Bird's Hill estate, the close (in the embryonic state) allows for two problems to be solved. It offers views to a maximum number of houses and an economical plan, i.e. one without too much space to be maintained. The 1905 sketch clearly reuses the same solution to answer Henrietta Barnett's wishes. But, even if one finds again in the 1909 plan an identical concern, especially along the park, it is difficult to find the same close in its final state as the evolution of the close of Bird's Hill. If the economic argument (highway maintenance costs) has certainly had an important role to play, one cannot forget the contribution of the idea of neighbourhood and the influence of the rural architectural tradition of the period.
38 The land belonged to Garden Suburb Hampstead Limited, which leased it out for building. The great majority of houses were built by building societies, which financed private builders who used architectural designs from an established range. Out of the total value of construction, the societies had constructed 67%, the Garden Suburb Development Company Ltd had built 25% worth and the Improved Industrial Dwelling Co. (a society for building cheap housing) 1,000,000F – less than 10% by value. The fame of Unwin and Parker, the experimental side of the enterprise and its location in a wealthy district have made it easy for the middle classes to acquire the greater part of the houses.

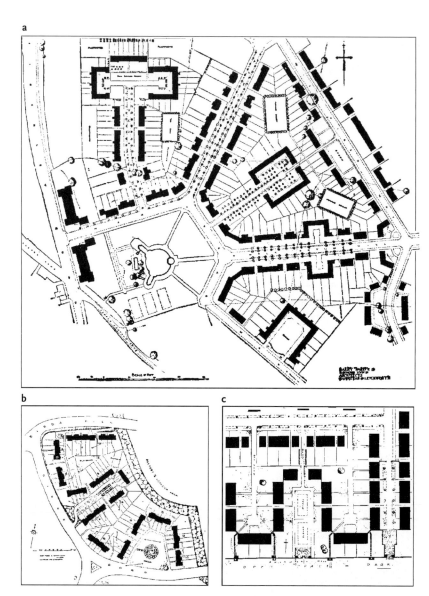

Figure 11
R. Unwin: the role of views in the design of the close (from *Town Planning in Practice*).
a. Hampstead Garden Suburb, plan of the access square onto Finchley Road.
b. Letchworth: Bird's Hill area.
c. Theoretical plan showing how it is possible to ensure the view towards a green space or a park for a large number of houses, through the layout of the close

a

b

Figure 12

Hampstead Garden Suburb: central square.
a. Drawing by E. Lutyens.
b. Cadastral plan of 1975, showing, beyond the original plan, the layout of radiating streets, which extends the classical composition of the square.

reading of the plan, it is nevertheless very noticeable to the visitor and from the appearanace of its inhabitants.

Subsequently, Hampstead Garden Suburbs developed considerably towards the northeast beyond the original plan. In this extension one can observe the systematic use of Unwin's tools: closes, setbacks etc. But there is a considerable reduction of the picturesque treatment, which is what gives the place its character. The inherent classical monumentality of Central Square, designed by Lutyens, produces a majestic composition of radiating streets, which seems out of scale with the small surrounding row houses. This axiality and symmetry of the composition and its clash with the adjoining tissue clearly bears witness to the conceptual differences between Unwin and Lutyens.

HEATHGATE: FROM THE PARK TO THE CENTRE

'Many ancient towns derive exceptional beauty from their enclosure by ramparts or walls. To this enclosure is due in no small measure the careful use of every yard of building space within the wall which has led too much of their picturesque effect. To this is due also the absence of that irregular fringe of half-developed suburb and half spoiled country which forms such a hideous and depressing girdle around modern growing towns.' Raymond Unwin adds, '... we should secure some orderly line up to which the country and town may each extend and stop definitely...' At Hampstead there is a long wall between city and park. Here the city begins and ends. This symbolic replication of a fortification is the allegory in stone of the need for a limit. Here the difference between city and countryside is formalized with clarity. And, if it is but an allegory, it is not the wall that stops the city, but the status of the park. The place sends you to walks in the boulevards or on the fortifications. The message is clear and precise. Along the wall is a path planted with trees, the last infringement of the city on the countryside; in this ambiguous place, where one does not know whether one is inside or outside, the city offers its organization and the countryside its trees.

From the sunken park one has to go through a gate in order to penetrate into the city. After some steps and a square, a setback and a narrowing, one emerges into Heathgate. There is a concern for the path and the sequence of views. Then, from the gate in Central Square, it is all a subtle game of recesses and gaps, with the church of Lutyens to mark the axis.

Heathgate is, therefore, a beautiful demonstration of Unwin's theories: overall thinking at the scale of the city (edge, barrier, gate, axis...) together with a picturesque treatment of the architectural detail. Because centrality has its own morphological rules, towards Central Square the density increases through the use of row houses and continuous façades. A game of making differences through the historical tradition of making the centre distinctive has influenced Lutyens and the treatment of the square

is pure classicism. However, he does not completely escape the medievalist picturesque influence in his church, which is Arts and Crafts romantic. There is a hierarchical application of the rules – those concerned with the overall layout are not the same
as those governing the local details.

Beyond the didactic bravura illustrated by Heathgate and Central Square,
Hampstead Garden Suburb appears to be like a catalogue of solutions to two problems: the route and the neighbourhood unit with the formal answer being the close.
The attempt to systematically answer the first problem takes its inspiration from
Camillo Sitte. The layout of streets, squares and crossroads always obeys the laws
of the medieval picturesque so that a street must always end with a significant
blocking point.

The close is a group of houses around a blind alley or a small cul-de-sac square. This
cul-de-sac generally emerges into a street and one can consider the houses, which, on
the street, announce or close the cul-de-sac, as part of the close. Once this system is
defined, there is an indefinite number of possible variations and Hampstead is an
essay in the typology of the system or, at least, of its implementation.

THE SPATIAL PARTICULARITIES OF THE CLOSE

The systematic experimentation carried out by Unwin in Hampstead allows us to
have at our disposal a great number of variations on that particular component of the
garden city: the close. One goes from the tightly enclosed and unified type at
Waterloo Court to the more complex one at the edge of the street and of the cul-
de-sac such as Asmuns Place.

Waterloo Court, which is the only important work of the architect Baillie Scott in
Hampstead, presents itself like a closed square courtyard made up of houses connected to form a single building. This development at the edge of the courtyard shows
buildings derived from the tradition of rural architecture rather than the product of a
new approach to a block of houses.

The close on Hampstead Way presents itself as a rectangle enclosed by buildings on
three sides. The two houses that end the sides towards the street are turned around 90
degrees, in order to open the close and block the sides. On the other side of the street
there is a special grouping of ten houses (three, then a detached one, two on the axis of
the close, slightly protruding, then a detached one and then again three) that
responds to the courtyard typology. This close works as a courtyard open to the
street, a variation on the theme of the farmhouse courtyard taken up again at
Waterloo Court.

This variety was taken even further with a close that was never built. It would have
been rectangular, closed on three sides; however, the row of houses would not have

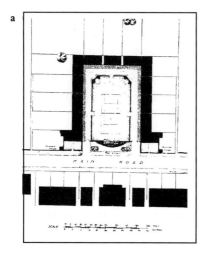
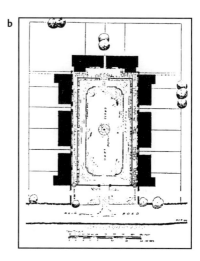
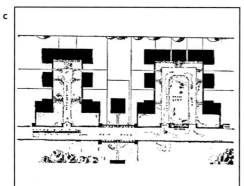
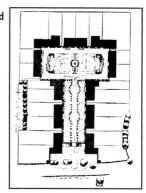

Figure 13

Unwin: typological variations on the theme of the close, from *Town Planning in Practice*.
a. Close off Hampstead Way.
b. Close off Main Road.
c. Associated closes off Main Road.
d. Unbuilt T-shaped close, of a type to be used for Asmuns Place.

been continuous, but made up of groups of two semidetached houses. In Morland and Romney Closes, the rectangle begins to be broken up more and more, but a wall between the houses ensures the continuity of the façade on the courtyard, thus preserving the distinction between the back and front spaces and also perhaps preserving, through the image of the courtyard, the original architectural reference.[39]

39 J. D. Kornwolf, *M. H. Baillie Scott and the Arts and Crafts Movement, Pioneer of Modern Design* (London: Johns Hopkins Press), 1972.

We have another variation on the type that abandons the rectangle in favour of the T shape. There was a similar nonrealized project where, starting from the street, one would find two L-shaped houses, set back from the street alignment, in order to obtain a small entrance square. Six groups of two semidetached houses would then form the street, which would emerge into a rectangular courtyard closed on three sides by semidetached houses. Between the houses a wall would ensure the continuity of the enclosure. This would be a much longer close than the previous ones and seemed to increase the degree of privatization of the courtyard space since it would be much deeper in relation to the street.

Asmuns Place appears to be a variation on this type. On the street (Hampstead Way) a setback announces a close; the cul-de-sac slopes slightly up and then, after two semidetached houses, it makes a small bend before one then enters the close proper. The right-hand side of the T is enclosed by ten houses connected in two groups, the first of six and the second of four. An interruption marks a courtyard with a double row of four houses. One emerges then into the end of the close, which is a rectangle built on three sides with a setback on the side opposite the entrance. A wall here ensures the continuity of the façade. This façade differentiates two spaces: the front one on the cul-de-sac and the back one, which cannot be seen by passers-by on the street.

The cul-de-sac, as its name suggests, is a place where one does not enter by chance, because it does not lead anywhere other than to private houses. This restriction, a reduction of the street to a service access, clearly defines the front space: it belongs to the residents and it does not connect to a more global level in the route hierarchy. It is tempting to define it as semi-public, because the people who use it are those who live there. Nevertheless, inside the front space there is a new distinction to be made: on one side there is the street and the pavement and, on the other side, the space is in direct contact with the house. A strip of land, the width of the lot becomes the responsibility of the resident. But it is difficult to see where each piece of land begins and ends and this can be attributed to a particularity of the English tradition. There is a global appropriation, which transforms this front into a common garden in which there are some subtle markings, which make it possible to identify the territory of each resident. This socialization of the space is not a general one and it follows the evolution and the changes of the complex history of the social groups making up English society. The front space is a flowery scene where the informed eye can read the history of the agreements and disagreements within these groups.

The back gardens are usually well isolated from the front. If some are accessible only through the houses, one can gain access to the end of the garden through a small path servicing some allotments, which in some cases pass between the house and the garden. In the first case the entrance to the path is through a small door in the wall (privatization of the place). This path is surrounded by high hedges, which are interrupted at times by small doors, while each garden is separated from the

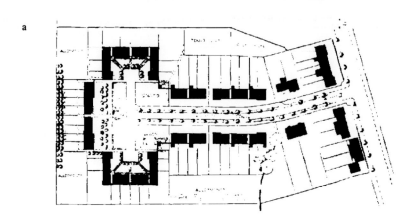

a

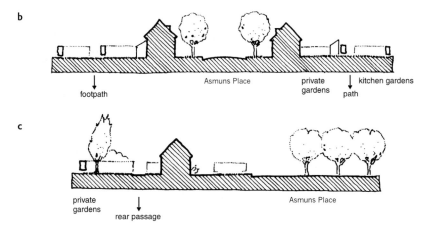

b

footpath   Asmuns Place   private gardens   path   kitchen gardens

c

private gardens   rear passage   Asmuns Place

d

Figure 14

Hampstead Garden Suburb: Asmuns Place.

a. Plan of the close published by R. Unwin in *Town Planning in Practice*.

b. Section, perpendicular to the road. The layout allows a clear distinction between front and back.

c. Section through the centre of the road showing the cut created in the back by the common passage between the cottages and the gardens.

d. The interior of the close at the time of construction.

next one by a hedge. The back–front differentiation is here clearly noticeable: drying laundry, a small shed, a space for storing unused artefacts, and a corner of the garden where a piece of lawn is kept for a table and chairs. The family functions of the garden are moved here from the front socialising space. The scheme resembles the French single-family housing, described in the work of Raymond et al.,[40] with the difference that the front is less of a private space and more of a collective one.

In the second case, the existence of a back passage crossing the gardens links these gardens into a collective image. The appropriation is more discreet, obeying some common rules. Besides, one can say that the front gardens, of a reduced size, give a much greater impression of privacy than those of houses that have private back gardens. All these observations bear witness to the relationship between differentiated spaces and also to a differentiation in attitudes towards these spaces. The close, if it negates the street as public front space does, at least reproduce the back–front contrast familiar in the traditional tissue, even though this front does not relate to the whole city, but rather to a community of neighbours. To this spatial contrast, symbolized by the wall that connects the houses and the subtle game of the entrances to the back paths, corresponds a contrast in use. If we assume this hypothesis, then we can see how in this type of grouping the rear passage begins to create an inversion of the scheme and we find the rear gardens providing the private representational space. A neutral public space ensures that an image of quality is maintained for the ensemble on the close.

WELWYN GARDEN CITY

Welwyn Garden City is 22 km from London, just beyond Hatfield New Town on the main road north – the A1. Served by trains, Welwyn is part of the ring of new towns that, in the Greater London plan, were intended to be the key to the growth of the British capital.

After World War One, a campaign was begun by Howard and his friends, W. G. Osborn, C. B. Purdom and F. J. Taylor,[41] for the creation of new garden cities, this time financed by the government. The strength of this campaign came from the success of Letchworth (1904) and from the necessity to build housing rapidly around London. In 1919, Parliament voted funds for reconstruction with which the financing of the new garden cities became possible. But the Ministry of Housing, convinced of the need to build rapidly the largest possible number of houses, became uninterested in garden cities.

40 See H. Raymond, N. Haumont, M. G. Raymond, A. Haumont, *L'habitat pavillonaire* (Paris, ISU/CRU), 1966.
41 From 1917 onwards a series of associations and societies were created in order to prepare for the start of the new garden cities. During the same period and together with these societies an advertising campaign was run through many publications. Thus in 1917 *The Garden City after the War*, by C. B. Purdom, was published and in 1918 *New Towns after the War*, by E. J. Osborn and W. G. Taylor; C. B. Purdom published in 1925 *The Building of Satellite Towns, A contribution to the Study of Town Development and Regional Planning* (London: Dent & Sons Ltd, re-edited and completed in 1949), which is an extremely well-documented book on Letchworth and Welwyn).

Howard was convinced that it was time to start building the second garden city without waiting for state aid, and in the summer of 1919 he began to buy the land needed. With the help of friends, he acquired 1.458 acres for a cost of £51,000 and, when it appeared that this was not enough, he raised capital through a new company called Second Garden City Limited, which enabled him to buy rest of the land needed, Sherrards Woods. On 29 April 1920 Welwyn Garden City Limited was founded with a capital of £250,000, in shares mainly sold to industrialists.

The first plan was designed by Crickmers, but Howard preferred to create an office within the company and appointed as chief architect Louis de Soissons, a young architect known as one of the most gifted of the new generation. Construction started straightaway with road works carried out on existing paths. The main avenue was created together with some other streets and the industrial zone was laid out and serviced. The first houses, built by direct labour, were occupied by Christmas 1920, and then, in November 1922, 50 more houses followed with 95 more in May 1924.[42] The first houses were built under the Addison Act of 1919, but the Housing Act of 1921 would provide the greater part of the funds.[43]

THE GENERAL PLAN

'As the designer walks over the ground to be planned, he will picture to himself what would be the natural growth of the town or district if left to spread over the area. He will try to realise the direction which the main lines of traffic will inevitably take, which portions of the ground will be attractive for residences, and which will offer inducements for the development of shops, business premises, or industries... there will arise in his imagination a picture of the future community with its needs and its aims...' (Raymond Unwin, *Town Planning in Practice*, p. 149).

This view of the site, considered as a framework that has the necessary elements to structure urban growth, is clearly noticeable in Welwyn. First, there is the use of the existing routes, such as Handside Lane or Bridge Road, which, at the beginning, were nothing but stony rural paths, along which the first constructions were built in an extension of the historical growth pattern. Then there is the use of existing trees, like the two that block the axis of Guessen Walk, where there is a magnificent chestnut tree, around which gravitates the Quadrangle (designed by Louis de Soissons). There is also the overall study of the terrain, which determined the location of residential and industrial areas and, finally, there is the bend of the railways, which made possible Louis de Soissons' brilliant axial composition.

In looking at the plan for the centre of Welwyn, it is difficult not to think of some axial compositions to which we became accustomed through the Beaux Arts' Prix

42 See references below p. 204.
43 For financing details, see C. B. Purdom, op. cit.

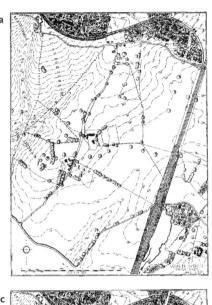

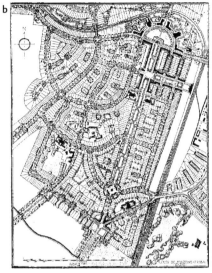

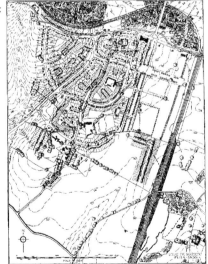

Figure 15
Welwyn Garden City: site layout by Louis de Soissons.
a. The initial site with the intersection of the railway line to the east, the sharp change in the relief to the west and the wood and the roads to the north. A path connects two farms.
b. The plan by Louis de Soissons. The great Beaux Arts composition, marked by the sequence town gate/rond-point/parkway/centre, leading to the station to the east, is combined, following Unwin's principles, with the picturesque layout of secondary streets and closes.
c. The executed plan in 1924. From the start of construction the incapacity of dealing with the centre is visible, as well as the deviation of the main axis, which no longer plays the structuring role initially assigned to it.

de Rome. Here there is a grand unfinished axis, which locates and sets off the administrative centre. Onto this some finite compositions are attached that thus determine a central point, which is not the activity centre, but is a place from where one can read several focal points. Thus, the first principle of Julien Guadet's architectural composition is respected: 'The first principle [that] must remain present in our mind is that a composition has one direction and that it must only have one. Its axis is only finished in one and only direction... We want to understand a plan from the first glimpse and what above all we value in a work is clarity, frankness and decision.'[44]

THE NOTION OF NEIGHBOURHOOD

A simple analysis of the plan makes it possible to distinguish between the neighbour-hoods. The commercial centre is dense with an orthogonal grid with the administrative centre as the key to the monumental axis. The station intrudes as a deeply penetrating presence in the city and the residential neighbourhoods of single family houses are composed according to the rules defined by Unwin, with the closes carefully composed arrangements of visual sequences. This reading, carried out at the level of each of the four zones, defined in Welwyn by the railways, can be done at a global level. One zone appears as the centre, and there is an industrial zone and then two peripheral residential zones. The notion of hierarchy is respected at the cost of a more or less segregationist plan. The grand idea of community has disappeared in the search for a functional urban logic.

BARRIER, LIMIT, MARKER

As in Hampstead, the city is bounded. The passage from the countryside to the town happens through special gateways, such as a row of trees signalling the vicinity of inhabited areas, and then a square, followed by dense building, heralding the city.

Thus Louis de Soissons systematically uses the tools of urban composition tried out in Hampstead by Unwin. While avoiding the exaggeration of the picturesque effects and the variations on the closes, he manages to superimpose two visions of the city: that of the 'medieval' town with its great variety, and that of the 'classical' city, with its rigour and its reassuring unity. This superimposition establishes a necessary hierarchy between the centre and the residential districts. The southwest neighbourhood (by the station) clearly formalises this play between two urban arguments and the conflicts it brings about; the central avenue (Parkway), a green rupture between elements, which do not have the same systems of reference, is thus a transition between two neighbourhoods.

This system of contrasts could have been effective if an enlargement in scale had not transformed the avenue into a park. There are now many 'cities', or rather one city, made from exploded elements. The brutal application of a zoning scheme, with, as a consequence, the absence of any overlap between the parts, made the efforts in trying to create a clear morphological identity seem fruitless.

---

44 Julien Guadet, *Éléments et théories de l'architecture*, Paris, Librairie de la construction moderne (no date).

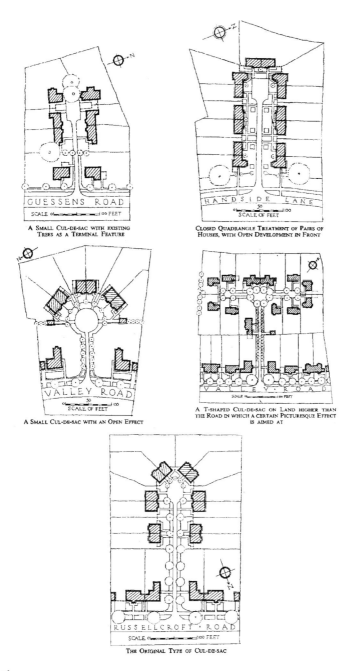

Figure 16

Welwyn Garden City: typological variations on the theme of the close.
A comparison with Unwin's variations shows the explosion of the original spatial type. The close is no more the reinterpretation of the courtyard of the manor house or of the farm, but a way of grouping a series of semidetached houses.

a

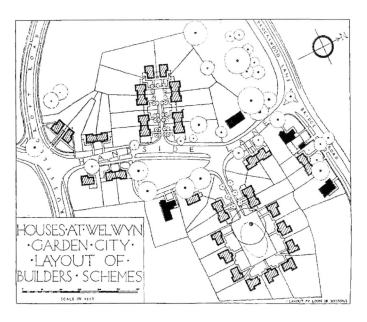

b

Figure 17
Welwyn Garden City, the Quadrangle and Handside Walk.
a. The Quadrangle, internal view of the close.
b. Initial plan.

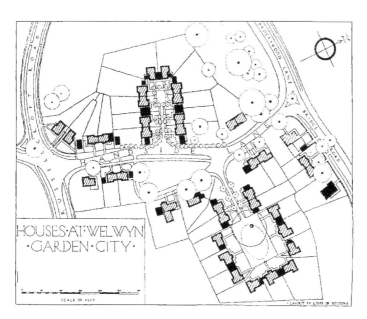

c. Situation in 1975 of the layout, showing extensions. The building of garages, outhouses or walls (in black) between houses re-enforces the continuity of the enclosure between the space of the close and the back gardens.

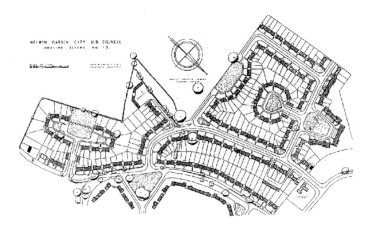

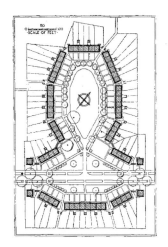

Figure 18
The close, continuation and reduction of the type.
The increased dimensions and the repetition of identical houses in the closes and in the neighbouring streets lose the specific character of the close. The garden city slides into a picturesque plot subdivision of semi-detached houses.

The implementation also produced other important changes. First was the growth of Welwyn beyond the limits decided by Louis de Soissons and Ebenezer Howard, an extension that, for economic reasons, was carried out rapidly and without taking into account the original logic. It makes the notion of barrier and entrance appear invalid. But the most regrettable thing is the disappearance during implementation of the systematic utilization of the close as a unit of intervention. Thus, the lack of care given to the local level reduces the close to a cul-de-sac, often determined by the overall street layout and most of the time deprived of its main characteristic, which is the existence of a collective space strongly demarcated in relation to the public and private spaces. The close thus represents nothing more than the disappearance of the street.

THE CLOSE: PURSUIT AND REDUCTION OF A TYPE

The two closes designed by Louis de Soissons – Handside Walk and the Quadrangle – together with the small triangular square from which they emerge, form the ensemble, which, in Welwyn, can be considered to be that which makes the most concessions to the picturesque. This is perhaps due to the consequence of the use by Louis de Soissons of the existing path and trees.

Handside Walk is a rectangular close, open to the street and formed by semidetached houses and closed at the end by two houses located at each side of the central axis. The houses are separated by gardens. The Quadrangle is a rectangle surrounding a very beautiful tree, which existed before the construction of the garden city. This rectangle is formed by detached houses, separated by gardens, and is closed by two groups of semidetached houses. Here, contrary to Hampstead Garden Suburb, where special care had been given to the differentiation between backs and fronts, there was originally some permeability of space. In fact, no wall connected the houses in the Quadrangle and even the back gardens of the first two houses of Handside Walk could be seen from the street. The modifications that this omission has provoked seem significant to us.

In the Quadrangle all the interior façade has been treated as continuous by the construction of garages, outhouses and walls. If the construction of garages can easily be explained by the appearance and general use of the car, the origin of the outhouses and, more significantly, of the walls cannot be of the same nature. The front space defined in this way seems to be an example of the same type of collective appropriation as has already been observed in Hampstead Garden Suburb, with the changes that result from a different population. This type of change is even more noticeable in Handside Walk.[45]

In Handside Walk one can notice the same phenomenon of the enclosure of space as in the Quadrangle. A hedge prevents any visual communication between the street and the back gardens of the two houses forming the entrance to the close. It has a secondary effect of shutting off the entire close, which makes the interior space seem to be ideal collective appropriation by the surrounding houses. This observation should

45 Welwyn residents were surely less well off than those of Hampstead Garden Suburb. This can be explained by the wish to build an economical city, a wish that was aided by state subsidies and by the repetitive character of the construction (in fact there are fewer types of house and, in addition, the closes or the neighbourhoods were built as wholes and were let only when they were all finished, which was not the case in Hampstead Garden Suburb). Another reason is the relative distance from the centre of London. This prevented the intensive speculative activity that happened in Hampstead. A third reason is the character, or rather the absence of character, of the architecture of Welwyn: too much or not enough systematically to tempt an intellectual elite.

be compared with Wilmot's observation on Dagenham, where he emphasises the existence of community activity inside some closes.[46] It is thus tempting to correlate the special morphology of the close with these types of collective practice. The closed space of the close at least forms a space that is specifically suitable for supporting any group activities that may be characteristic of English culture (see Wilmot's studies on matrilocality).

What is quite clear here, and confirms the observations with regard to Hampstead Garden Suburb, is the necessary existence of a spatial differentiation that provides a third type of space between the public realm and private space. When the spatial arrangements do not take this necessity into account residents themselves, as a consequence, modify their space, when this is possible. This also means that one of the qualities of the design of Welwyn is that it allows for these modifications.

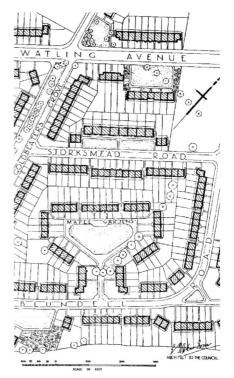

THE CLOSE: FROM PUBLIC TO PRIVATE SPACE

To reduce the block to the close could seem arbitrary. In fact, in both Welwyn and Hampstead Garden Suburb, the block exists beyond the close. But the close introduces a new hierarchy in relation to the traditional tissue and the space of the cul-de-sac produces a level of unusual relations and allows different activities to take place. The setting apart of the front space vis-à-vis the city is fundamental. It means that the close has some autonomy so that it is tempting to consider it as a separate unit. In Hampstead Garden Suburb as well as in Welwyn, the block is the combination of individual plots and of closes. This combination, first, obeys some general rules with respect to the density and the walkways. Secondly, it attempts to respect the difference between the private and the public domain. It is at this level that the close operates as a sub-

Figure 19
A London County Council housing estate.
The formal building typology of the garden cities is used in the 1920s on all residential developments of low density, built at the edge of cities.

46 P. Wilmot and M. Young, *The Evolution of a Community, A Study of Dagenham after Forty Years* (Routledge and Kegan Paul), 1963.

division by functioning as a unit. The interior space of the close contrasts with the specifically public space of the street through an element of enclosure such as a narrowing of the space between buildings, a hedge or even a gate. The public–private contrast functions again in the interior of the close, but is reduced due to the collective appropriation of this space.

Thus the close takes away from the street a whole series of important activities, reducing it to the technical role of a route that allows for movement only. If this reduction of the street is not entirely due to the close, it is at least the most important factor in this process. Monopolising a certain number of practices and reducing and transforming them, the close formalizes this privatization of space, which follows the privatization of ways of life both in England and in France. And the grouping that it induces, mainly among the most disadvantaged classes, where the group is a practically and culturally vital extension of the family, does not contradict this assertion: confined to the close, they are rather the reflection of its autonomous character. But, apart from the close or even with the close, Hampstead Garden Suburb and Welwyn represent the traditional scheme of contrasting space that is still differentiated, and can be appropriated and modified.

The garden city carried out wonderfully the transition between a space where public life is privileged, so that private activities need a lot of support, and a space that, by privileging private activities, demands that the public space must be carefully supported. Thus, the garden city, by its skilful design, goes to the heart of English culture with its love of nature reduced to the private garden (and gardening). It brings to the neighbourhood community a group vitality that meets the needs of capitalist urbanization and, at the same time, provides a technical answer to urban growth and the social answer to the necessary reproduction of bourgeois cultural models.

CHAPTER 3
THE EXTENSION OF
AMSTERDAM: 1913–34

> The housing problem can only be resolved by mass production. In
> order to find a viable solution one has again to go back to housing
> blocks, but at a larger scale than previously.
>
> H. P. Berlage

With the choice of Amsterdam, we are following a double aim: on the one hand to investigate one of the last moments of traditional city planning and, on the other, to evaluate the role of architecture in the planning of this city.

Traditional city planning should not be contrasted with modern town planning, as Siegfried Giedion has done,[47] leading to a rejection of all that does not have the imprint of CIAM (Congrès International d'Architecture Moderne). The development of Amsterdam is modern, and even progressive, because of its objective, which was the building of mass housing (South Amsterdam alone represents around 12,000 houses) as well as the means set up to achieve it, which included public expropriation and long-term planning. However, these new initiatives were not carried out in defiance of the existing city. Neither in the overall plans nor in the treatment of details is the reference to the city forgotten.

The part played by architecture here is paramount, sometimes even obsessive. It is worth considering this often-neglected aspect. More even than the plan by Berlage, which has been extensively discussed, it is the Amsterdam School that interests us. It was a movement that was denigrated by the Stijl and forgotten by the architectural historians, who only saw in it the Dutch and delayed version of the Jugendstijl.[48]

Beyond the games played with brickwork and decoration, the work of the Amsterdam School seems to us rather more of a series of experiments on the urban block with a starting point in a reflection on housing cells and their combination.[49] Set up in this way, this study is no more a discussion of styles, but it highlights the problem of an urban architecture, where the façade is not the simple disclosure of an interior, but the place of a conflict, a compromise between two scales, that of the house and that of the city.

---

47 S. Giedion (1941), *Space, time and architecture*.
48 Nikolaus Pevsner and Henry-Russell Hitchcock, who are among the few who wrote about it, do not see in it anything apart from the decorative aspect of the brickwork and the treatment of corners.
49 Proving this, Giedion notes, 'J. J. Oud was the first to use the internal courtyard to give a more human aspect to the large housing blocks of his Tusschendiken project (1919)', and ignores the earlier Amsterdam experiments.

In order to demonstrate this approach, we have decided, after an investigation of the planning developments of the 1910–40 period, to limit our discussion to the following two sectors: the first, a relatively small one, is the quarter of Spaarndammerbuurt; the second, a larger one, is the extension towards the south of the Berlage plan of 1917. In fact, the east districts (Insulinde) and the west district (Mercator plein, Hoofweg) only confirm, with some minor departures, our observations on the two sectors chosen. The garden cities of the north (Buisksloterham, Niewendammerham) and those of the southeast (Watergrafsmeer), while offering interesting comparisons with the London garden cities, seem to us rather marginal with regard to our investigation and

Figure 20

Amsterdam: the south Amsterdam plan – to the right M. de Klerk, to the left F. Zietsma.
'The miracle of the creation of a collective architecture... The isolated and one-family house type lost its importance in favour of a group of buildings sited along a street and belonging to a larger group, which contained a network of roads, conceived as a whole and carried out by different architects' (Bruno Taut, 1929).

do not offer the historical experience of those English garden cities from which they derive.

THE PARTICULARITIES OF CITY PLANNING IN AMSTERDAM

DEMOGRAPHY AND HOUSING IN AMSTERDAM IN THE NINETEENTH-CENTURY

From 1850 to 1920, after emerging from a long period of economic stagnation, Amsterdam's population grew by almost three times from 230,000 to 683,000 inhabitants. The development of colonial commerce combined with the first effects of industrialization to give the Low Countries a prosperity that had been impossible[50] in the previous century, which had been dominated by the maritime wars with England, followed by the blockade by Napoléon I.

In order to take advantage of this expansion, the city of Amsterdam had first to modernize its port, which had been made inaccessible by the sandbanks of the Zuiderzee. The North Holland canal (Helder canal), completed in 1825 but built with too small a width, did not have the expected effects, so the North Sea canal (from Amsterdam to Ijmuiden), executed from 1865 to 1875, can truly be considered to mark the starting point of the modernization of the city. This was to be implemented by the 1875 plan of Kalf, an engineer, which was the first extension project since the building of the three canals.[51] In fact, the city had not increased in size since the seventeenth century, with a population still housed within the perimeter of the old city.

Taking into account the constraints of Holland, Kalf proposed a ring of development around the agglomeration, which adopted, for the layout of streets, the irrigation grid of the pre-existing rural plot subdivision. This meant abandoning the radioconcentric plan in favour of one that extended orthogonally in two directions. Exclusively concerned with the layout of roads, Kalf left the construction of the buildings in the hands of speculative developers. Because of this policy, a contrast developed between the bourgeois neighbourhoods, mainly sited around Vondelpark (carried out by private initiative in 1863), and the working-class districts.

These, in spite of some clearly smaller parks – Oosterpark, Sarphatipark – also represent speculative developments where maximum profitability was sought. As a consequence, there were some very small houses (20 square metres, one room per

---

50 Even though the figures differ depending on sources, the demographic growth of Amsterdam can be seen from the following table:

1800	220,000 inhabitants	1890	425,000 inhabitants
1850	230,000 inhabitants	1900	528,200 inhabitants
1860	250,700 inhabitants	1910	590,900 inhabitants
1870	273,900 inhabitants	1920	683,000 inhabitants
1880	330,000 inhabitants	1930	750,000 inhabitants

51 The project of Van Niftrick, presented to the municipal council in 1867, was not proceeded with.

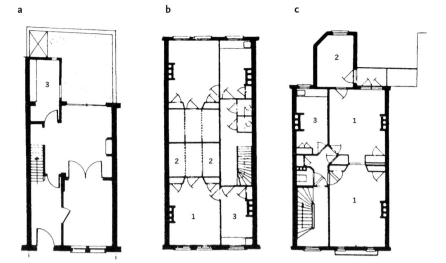

a   b   c

Figure 21

House plans in Amsterdam at the beginning of the century.
a. Traditional social housing (rooms off outside corridors).
b. Alcove type housing, c 1890.
c. Working-class housing, after the 1902 law, 1. living room, 2. beds, 3. kitchen.

family, back to back) with bed cubicles in recesses in the kitchen. These were known as 'alcove housing'.

The neighbourhoods of Spaarndammerbuurt, Staatliedesbuurt, Kinker, Dapperbuurt, Pijp and Oosterparkbuurt were built in this way and little by little occupied all the remaining free land between the enclosure of the three canals and the limit of the communal territory. With demographic growth continuing, the pressures for the densification of this type of housing became extreme, leading to the appearance of makeshift dwellings in the courtyards of the old quarters, and overcrowding of the already small cells in the new ones. In both cases all available spaces – attics, cellars etc. – were utilized.

Starting in 1852 with some philanthropic societies and from 1868 with some working-class cooperatives, there was an attempt to find a remedy to these conditions. Among these were the Rochdale (sic), Eigen Haard, Eigen Woningen and De Dageraad cooperatives, which would be involved later in the South Amsterdam plan. However, in spite of financial support from the municipality, the amount built was inadequate in relation to the extent of the problem. This situation, which was to be found at the same period in the other main Dutch cities, could not have been resolved without the intervention of the public authorities.

This happened in two ways. From 1896 onwards, at the same time as it increased its territory, mainly in the southern part of the city, there was municipal intervention. There were measures favouring social housing such as grants of land for its construction according to projects prepared by the technical services and by the municipal architect. This action coincided with a number of decisions intended to halt land speculation. The city became involved in the systematic acquisition of land in order to have an effect on the property market and, modelling itself on the English example, it adopted a system of 99-year leases.

There was also governmental and parliamentary intervention, which resulted in 1901 in a law on housing, the 'Woningwet', which was accompanied by the necessary credits for its immediate implementation. From 1902, communes with more than 10,000 inhabitants had the right, the duty and the means, in the form of 50- or 75-year loans and state support for:

- the establishment of development plans;
- the expropriation of land occupied by insalubrious housing and the acquisition of the necessary land for the construction of social housing;
- building directly or through recognized associations (working-class cooperatives, low cost housing societies) managing social housing.[52]

In parallel, some measures were taken in Amsterdam in order to help the societies for the construction of social housing in the form of construction and management subsidies (1916). In spite of these measures and in spite of the construction of 40,000 houses in eighteen years (1906–24), the municipality estimated a lack of 15,000 houses in 1924. About 10 per cent of the population continued to use the 'alcove homes' or 'cellar homes'.

TECHNICAL CONSTRAINTS AND LAND CONDITIONS OF CITY PLANNING IN AMSTERDAM

Demographic pressure and the endorsement by the public authorities of social housing were the origins of the law on housing, as we have seen. This law, whose progressive character has been widely noted, defined a framework in favour of housing construction and urban growth. It is difficult to understand the practical modalities of its application without taking into account the technical constraints typical of Dutch city planning; these have given a particular aspect to land problems in Amsterdam.

The land problem comes first, since Amsterdam, like many other cities in the Netherlands, is situated below sea level. This means that not only the construction of buildings but the very existence of land depends on a technical intervention. Land is obtained little by little through drainage and by the reclamation of land (polders) through successively isolating sections by dykes (dams). This land, which was first

---

52 The commune directly took on board housing construction from 1917. Its major effort went to individual housing in garden cities, while urban housing was left to individuals or societies. For the period 1906–23 the following figures are available:

	PRIVATE HOUSING	SOCIETIES' HOUSING	COMMUNES
Individual houses	303	82	2,386
Duplex housing with independent entrance	1,989	2,282	1,564
Apartments	23,309	9,429	760
Total	25,309	11,793	4,710

It should be noted that, starting from 1917, the greater part of housing built by societies or individuals benefited from subsidies and loans and was under strict control. For 1922, the portion of the non-aided housing corresponds to less than 2% of the volume of house building on site. From: *Amsterdam: developpement de la ville, habitations populaires*, Municipality of Amsterdam, 1924.

cultivated and then, in the period that concerns us, built upon, bears the imprint of its patient stabilization, inscribed in the layout of the canals and drainage channels.[53] The security of land depends on the solidity of each element; this system needs rigorous control by the municipal authorities. One constantly has to watch over the dykes, whose rupture can, in a few hours, cause the inundation of hundreds of hectares. It is necessary to check before construction takes place that land is sufficiently stabilized and a minimum of five years is essential between the enclosure and the construction of buildings.

Then water- and sewage-disposal problems follow and it is necessary to ensure, through a complicated system of locks, the daily renewal of the city's waters. In Amsterdam the canals, which collect used water and domestic refuse are daily cleansed by the water of the Zuiderzee. The first drainage system, reserved for the floodgate waters dates from 1870 and concerned only new neighbourhoods. The decision to establish a whole network for all waste water and to connect to it the canals of the old centre dates from 1907. Until that date, at each tide one had to coordinate the action of multiple locks in order to retain fresh water at the time of the incoming tide, to introduce the sea water progressively into the canals along a well-defined circuit, and then discharge the polluted water into the Ij at the time of the outgoing tide. In addition, the Amstel had to be isolated in order to prevent the salt water of the Zuiderzee from returning to the river at high tide and reaching, upstream from the city, farming and agricultural land (the closure of the Zuiderzee was completed in 1932, the lock that isolates the Ij from the Zuiderzee following the Kalf plan).

All this has required competent technical services in order to ensure the maintenance of the works and, through providing these services, the municipality controlled the land for many centuries. The nature of the land makes organization obligatory and means that decisions on building construction are taken out of private hands. The difficulties encountered in making land usable encouraged the concentration of buildings, because their concentration guaranteed stability.

The resulting urban structure is very clear: a dense tissue cut by a network of carefully structured canals, which allow for an economical and logical distribution of space. The building typology is simple. With the exception of some public buildings constructed in stone, local materials, wood and brick, were used. The building structure, fixed by the span of a timber beam, is narrow (between 4 and 5 metres). The stable land is reached through some 10 metres of sand and mud, with piled foundations, which allow for weight concentration. There then emerged a type of multistorey construction, which continued, with some stylistic variations, until the beginning of the twentieth century. This type provided all the current functions: housing, trading and storing goods, commerce and small scale industry. The gable, which faced the

---

53 Toponymic study shows clearly the recognized origins: dam – *dam* or *schans*; embankment – *kade*; ditch – *dijk*; basin – *gracht* (a canal that allows traffic and unloading).

street, with its beam and its pulley, allowed easy access for the goods to the lofts as well as for objects and furniture to the flats; the narrow and unattractive staircases were only for people. Since the stability of each building depended on the solidity of its neighbours, since the seventeenth century the construction, and especially that of foundations, was subject to control by a municipal commission.

The more specialized buildings, such as the large warehouses of the eighteenth and nineteenth centuries and the collective homes (*beguinages*), do not escape these rules, but are activated by the addition of identical elements. The same procedure gives rise to ordinary buildings as well as to highly-specialized ones, with the exception of the prestige buildings. There is no difference in the structure between a group of buildings deriving from single initiative and an ensemble project for a whole block. The speculative housing of the end of the nineteenth century, the *revolutiebouw*, which can still be seen in the neighbourhoods of Pijp and Dapper is an example of this process.

One can understand that in such a context the application of the 1901 law happened relatively rapidly, because people were prepared better than elsewhere to accept a municipal authority, which was only extending its traditional role. Besides, even before the promulgation of the law, the municipality of Amsterdam had taken some measures that were to facilitate its application, progressively going from the control of land preparation to the complete implementation of schemes.

The year 1896 was important in this context. Faced with the extent of the works to be undertaken, which were a consequence of its economic and demographic development, Amsterdam increased its territory. On 1 May 1896, with the annexation of Nieuweramstel, the area of Amsterdam increased from 3,250 to 4,630 hectares. The plan of Berlage, which began life on the drawing board in 1903, corresponds to the urbanization of this new territory.[54] In the same year the city introduced the empty teutic lease. This meant that it retained the ownership of the land it helped make buildable, believing that, in a period of increasing land prices, the development brought about by the works must bring benefit to the public, represented by the municipality, rather than contribute to private profit. At the same time the city managed directly some firms, which had once been exploited privately, such as water distribution, telephone facilities, gas and public transport. This meant that the decision of the municipal authority to manage urbanization directly in all its forms was further confirmed by the possibility, with the housing law, to manage housing in the same way.

SPAARNDAMMERBUURT: AN EXEMPLARY EXPERIENCE

The area of Spaarndammerbuurt represents an interesting example of the extension of Amsterdam at the end of the nineteenth and beginning of the twentieth centuries.

---

54 On 1 January 1921 Amsterdam grew to 17,455 hectares (with the annexation of Waregraafsmeer, Sloter, Buiksloot, Nieuwendam).

Triangle in plan, it is situated between the western docks of the port and the railway line between Amsterdam and Haarlem (1839) and it can be considered to be part of the development of those working-class districts connected with the 1875 plan. The first built area, in the south of Spaarndammerstraat, reproduced the common type of the working-class buildings of the period, very similar to those in other districts, where the municipality adopted the road infrastructure following Kalf's plan. The realization of the buildings, which was left to private initiative, was the concern of the *revolutiebouwers*, small developers who, aiming at maximum profit in the second half of the nineteenth century, undertook the greatest part of the construction of social housing. For many years the northwest portion of the triangle remained empty. In 1881 the building of the central station by P. J. H. Cuypers (1827–1921), the architect of the Rijksmuseum, and A. L. van Gendt led to the extension of the railway and accentuated the isolation of the district, which, up until then, could have been considered as an extension of Jordaan. Very likely it was the reorganization of the port of Amsterdam in 1910 and its extension towards the west that led to the completion of the urbanization of the district. This portion, which is the only one that interests us here, was carried out in very different conditions from the previous blocks, because the 'Woningwet', the 1901 law on housing, was applied from 1905 onwards. It seemed likely that advantage was taken of this opportunity to experiment on a modest scale, with the solutions that were to be extensively applied later on in the implementation of Berlage's plan. The first hint of what we are going to discuss concerned the choice of architects.

Two of them are in the direct tradition of Berlage and belonged to the group Architectura et Amicitia. H. J. M. Walenkamp (1871–1933) built the Zaanhof estate in 1919. The other architect was K. P. C. de Bazel (1869–1923), an experienced architect, who appears as the second-in-charge after Berlage in the fight for a modern architecture in Amsterdam and who built the whole of the Sparndammerdijk/Uitgeestraat and Zaandammerplein housing.

But the first housing estate built around the Sparndammerplantsoen was carried out by a much younger architect as his first major work. Michel de Klerk (1884–1923). This architect, who was later to become the leader of the Amsterdam School, had already attracted attention with his participation in the Scheepvaarthuis project of 1911 with J. M. van der May (1878–1948) and P. L. Kramer (1881–1961). He had designed a small block of flats for a private client near Vondelpark (J. Vermeerplein). For the same client, the developer K. Hille, he drew up the plans for a block of social housing at the edge of Spaarndammerplantsoen, the first part of a larger estate. The economic difficulties brought about by World War One led the cooperative Eigen Haard to take up and continue the initiative, with de Klerk retained as architect. The design seems to link the realization of social housing, in the conditions previewed by the 1901 law, with experimentation in architecture.

Even more than the Scheepvarthuis, which remains influenced by the Jugendstijl, the realizations of de Klerk in Sparndammerbuurt constitute the first built manifesto of the Amsterdam School and its first point of reference. And it was to the de Klerk, Kramer group that, from 1920 onwards, one of the first estates of the Amsterdam South plan was entrusted, the Dageraad, which still shows the wish of Berlage and of the municipal authorities to combine, this time on a large scale, the development of the city and the building of social housing with the definition of a new architecture.

One has to remember, at this point, the role played by the theosophic circle Arquitectura et Amicitia, led, from 1893 to 1917, by Bauer, Kromhout, Bazel, Walenkamp and Lauweriks. This generation, between fifteen and twenty years older than the Amsterdam school and often called the Berlage school, had been impregnated with the socialising ideals of the Arts and Crafts and had connections with the German and American theosophical movements, which had taken on three tasks:

- to spread architectural culture through its journal, *Architectura*, later in 1918 called *Wendingen*, by organizing conferences, trips, debates, etc.;
- to reorganize the profession with the creation of the BNA (Union of Dutch Architects), where de Bazel became the first president;
- to enter into the municipal institutions (technical services and commissions for architecture), which was made easy by the arrival of the SDAP (the socialists) in power at the town hall in 1902.

The architects of the Amsterdam school, whose leaders were also theosophists, naturally and progressively took up these posts from 1912 to 1917.[55]

ARCHITECTURE AND URBAN SPACE

If we examine the various stages of implementation of the neighbourhood, many lessons can be drawn from them. Kalf's plan, which was pretty basic, took up again the layout of the principal roads and the directions of the canals of the rural subdivision (irrigation, drainage), and defined the framework of the speculative housing development, carried out between 1875 and 1877 at the same time as the extension of the docks. The axis of the area, the Sparndammerstraat, built on the northeastern part of the dike, divides the district in two parts: the docks to the north, with some houses, and the main housing development to the south.

With the extension of the port in 1910, the municipality decided to complete the construction of the neighbourhood in order to build homes for the needier classes.[56]

---

55 G. Fanelli, *Architettura moderna in Olanda 1900–1940*, Marchi e Bertolli, 1968. *Nederlande Architectuur 1893–1918: Architectura*, exhibition catalogue from the Architecture Museum, Amsterdam, 1975.

56 The decision to build 504 dwellings on four floors, which were to be let at a price below the cost price (2.40 florints rent per week, when the flats should have brought in 3.66 florinths per week, considering the cost of construction in 1914), was abandoned in 1917 as a consequence of the rise in prices after the war. From: *Amsterdam: developpement de la ville, habitations populaires*, op cit.

The available land, bounded by the railway towards the southeast and by the dike to the north, was exploited in a completely different way from the 1875 housing development. The repetition of the minimum-sized block on a regular grid contrasted with an attempt by the architects to outline some differences in the urban space in order to more clearly define the district.

At first this attempt concerned itself with the organization of roads and the location of facilities. The new centre of the district was defined by a square (Sparndammerplantsoen), carried out by de Klerk between 1914 and 1917. On the axis of Knollendamstraat, this square introduced an axis perpendicular to the original axis (Sparndammerstraat)[57] and began a shift of the centre of gravity of the neighbourhood. The establishment of businesses (on Oostzaanstraat) and new facilities (on Oostzaanstraat, Hembrugstraat and Wormerveerstraat) confirmed in practice this modification of the structure of the district.

The differences can be summarised in the following table:

Old centre	New centre
Street	Square
Predominance of shops	Predominance of public facilities

Secondly, this attempt concerned itself with the quality of the urban spaces defined by the project. In relation to the buildings of the nineteenth century, the realizations of the 1913–21 period represent a clear typological innovation. The block is no more conceived as an interchangeable unit, the consequence of cuts based on the assembling of minimal plots zoned uniformly for 'alcove' dwellings, with, possibly, some commerce on the ground floors (Sparndammerstraat). The block became a more complex organization of an area of urban land, ensuring in morphological terms the continuity of the tissue, stressing the reference points, allowing for the integration of different functions (habitat, commerce and infrastructure) and creating a variety of spaces.

The design of façades played an important role. In the realizations of the Amsterdam school, façades are determined by the external spaces to which they refer as much as by the internal disposition of the building they enclose. This led the designers to be condescendingly called 'façade architects' by those espousing a rigid modernism (Giedion). The monumental treatment of the square defined it as a special place. The post office, at the top of the block bordered by Zaanstraat, Oostzaanstraat and Hembrugstraat, played the role of a landmark and 'adorned' the square, while the technical school, on the axis of Krommeniestraat, restricts the perspective and, as a monument or facility at the scale of the district, expresses its difference from the primary schools inserted in the neighbouring blocks.

57 The original design of the square, before the interventions of A. van Eyck, made this clearer.

Finally, the relationship between blocks is marked by the common symmetries, some inflections and some correspondences, which demonstrate that the choice of special reference points is not the outcome of an isolated thinker, but the consequence of a consensus of ideas. One only has to note how the entrance of the Zaanhof (by the architect Walenkamp) is linked with the Hembrugstraat, with the concave part of the de Klerk block, or the connections of the blocks by de Bazel (around Zaandammerplein) are linked with the neighbouring streets and blocks.

It is worth observing here, how, when examining these works, one tends to judge the architects of the Amsterdam School differently from the norm. De Klerk, especially, is very often presented as an artist of exaggerated sensitivity, seized by a sort of formal delirium. The historians do not remember anything of his architecture other than his exuberance, his unusual silhouettes and his complicated brick detailing. Certainly, this exists, but the image of a solitary individualist, such as Gaudi, risks masking the reality, which is here of a profound modesty. It is the modesty of the architect facing an urban context.

The fantasies of de Klerk, Kramer and de Wijdeveld are always in correspondence with the special parts of the tissue, which they emphasise. This is not a solitary and isolated intervention, but the exploration of the city and the insertion of architecture into a context. It is also the modesty of an architect vis-à-vis other architects. In Sparndammerbuurt, where de Klerk was the first to intervene, it is hard to detect an agreement between the architects from the start. But in the implementation of the Amsterdam South plan, it is sufficient to observe the connections between the parts designed by different architects in order to understand what the word 'school' might mean: a deep adhesion to the same principles and specific agreement in their implementation, which manifests itself in the impossibility to distinguish the exact point where the intervention of one architect ends and the work of another begins.

FIVE BLOCKS

Further study of the Spaarndammerbuurt may seem superfluous unless one recalls our hypothesis that it is the case of a rehearsal, on a small scale, of the principles carried out subsequently. If we consider the five blocks built in the northwest, the main arrangements the detail, adopted later in the South Amsterdam plan, are dealt with here:

THE 'TRADITIONAL' BLOCK, MADE UP OF SEVERAL GROUPS OF BUILDING PLOTS

This is the case of the two blocks that define Spaarndammerplein, where different architects intervened (between 1913 and 1914): de Klerk for the monumental façades framing the square, others for other streets. Whatever the architects and groupings of them, there is a great difference between the fronts. On the streets or on the square the façades express an urban order, even a monumental one in some cases, while in the backs the private gardens of the lower dwellings and the balconies of the higher floors allow for extensions and alterations.

Some facilities were integrated into the blocks. The schools, located on Hembrugstraat and Wormerveerstraat, built by the architects of the technical services of the municipality, respect the logic of the block. The buildings on the streets respected the alignment and the courtyards at the back occupied the whole depth of the plot. The A block had an internal space used collectively with its exits on the street through porches (Oostzaanstraat and Krommeniestraat).

Where the block is conceived as a unit (block C by de Klerk, 1917),[58] the integration of the different functions (post office, school) was stronger. The heart of the block, beside the part occupied by the courtyard of the existing school, which occupied the biggest plot, is composed of a series of small independent gardens belonging to ground-floor dwellings. A small lane services these gardens starting from the common courtyard located behind the post office. Some dwellings have their entrances through this open-access courtyard; the difference between elevations is here less than in the garden zone or in the previous blocks. In a still embryonic way the public begins to penetrate into the interior of the block.

In the case of the two estates, Zaanhof and Zaandammerplein (D. Walenkamp, 1919 and E. de Bazel, 1919–21), the last built portion of the quarter, we find a decomposed block. In these two examples the large block is equally orientated towards its centre, formed by a public square, as towards the streets that define it. The 'layer', formed by a double thickness of building, could be considered by itself as joined up block, but it seems to us that the strongly defined unit of each of these compositions leads rather to the concept of just one block of a particular type: the *hof*, which links to the Flemish béguinage tradition and reinterprets the English experience of the close.

This is clearly visible in the Zaanhof estate, which locates a ring of high buildings on the streets while the internal space is surrounded by low buildings, which recall the small houses of the béguines. It is really only an appearance, not the reality, because each unit, which we call a house, is in fact the superimposition of two dwellings.

Planned before World War One and partly built during that period, the completion of Spaarndammerbuurt remains modest in scale when compared with subsequent realizations.[59] But the new outlook on the block on this occasion forecast, even before

---

58 There is scope for thinking with Henry-Russel Hitchcock that the different buildings carried out by Michel de Klerk had been designed together since 1913, having started with the northern edge of the square, then the southern edge and then the block of the post office itself, built in several phases and including the school. From H.-R. Hitchcock (1958), *Architecture, Nineteenth and Twentieth Centuries* (Harmondsworth: Penguin Books), and several numbers of the magazine *Wendingen* (Amsterdam).

59 The number of dwellings drops progressively from 3,772 built in 1913 to 737 in 1920, because of the war. From this last date onwards the pace of the economic activity increases: 3,178 dwellings in 1921, 6,385 in 1922 etc. From: *Amsterdam: développement de la ville, habitations populaires*, op. cit.

a

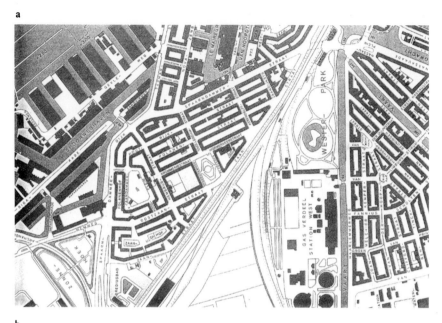

b

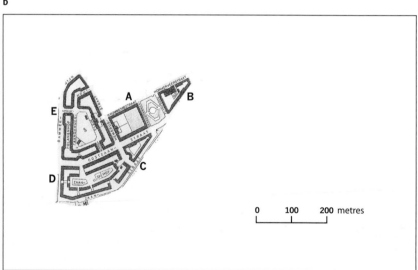

0   100   200 metres

Figure 22

Amsterdam: Spaarndammerbuurt.

a. Plan of the area.

b. Sectors designed by the following architects: M. de Klerk (A. 1913, B. 1913–14, C. 1913–17), H. J. M. Walenkamp (D. 1919), and K. P. C. de Bazel (E 1919–21).

a

b

c

Figure 23

Monumentality in domestic architecture. De Klerk: working-class housing in Spaarndammerbuurt.
a. General view.
b. Detail of the entrance of the west façade.
c. Detail of the entrance of the east façade.

the first attempts by J. J. Oud in Rotterdam, a change in the status of the internal space, which would, after the realization of Berlage's plan, lead to its destruction.

THE EXTENSION TO THE SOUTH AND THE NEW AMSTERDAM URBANISM

THE BASIS OF THE BERLAGE PLAN

It is not in the scope of this study to discuss in detail Berlage's plan, nor the difficulties of its realization. However, it would not be possible to study the blocks in detail without defining their context, i.e. without some investigation of the overall structure proposed for the southern quarters and examining two problems: the connection with the existing city and the layout of the new quarters.

The nineteenth-century development, based on Kalf's plan, shows the preference for an orthogonal system and the abandonment of the radiocentric layout. The solution to the geometrical problem lay in the mastering of the junction of the two directions of this new system. Evaded by Kalf, the problem was solved in a monumental way in 1889 by Eduard Cuypers with the Rijksmuseum and the development associated with the surrounding avenues and esplanades. Nevertheless, this local action left unsolved the problem of the connection of a new tissue with the nineteenth-century developments.

The first Berlage project (1903), based on the idea of a garden city separated from the existing city by a park, was rejected because of its insufficient density. The second project, presented in 1916, was approved by the municipal authorities in 1917 for the portion within the internal administrative perimeter of the city (the 1896 limits); the territorial extension of 1921 allowed it to be extended to completion.

Globally, the extension to the south presents itself as an autonomous whole, which is connected to the old city across the nineteenth-century quarters. Berlage deliberately ignored the orthogonal grid of Kalf's plan, the rural plot subdivision, and organized the new quarters as a city, which has its own structure defined by the large scale layout of the roads and which seeks to achieve an order similar to the canal order of the old city.

The autonomy of the new quarters, which appeared clearer in the project than in its realization, is confirmed by the position of the proposed Minerva station, meant to be at the southern edge of the plan, which was never built and which would have given meaning to the principal axes. The new station is related to the old one to the north of the old city, while Minervalaan relates to Damrak. The Amstelkanaal surrounds the new city in the same way as the bastioned enclosure of the seventeenth century closed the city. Berlage takes here up again the same principles as in the extension plans of the Hague (1908) and Purmerend (1911): a clear structure of the new quarters, a clear-cut separation from the old development and a station opposed to the old city.

a

railway   Oostzanstraat

b

c

0   10   20
|__|__|__| metres

d

Figure 24

M. de Klerk: Block C in Spaarndammerbuurt, successive sections showing variations in the internal spaces.
a. School courtyard in the centre of the block.
b. Central lane and private gardens.
c. Entrance in the back court of the post office.
d. Block seen from Zaanstraat, the post office.

a

b

c

Figure 25

M. de Klerk: Block C in Spaarndammerbuurt.
a. Façade on Zaanstraat.
b. Rear façade of the dwellings on the Zaanstraat: the balcony, protected from street views, is the substitute for the back garden.
c. Drawing by M. de Klerk for the Hernbrugstraat façade.

a

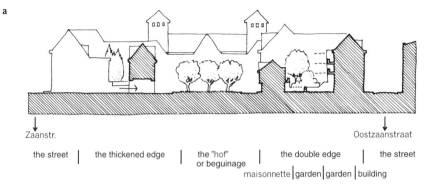

Zaanstr.				Oostzaanstraat
the street	the thickened edge	the "hof" or beguinage	the double edge	the street
			maisonnette │garden│garden │building	

b

Figure 26
H. J. M. Walenkamp: Block D in Spaarndammerbuurt.
a. Overall section.
b. The internal space: Zaanhof, the low houses are grouped around the square and re-interpret the traditional Flemish *béguinage*.

If we examine all the projects for the extension of Amsterdam,[60] where the southern part is but just one element, the negation of the nineteenth-century city planning appears even more evident.

60 The report on a similar plan of the projects established in the different quarters, published in the collection edited on the occasion of the seventh century of Amsterdam, confirms our earlier hypotheses on this point.

The old city became the centre for a pattern that comprised four satellite sectors: West Amsterdam, on the area of Watergraafsmeer, where the garden city built by D. Greiner, is but a minimal portion; Amsterdam South, the object of our study; Amsterdam East, on the area of Boos en Lommer, where the main axis, Hoofweg-Mercatorplein, was built from 1925 onwards; and Amsterdam North, which connects the garden cities of Buiksloterham and Niewndammerham. The segments of this pattern are separated by major barriers: the Amstel, the Wondelpark in the south, the Ij and the port infrastructure to the north – the developments of the nineteenth century.

CONTINUITY AND RUPTURES

Two clearly defined parts are apparent that are separated by canals (Boerenwetering, Overdam) and by the Beatrixpark. To the east there is the plan in the shape of a Y connected to the Amstel and, to the west, a grouping, whose structure is not very clear today, which is dominated by the Minervalaan/Stadionweg crossing.

The continuity of the southern quarters with the nineteenth-century city is ensured for functional access reasons: the continuity of roads and sewers. To the east, the system of secondary roads – Rijnstraat, Maasstraat, Scheldestraat – roughly parallel to the Amstel ensures an adequate connection with the radial roads of the old city and serves as a support for the commerce and facilities of the district. To the west, because of the change of direction of the nineteenth-century quarters and the barrier of Vondelpark, the connections are more difficult and give rise to a series of crossroads in the shape of Y to the north of the Amstelkanaal (a system formed by Beethovenstraat/Coenenstraat/Ruloffstraat/Roelofhartplein/Jacob Obrectplein), or by monumental changes of direction (Minervalaan, Olympiaplein).

In this way the plan shows the image of a double system, which combines monumental effects: to the east a crow's foot, a trident to the west and more discreet continuities with the old linear layout to the east (and perpendicular to the monumental axis), more punctual to the west, leading back to Lairesstraat.

Even though Berlage's plan begins more to the north, we have located on the Amstelkanaal the rupture between the nineteenth-century city and the extension to the south. The toponymy confirms the morphological analysis stopping on this line the old south (Oud Zuid), different from the new south (Niew Zuid). In fact, when Berlage took on his extension, the city did not present a homogeneous face. For technical as well as aesthetic reasons, the first task was to deal with the completion of the old south before starting the implementation of the new south.

These technical reasons were: the Amstelkanaal, which plays an essential role in land drainage and defines the southern edge of the immediately constructible zones. Once the project was approved (1917), the blocks situated to the north were first completed, because, in order to ensure land stability, it was forbidden to leave gaps. These were all

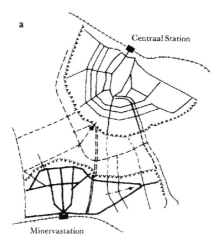

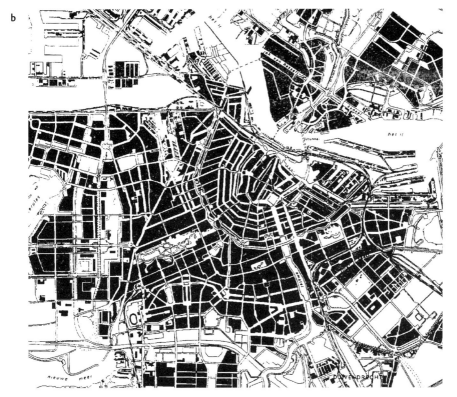

Figure 27

Amsterdam: plan of the districts south of the historic centre of Amsterdam.

a. Plan of Berlage's scheme of 1916.

b. Present situation. Even though Berlage's plan was not entirely carried out, the essential elements of his scheme are visible today.

75

a

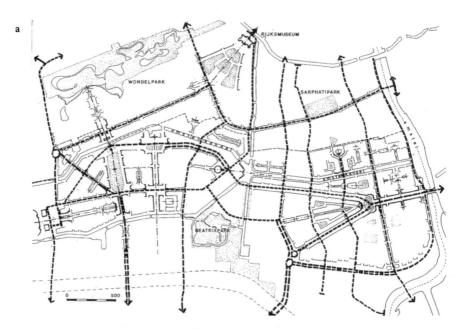

b

Figure 28

Amsterdam: the Berlage Plan as executed (1917–40).
a. The geometrical adapted to the site.
b. The present state (1975 cadastral plan).
The secondary roads extend the nineteenth-century layout.

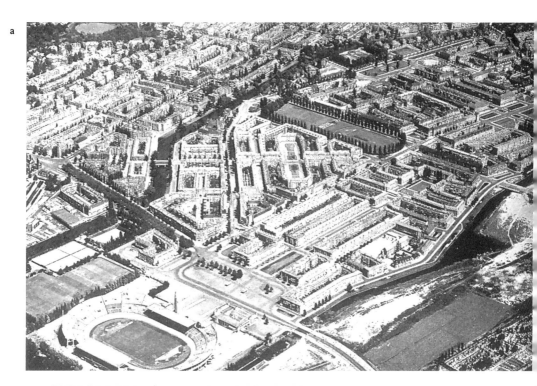

a

b

Figure 29

South Amsterdam: the Berlage Plan in 1940.
a. Area of the Olympic stadium (west part).
b. Amstellaan area (east part).

small projects carried out at the edge of the nineteenth-century city between 1917 and 1920 on a line comprising Krusemanstraat, de Lairessestraat, Baerlestraat, Roelofhartstraat, Lutmastraat and Tolstraat. From this line and on the Amstelkanaal, a series of larger operations were launched in 1920–1: Bertelmenplein (van Epen), Harmoniehof (van Epen), followed by Schwarzenplein/Henriette Ronnerplein (de Klerk, Kramer, etc.), Smaragd (van Epel and Gratama).

For aesthetic reasons Berlage was concerned to surround it with a clear space and hide the old layout. The Amstelkanaal became a promenade, with both banks developed. Locally the squares were improved: Roelofhartplein, Cornelis Troostplein and de Kejserplein organize the old and new tissues and bring the barrier to a line, where the Amstelkanaal is visible and can be controlled.[61]

Next, the portion between the Amstelkanaal and the base of the Y (Rijnstraat/ Vrijheidslaan north, 1921–4) was started, followed by the Marathonweg (1922–4). This phase, which was marked by the 1924 International Town Planning Conference, was then followed by a slack period, when few building sites were operating. The Amsterdam Olympic games (1928) were the occasion for relaunching the implementation of the south plan. The monumental axes, the southern and central portion of the Y (1927–8), Minervalaan (1928) and the stadium district (1927–8) were completed.

The consequences of the 1929 crisis brought a new halt to construction activity, apart from the launch of a few projects. Building activity started again from 1933: the completion of the eastern sector between the Y and Kennedylaan (1933–9) and the completion of the nonmonumental parts of the western sector. Some parts, such as the edge of Beatrixpark, were not completed until after World War Two. The various interruptions were to be marked by changes in the architecture. If the first phase (1918–24) showed some realizations conforming to Berlage's plan and was recognized by the exuberance of architects such as de Klerk, Kramer, Staal, Wijdeveld and Van Epen, the second one (1926–39) rather implemented serial developments, with a systematic application of blocks, layout principles and dwellings distribution by less well-known architects: Rutgers, Warners, Westerman. Finally, during and after the crisis, the Amsterdam School suffered from attacks by the functionalist architects. The first demonstration of this is the school of Duiker (1930), who introduced a different concept of the block. This concept, which was tentatively shown at the edge of the south plan by the open blocks of Kennedylaan, was to flourish in the Boos en Lommer district (Landlust).

MORPHOLOGICAL STRUCTURE AND ARCHITECTURAL MODELS

Less sensitive in its implementation than in the project, the south extension is principally conceived as the superimposition of a large scale layout on a neutral

---

61 Beside the important interventions on the edges of the Amstelkanaal (1918–20) the 're-infilling' was carried out in two periods. One came before the launching of the large works (the period 1917–21, of which we have already written) and the completion of older projects, such as the Willem Park Estate and some punctual interventions (1910–20 period). Another portion was carried out later, such as the completion of the Roelofhartplein (1925–9).

road network, connected to the old tissue in the eastern sector. This structure, which links the global and intermediate levels, makes the division between the eastern and western sectors legible; it also marked social differences with a working-class majority to the east and more bourgeois districts to the west. As discussed above, this difference is emphasized by the house types and the participation of different architects.

The monumental system is based on simple, classical figures: symmetry, alignment and façade arrangements. The treatment of corners emphasizes symmetry and indicates the hierarchy of the respective roads. This system stresses the autonomy of the southern districts on the plan of location and distribution and does not refer directly to any facilities except for the stadium (and the proposed Minerva station). The secondary system ensures continuity, but, with the exception of Rijnstraat, its perspectives are deliberately broken. As a support for the facilities (churches, administrative buildings) and commerce, it is not globally legible, but continuously refers back to the monumental system, especially so in the corner treatment.

Both these two systems define a grid framework occupied by groups of blocks. The position of self-contained projects, i.e. those belonging to a defined detailed plan, reveals some spatial models, which do not only follow the orientation of Berlage's, but seem to propose a language common to all architects working in the southern sector. The exceptions are those functionalist tendencies that emerged after 1930.

The grid, resulting from the superimposition of the two systems, was not uniformly applied. At times the interventions conformed to the monumental system, and the same architect was put in charge of the buildings surrounding a square or on both sides of an avenue. At other times the interventions led to some self-contained groupings, with their own character and, usually, centred on an internal square accommodating schools with little connection to the overall structure. Their local character is shown by porches, passages under buildings, twists and turns, which separated part of their road system from the overall network. With the exception of the Marathonweg/B. Kochstraat, these interventions are never on the axes of a secondary road, i.e. the middle level appeared as a resulting outcome and did not have a generative role in the development of the tissue.

THE AMSTEL BLOCK

THE A PRIORI AND THE A POSTERIORI BLOCKS

In assessing the interventions and the plot subdivisions, it is noticeable that the block is not a unity in the architectural project. Except for a few cases, it was always carried out in several parts by different architects, who tended to build on both sides of the road rather than a whole block. Nevertheless, in Amsterdam, one would not be able to reduce the concept of block to the resulting a posteriori subdivision. The Amstel block imposes itself as a recognisable type, i.e. a common tool or spatial organization

Figure 30
South Amsterdam: characteristic urban space.
a–b. Monumental landmarks.
c–d. Intimate spaces.

about which a consensus has been established and where it is possible to list its qualities and describe its evolution.

This consensus is shown in the way different architects work side by side, a common modesty towards the urban space and a sensitive treatment of street façades, where the effects are never gratuitous, but always refer to an urban location (e.g. corner symmetry) and where the juxtapositions are the result of a consensus. There is a corresponding modesty towards the internal space of the block and a respect for the plot structure agreement on the orientation of the façades, etc. The basis, set out by Berlage's plan and the recommendations of the building developers[62]on the organization of the dwellings and their plans, certainly facilitated the architects' work and produced a consensus. But it is not possible to explain only through external constraints the aspect, at times regular and at times varied, of the adopted layouts. The Amsterdam School, besides being in possession of a formal repertory, which is its mark and to which one is inclined to limit it, is perhaps the last movement favouring an urban architecture. In Amsterdam this urban architecture is founded on the concept of the block.

The blocks, built in a group by one architect or resulting from the grouping of buildings carried out by different designers show precise qualities, which we can link together to form an abstract object: the type. The Amstel block is formed by a continuous perimeter of buildings, which encircle a central – usually rectangular, unbuilt space, its width varying between 40 and 45 metres up to 60 metres in some cases. Its height is of four floors, sometimes three. A supplementary attic floor contains the 'cellars', prohibited in the basement. The buildings are made of brick. Overall, the block juxtaposes two opposing concepts:

- long sides/corners;
- edge/centre (or exterior/interior).

These contrasts determine a different status for each segment of the space and this status is morphologically expressed and reinforced in practice.

THE CORNER PROBLEM

Because of its size, the block poses a delicate problem for solving the ends because: it is too narrow for easily ensuring continuity around the corners. Two solutions are used: one is not to build on the short side and to prolong the row of houses up to the street; the other consists of returning a series of plots on the short side of the block.

Up to 1917 this latter solution was the more frequently used. It created a rupture in the continuity of façades and made the end different from the long sides of the block. This difference, the fact that the end building could open up on three sides, favoured unusual buildings, but did not meet with the desire of the architects of the Amsterdam School to resolve completely the architectural problem in relation to the urban space. The problem was quite clear here: to ensure the continuity of façades while, especially on principal roads, stressing that special point of the tissue, the corner.

62 The building contractors applied the prescriptions of the housing law of 1901. The 1905 municipal by-laws, following the law, fixed the number of floors to four for the whole of the city, in order to avoid the superimposition of too large a number of families, to avoid any suspicion of descent into a dangerous promiscuity; then (1912 by-law) its height was fixed to three floors in the Amsterdam North buildings, then to two (1919 by-law) for the garden cities. In parallel, the municipality established some model types in order to avoid 'flats', which were considered dangerous, because of the staircase common to several families, and to favour instead the overlapping of dwellings so that each had an individual entrance at ground-floor level.

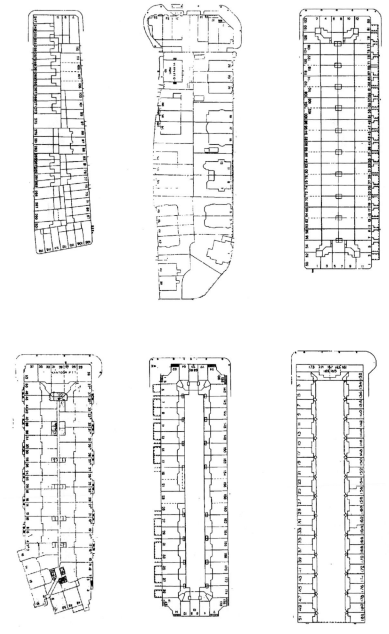

Figure 31

Variations of the Amstel block.

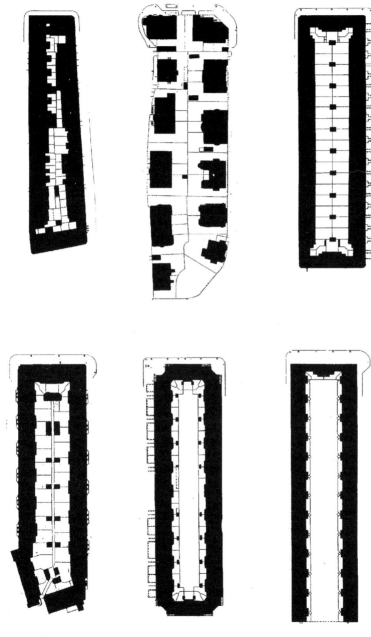

Figure 31 (Cont'd)
Variations of the Amstel block.

Because the block had been broken up by several interventions, the layout of the corner plots made it difficult to ensure a consistent façade treatment. The problem was eased when the same architect dealt with the whole block, or at least with a sufficient part of it to keep central, as the staircase layout was able to accommodate a change in direction over a sufficient number of plots. The principle of private gardens was retained and gave rise to a sometimes acrobatic layout in order to give access to a shed from all ground-floor dwellings. From the street side, the corner is celebrated with a variety of effects, such as raising the building or, in contrast, lowering the roofs, which may cover many floors, successive recesses in the façades, monumental treatments etc. This picturesque symmetry, used in Amsterdam, leads to a competition between facing blocks.

Because of these layouts, the corner dwellings are different, smaller cells, with special plans. Because of its strategic position in the tissue when combined with the particularities of the spatial organization, the corner is the chosen place for establishing commerce. The architectural treatment links up here with space planning by assigning a special status to crossroads.

PERIMETER/CENTRE

Driven by a wish to give each working-class family an individual dwelling, the housing units reproduce to the greatest possible extent the characteristics of the traditional Dutch house with a ground floor directly open to the street, a small garden at the back and a room on the first floor. In the blocks of Berlages's plan, the buildings provide direct access to all dwellings from the street, private gardens for ground-floor dwellings and balconies on the back for the upper-floor units. As far as possible, the duplex is preferred to the flat, because it reinstates internally the layout of the traditional house. The contrast between edge and centre indicates the pursuit of tradition. The morphological qualities refer to life as lived in the dwellings with precise qualities given to the different elements.

External	Internal
façade on street	façade and garden
continuous and special	fragmented and ordinary
accessible	nonaccessible
urban reference	reference to dwelling
representation	private life
exposed	hidden
the architect's input	the inhabitants' input

The centre, i.e. the group of gardens, plays a double role. In isolation, each garden is a private back space for the ground-floor dwelling; collectively the group of gardens forms a courtyard, which is not accessible from the upper-floor dwellings. The struc-

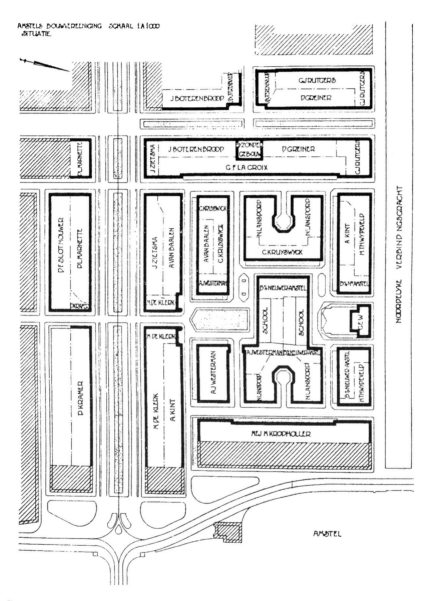

Figure 32
The distribution of the development between different architects.
If in Amsterdam the block is the basic unit of the tissue, it only rarely corresponds to the unit of the project. The division of interventions and their attribution to different architects is carried out following a logic that takes into account the control of public spaces: avenues, squares, crossroads, ends of perspective views etc. Here an area is shown near the Amstel, designed by a group of architects under the coordination of J. Gratama, former associate of Berlage.

ture of the built areas – strongly marked by the narrow alternating projecting bays, which correspond to the staircases and the kitchens, and wide bays, corresponding to the balcolnies – helps identify the individual dwellings. Appropriation is shown by the definition of the gardens or of their substitutes (the balconies) through objects, decoration, paving, flowers etc.,[63] and goes as far as the construction of penthouses, greenhouses and sheds for tools or domestic animals, linking with the Dutch tradition of the hut at the end of the plot. Sometimes this last element is taken on board by the architect and constructed in order to be permanent.

On the street, the façade, dominated by the composition of the architect, makes reference to the urban quality of architecture. In spite of this, the mark of the inhabitant inserts itself discreetly in the window composition. The living room, which in Holland is often open-plan, even in modest dwellings, is indicated by a more important bay than the other rooms. The façade is dealt with in its thickness on the principle of the bay window. This intermediate space, sometimes reduced to a minimum overhang, functions as the place where one shows oneself. The division of the bay into fixed and opening parts favours this: shelves with souvenirs, curtains and panes, which frame the views, cactus etc., turning the window on the street into a veritable shop window. Indeed, in the local shops, the shop window has the same dimensions as a living room window. Because the organization of the plan lends itself to transformation, the ground floor can easily be transformed into a shop. On the contrary, some badly placed shops have become dwellings. Borssenburgstraat and Amstelkade, among others, are examples of this practice.

THE LOSS OF DIFFERENCES

The organization that we have just described is repeated with minimum variations on the whole of the Amsterdam south plan, as in other parts of the city and in other cities. It appears to be a constant, something that had only few exceptions before 1930. Among these, we will consider here those that relate to the status of the central space, because its evolution, already forecast at Spaarndammerbuurt, would lead to important modifications after that date.

The need for the back garden to function like that of a traditional house led to the creation of a lane, which allows for direct access to resolve the problem of bicycles. The internal space is no more formed only by elements pertaining to each dwelling, but there is now a collective space: like the lane servicing some common spaces (maintenance, storage). Although protected by a covered passage or by a barrier, the internal space becomes more generally accessible.

---

63 The status of the back garden is multiple. It can be an additional room in the open air, marked by paving, a bench, some statues, as representations of nature and of places for gardening, a space for storage and odd jobs (toolshed, clothes drying, hutches). Dutch tradition allows the integration of these different aspects in a very restricted, carefully organized and well-kept space. When in France, the contrast dirty/clean confirms the contrast between hidden/in evidence here, with the exception of the most marginal population, the dirty is repainted every year.

a

b

c

Figure 33
Internal spaces.
Completely isolated from the street, the internal space is a place for trees and silence, allowing for individual use, especially on ground floors (a, b). From 1930 onwards, the opening of the block and the creation of a common garden, accessible and visible from the street, lessened the differentiation between fronts and backs and sterilized the central space (c).

In parallel, another variation involved reducing the dimensions of individual gardens and creating a common space in the centre, usually planted, to reduce overlooking. This provided a play area for children, especially for those who lived on the upper floors, who, up till then, had been less favoured than those of the ground floor. This garden, which was accessible from the dwellings, is rarely accessible from the street.

These two modifications bring us a new concept of the block, where the centre, occupied by a collective garden, is accessible from the street through a passage, which can be controlled and kept closed. The reduced contrast between the exterior and interior makes for a more complex relationship of the perimeter (street façade/garden façade) and the centre.

Perimeter		Centre
street façade	internal façade and garden	
continuous and special	fragmented and ordinary	continuous and organized
accessible	nonaccessible	accessible and controlled
urban reference	reference to the dwelling	reference to the block
representation	private life	representation and collective practices
displayed	hidden and exposed	exposed
the architect's input	the inhabitants' input	the architect's input

The idea of the central garden appears also in complex organizations, where several blocks are associated following the principles tried out in the Zaanhof. The perimeter split in two with high buildings to the exterior and small houses around the garden. The Harmoniehof, carried out by Van Epen, is the most developed example of this idea. This model evolves to accommodate in its centre some facilities: a library at Cooperatiehof, a school and public baths at Smaragdplein. The difference between the interior of the block and a small square became blurred.

The third phase in the disintegration of the block happened after 1930, as part of the evolution process. The central space increased so that the individual gardens became simple balconies. At the same time, the duplex was abandoned in favour of the apartment, i.e. there was no longer a difference between the ground and upper floors. Finally, because of hygienic concerns, the south end of the block, which was exposed to the internal space, was suppressed. The role of representation/planting of this end became more important than simply that of a central space.

The last step was taken at Amsterdam south extension in 1934 with the buildings of artists' studios in Zomerdijkstraat by Zanstra, Glesen and Sijmons.[64] The building, a simple structure of six floors, was not conceived within a tissue, the built-up area did no more than give rise to an external space. The southern façade contained the access and the loggias or balconies, which were at the same time spaces for display as well as private extensions of the living rooms. The arrangement of space was based solely on a solar orientation.

The Hague, with the Nirvana building by J. Duiker (1926–9) and Rotterdam with the Bergpolder building by J. A. Brinkman and L. C. van der Vlugt 1932–4), had preceded Amsterdam in the practice of abandoning the concept of the urban block. The appointment of Van Eesteren to the direction of the town planning services (1930) well symbolises Amsterdam's rallying to the new ideals and the abandonment of the principles that, since Berlage, had guided the development of the city and its architecture. With the decline of the Amsterdam School at the beginning of the thirties, Holland no more had the driving role it had ten years earlier. For some years already it had been towards Weimar's Germany that the avant-garde were looking. Nineteen twenty-four had been for Amsterdam the opportunity of a demonstration for which the 'International Congress for the construction of cities' had given the pretext. Nineteen twenty-nine, with the second CIAM congress, if for only a short time, marked the importance of Frankfurt.

64 The case of the J. F. Staal tower on the Victorieplein (1929–32) is more ambiguous: limiting the monumental perspective, it offers very visible contrasting aspects, with the back looking out onto the almost private small square. There is the abandonment of the block, certainly, but also a clearly stated urban integration.

CHAPTER 4
THE NEW FRANKFURT AND ERNST MAY:
1925–30

Frankfurt was, once implemented, the dream of the architects of the Modern Movement. It showed what could be achieved with control over development, industrialized construction and social housing. In comparison with only thirty dwellings by Le Corbusier at Pessac, at Frankfurt 15,000 were built. It is also consciously experimented with the block, making it disappear and be replaced by another type of urban form – from which we are only now with great difficulty managing to escape. The link between municipal urban policy and architecture reached here a degree rarely equalled in other German cities. This is why we have thought it important to spend some time on it.

HOUSING POLICY AND CITY PLANNING IN FRANKFURT

The activity of Ernst May in Frankfurt corresponded exactly to the happiest period of the Weimar Republic, a time of economic prosperity. In order to appreciate the importance of the achievements in the field of construction, one has to consider Germany's situation at the end of World War One. As a consequence of the military defeat and the abdication of the emperor, the first crisis, a political one in 1918–21, witnessed the collapse of the economy in an atmosphere of brutality, marked by the repeated and violent confrontations between political groups that ended with the crushing of the revolutionary parties.[65] Then, while industrial production progressively improved, inflation accelerated to enter, from 1922 onwards, into a crazy[66] spiral. The political crisis was succeeded by a monetary crisis, which ended only in 1924 with the complete reorganization of the German finances by the Stresemann government through the creation of the Renten Mark, loans from foreign countries and the control of credit.

Dependent on the economic conditions, construction did not really recover until that time. Beforehand, political action and escape into utopia were the only possible routes for architecture.[67] If we take into account the war years, ten years separated the first

---

65 The repression of the socialists and the communists, who were anxious to establish a socialist republic in the image of the young USSR, consecrated the alliance of the social democracy and the right. In the large cities the climate called for a civil war, rioting (Spartakists and communists in Berlin in January 1919 and March 1919 and in Bavaria in 1919, the extreme right in Bavaria in 1920), a ferocious repression by the army and the militia of Noske (1,200 dead in Berlin in March 1919, 500 gunned down in Munich in April), murders (Rosa Luxembourg and Karl Liebknecht, Kurt Eisner, Gustav Landauer in 1919, Erzberger in 1921; Walter Rathenau I in 1922). For the relationships between the political situation and architectural movements, see B. Miller-Lane (1968), *Architecture and Politics in Germany 1918–1945* (Cambridge, MA: Harvard University Press).
66 At the beginning of June 1922, the dollar equalled 317 marks, in December 8,000, in June 1923 100,000, at the beginning of September 1923 100,000, in November 4,200 milliards.
67 For this see M. Tafuri (1972) in the magazine *VH 101* (Paris), pp. 7–8.

works of the Werkbund in establishing a theory of the industrial city – the Gros-Stadt – from the restart of construction. During that interval architecture changed its face. The international avant-gardes – de Stijl, constructivism, Dada – broke definitively with any neoclassical or neo-regional points of reference. From 1923 onwards, the Bauhaus moved towards the international movement while in France Le Corbusier and the Esprit Nouveau worked in the same direction.

Economic prosperity went together with faith in the technical possibilities of construction. The need for social housing was great since nothing had been built for ten years and this need prompted a search for new solutions. Industrialization was not only an abstract architects' dream, but the indispensable condition for a rapid resolution of the housing crisis, which had been made more urgent by the industrial reorganization and the population concentration that came as its consequence. The Werkbund, which regulated the relationships between architects and German industry, regained an important role after the war. It assembled, coordinated and created such opportunities for experimentation as the Weissenhof exhibition (Stuttgart 1922), which it organized.

In some social-democratic municipalities such as Frankfurt, the period 1925–30 demonstrated a considerable effort towards social housing and the tackling of urban problems. The dependency of the German economy on American capital (the loan of 1924) made Germany the first European country to feel the 1929 crisis. By 1930 the recession had arrived and with it the rise of Nazism, which put a final full stop to the experiments of the Weimar republic.

Frankfurt, as an important industrial city, had increased in population since the nineteenth century and, as a consequence, had seen the construction of new housing areas on the periphery following layouts which followed the haussmannien model. They included bourgeois buildings along avenues in light and airy districts and '*Miet-Kazerne*', containing small dwellings for the working class. The whole development was subjected to a process of speculation, which attempted to limit the application of Adickes laws (1902), which had given the municipalities the possibility of buying land and thus intervening in the housing market.

In spite of the incidents that marked the first years of the Weimar Republic, the working-class movement remained powerful and the unions continued to be well organized. Under their pressure the social-democratic municipality of Frankfurt established the objective of carrying out large-scale social housing developments and provided itself with the necessary technical means and land resources.

The town planning office, which was organized under the direction of the architect Ernst May, provided a public service of architecture and city planning whose duties went beyond providing sketch schemes and development control of projects. The concentration of powers and the means of implementation in the municipality avoided both a dispersal of responsibilities and any gaps between different levels of intervention. With the status of *Stadtbaurat*, Ernst May participated in making muni-

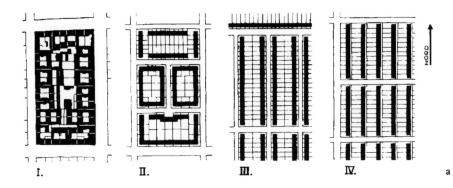

I.   II.   III.   IV.   a

b

Figure 34
Ernst May: *Das neue Frankfurt.*
a. E. May, layouts illustrating the evolution of the urban block (*Das neue Frankfurt,* 1930).
b. Siedlung Römerstadt.

cipal city planning policy and, in charge of the technical services, he implemented this policy through the master plan of Frankfurt.[68] This provided him with an opportunity to apply to his home town the results of his planning experiments in Breslau (1919–24). He ensured the implementation of those parts of the plan that corresponded to the urban extensions, while Adolf Meyer, the former associate of Gropius, was in charge of the town centre. In the interventions of Ernst May there is no rupture between decisions and realizations. The organizational skills and competence of the technical services allowed interventions to take place at all scales, including:

- land acquisition;
- planning of details: the plans of the main Siedlungen were the work of groups of municipal architects, who were sometimes associated with independent architects;[69]
- construction: the municipality established factories for prefabrication and carried out experiments with materials such as lightweight concrete;
- financing of construction (see below);
- management of implementation: technical assistance and quality control for the Siedlungen that were built by private companies and direct management of projects for municipal cooperatives;
- information for the public: as in Breslau, but on a larger scale, May founded a magazine, *Das neue Frankfurt*, which regularly presented the projects and the realizations in Frankfurt, but also the experiments in modern architecture of other German and foreign cities and devoted much space to international culture, including artistic experiments, theatre, cinema, pedagogy and sports.[70]

In addition to technical advice, the estate and finance service helped in the construction of social housing in many other ways:

- by land policies.[71] At the time of the launching of the Nidda project, the city already owned 45 per cent of the land and it proceeded to acquire the rest by expropriation or exchange. Land acquired in this way and on which speculation could no longer take place, was allocated for housing so that land costs (including services and a share of public infrastructure), project fees

68 Put in charge of the master plan of the agglomeration, Ernst May was constrained by the limits of the communal land; this explains the 'unfinished state' of some Siedlungen, but the principle of decentralization led him to regional planning and the creation of satellite towns in a zone that goes from Wiesbaden to Harau and from Darmstadt to Nauheim.
69 The technical services defined eighteen types of basic unit that could be extended. In order to respond to the immediate crisis, they constructed many small two-room dwellings, which, when later combined, could form larger dwellings (of four rooms), and they made some rooms of the family dwellings independent in order to allow subletting. See E. May (1930), 'La politique de l'habitation à Francfort' in *L'Architecte* (Paris), January; E. May (1930), 'Fünf Jahre Wohnungsbautätigkeit' in *Das neue Frankfurt* (Francfort), No. 7–8, February–March (also see in the annexe, p., E. May collaborators in Frankfurt).
70 Imitating Frankfurt, other cities started new magazines: *Das neue München, Das neue Leipzig, Das neue Berlin, Das Bild* (Hamburg); the first years of the *Architecture d'Aujourd'hui* (up to the beginning of the World War Two) owed a great deal to *Das neue Frankfurt*.
71 Land would be expropriated after arbitration at 3.5 MK per square metre against the 15 MK requested, the market gardeners giving up land situated on the sites of the Siedlungen for the new plots, grouped in the valley (the river had been channeled), which form green wedges between the old town and the extensions.

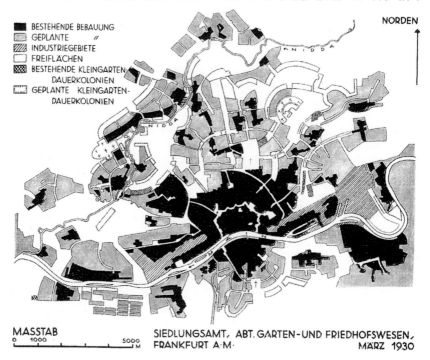

Figure 35
Ernst May, plan of Frankfurt (*Das neue Frankfurt*, n. 2/3, 1930).
The old city becomes the centre of an urban system, which integrates the nearby villages and the new areas of social housing.

and loan interests, represented less than 25 per cent of the total cost of the dwelling.

- financing and management. Although it never amounted to 100 per cent, the participation of the municipality was nonetheless very large; it acted directly, through the agency of municipal cooperative societies and through loans to private cooperative societies, which were often managed by unions. Public support was provided in the form of government loans at low interest rates (3 per cent, sometimes even 1 per cent), through loans from savings banks, through subsidies and through loan guarantees.

Faith in the principles and pride in the realizations culminated in the choice of Frankfurt as the site of the second CIAM congress of 1929.

THE SIEDLUNGEN OF FRANKFURT

Urgent needs lead to speed. In Amsterdam fifteen years had gone past between the decision to put Berlage in charge of the extension and the beginning of its implementation. In Frankfurt, a year after he was put in charge of the technical services May established a short- and long-term building programme, with a master plan for the whole of the agglomeration and detailed plans that allowed the start of the first interventions.

In three years (1926–8), 8,000 social dwellings were ready or on site, while a second programme, worked out in 1928, planned the building, in the three following years, of 16,000 new dwellings.[72] This programme was not just the response to a necessity: its implementation followed closely the master plan of Frankfurt, which defined the possible sites in relation to land policy and proposed, together with housing, industrial sites and green zones.

The principles guiding the master plan essentially were those of May's projects for the extension of Breslau (1921 and 1924), which were notable for their refusal to perpetuate a radio-concentric development pattern and a concern to introduce some green areas into the city. This dispersed development (*trabantenprinzip*) linked to the experience of Unwin in Hampstead Garden Suburb, in which May had participated. It also connected with the theoretical projects of 1922–6, which had seen the blossoming in Germany of the satellite cities schemes, influenced by the ideas of Howard, and the works of the Werkbund, such as those of A. Räding, B. Taut and P. Wolf, which were known from German and foreign publications.[73] This development pattern was concerned with the practice of zoning a concentration of industries along the River Main to the east and west of the old city with administration and commerce in the centre and housing on the periphery.

The Siedlungen were not conceived as the autonomous villages of a pastoral community following the model of the American 'colonies', which had inspired Ebenezer Howard. They were rather the housing districts of a large industrial city. A public transport network linked them to the centres and to the work zones and only a minimum of facilities, meeting the most basic needs, was provided locally.

May wanted to preserve the urban unity. Even though he criticized nineteenth-century city planning, he was nonetheless deeply connected to Frankfurt's history and its centre was carefully planned, as is demonstrated by the project for the quays of the Main. It was certainly not a 'Plan Voisin' for Frankfurt. The green zones, made up of rural land, areas of market gardens, forests and public parks, were for him a means to structure an agglomeration that was too large for continuous development, but whose existence was

---

72 The annual breakdown is the following:

1926	2,200 dwellings	
1927	3,000 dwellings	+ 200 temporary ones
1928	2,500 dwellings	+ 100 temporary ones
Total	7,700 dwellings	+ 300 temporary ones

The 1928 programme was brutally halted in 1930 with the dismissal of May following the shift of political power in the municipality.

73 See C. Purdom, *The Building of Satellite Cities*; P. Wolf (1926), *Wohnung und Siedlung, Berlin* (E. Wasmuth).

not to be denied. Discontinuous growth and typological innovation were the result of this logic of urban development, which derived its origins from the whole city. The Römerstadt Siedlung specifically shows the relationship, established by May, between the city and its extensions. Its name, which recalls its Roman origins, of which Frankfurt was proud, the 'rampart', which established a dialogue with the enclosure of the fortifications of the old city above the Nidda valley and the nineteenth-century suburbs.

THE PLAN FOR THE NIDDA VALLEY

Although only a portion of it was implemented, the Nidda valley project shows the clearest application of May's principles. To the northwest of Frankfurt before the first foothills of the Taunus, the River Nidda, flowing into the Main downstream from the city, creates a valley, which is quite shallow and partly liable to flooding. It is punctuated by the villages of Rodelheim, Hausen, Praunheim and Hedderheim. In 1925 the suburbs of Frankfurt reached the river at only one point, on the road to Hedderheim, leaving a large piece of land free between the villages and the city.

The work undertaken by May consisted of giving a form and status to this piece of land, which became a public park in the image of the large London parks. Around the park the villages, linked by the Siedlungen, formed a planned ring, punctuated by secondary open spaces. The gardens and the lanes formed a continuous system, independent of the road system, which anticipated the seven-routes theory, which Le Corbusier was to apply thirty years later in Chandigarh.

May tried first to define clearly the edge of the park. The Römerstadt, Praunheim and Westhausen Siedlungen enclose it to the north, but the project planned to isolate the park from the nineteenth-century suburbs with a belt of small Siedlungen in order to control completely the edges of the city. The Höhenblick, Raimundstrasse and Miquelstrasse Siedlungen can be understood only as part of a global vision, since, located at the edges of the development, they are the initial section of this new 'front' on the park. The project of the Nidda valley, in fact, started on the nineteenth-century boulevards as an extension of the botanical garden and of the Grüneburg Park.

The present city gives only a faint idea of what had been envisaged. The northern portions of the Praunheim and Römerstadt Siedlungen have not been implemented and the recent commercial centre of Norweststadt contradicts May's project. The central free space has remained a no-man's-land, encroached on by the uncontrolled fringes of the new development. Only the treatment of the right bank of the Nidda, for a length of not more than 500 metres, makes it possible to reconstitute the whole. In order to explain it better, we will examine in more detail the Römerstadt and Westhausen Siedlungen, discussing the overall plan and the linking of the districts and the treatment of roads and edges.

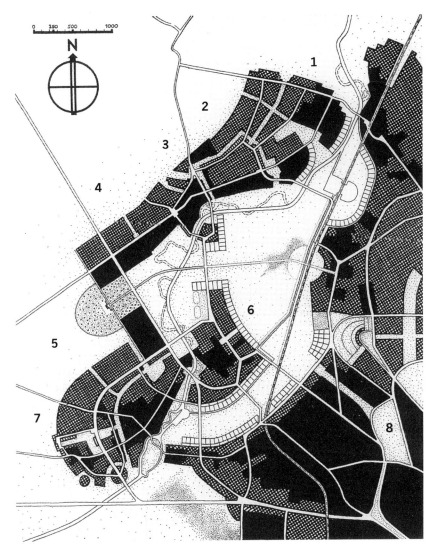

Figure 36
Development plan for the Nidda Valley (*Das neue Frankfurt*, n. 2/3, 1930).
In black: old built-up areas and executed *Siedlungen* hatched the planned interventions.
1. Hedderheim (village).
2. Römerstadt (*siedlung*).
3. Alt Praunheim (village).
4. Praunheim (*siedlung*).
5. Westhausen (*siedlung*).
6. Hausen (*siedlung*).
7. Rödelheim (village and *siedlung*).
8. Botanical Garden.

THE RÖMERSTADT SIEDLUNG

The first portion of a larger whole, which was not completed, Römerstadt was built from 1927 to 1928 for the Gartenstadt A. G. Society and consisted of 1,220 dwellings.[74] As with the Nidda project, Ernst May directly participated in the project with H. Böhm and W. Bangert for the overall plan and C. H. Rudloff for the architecture of the buildings. The architects Blattner, Schaupp and Schüster were put in charge of school buildings.

The Siedlung is located between the 'In der Römerstadt' route, which connects the villages of Praunheim and Hedderheim, and the Nidda. The overall principle is simple. Perpendicular to the route, there is a spine road on which the facilities, such as commerce and schools, is grouped. On both sides there are streets lined with dwellings, which are parallel to the valley and slightly tiered. They are interrupted by paths leading on to esplanades planted with lime trees, and which form a number of belvederes above the market gardens laid out on the banks of the Nidda. May adapted this scheme in order to fit it to the site and differentiate the districts, in accordance with Unwin's picturesque principles.

The spine road, the Hadrianstrasse, formed two successive bends, whose internal portions were occupied by continuous buildings, and, opposite them, the perpendicular of streets were laid out to a staggered plan. These dispositions of opposing bends and abrupt corners, which interrupted the perspective, accentuated the private character of these secondary streets. On both sides of Hadrianstrasse, these streets belonged to two different types of geometry: a continuous and curving street to the northwest (im Heifeld, an der Ringmauer) with a fragmented and rectilinear geometry to the southeast (Mithrastrasse, im Burgfeld). These are two different ways to indicate that they were local service streets. In the interior of these two districts there are a number of defined units. These are a series of row houses or apartment buildings linked to gardens, separated by paths leading to the belvederes. These are variations on the theme of the block.

The rows of low two-storey houses, clearly oriented in relation to the streets, give rise to an internal space, which is occupied by enclosed private gardens in the northwest portion and traversed by a lane in the southwest portion. In the last rows on the edge of the valley, the gardens face an alley, which forms a promenade

74 The allocation of the dwelling sizes in Römerstadt is:

Number of rooms					m²	Monthly rent (1930 marks)	Dwelling type
1	2	3	4	5			
	240				48	52	Flat
		308			66	69	Flat
			226		75	90	Single family house
			395		88	100	Single family house
			49		106	125	Single family house
				9	130	160	Single family house

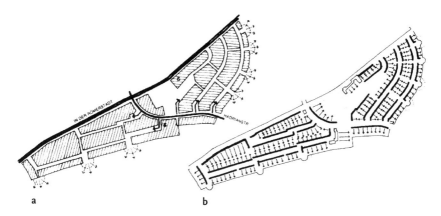

a   b

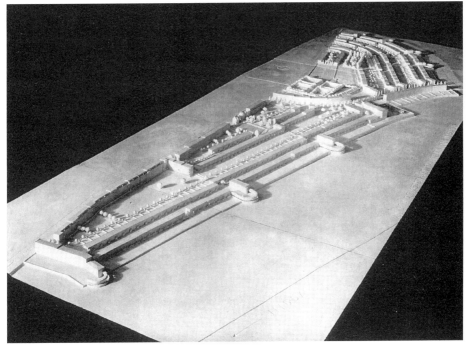

c

Figure 37
Ernst May, Siedlung Römerstadt.
a. Layout of planned units.
b. Status of spaces. Although the buildings are isolated from each other, the whole layout works as a 'traditional' tissue, clearly showing differences and oppositions.
c. The bastioned rampart at the edge of the valley corresponds to the enclosure of the old town (photo of model).

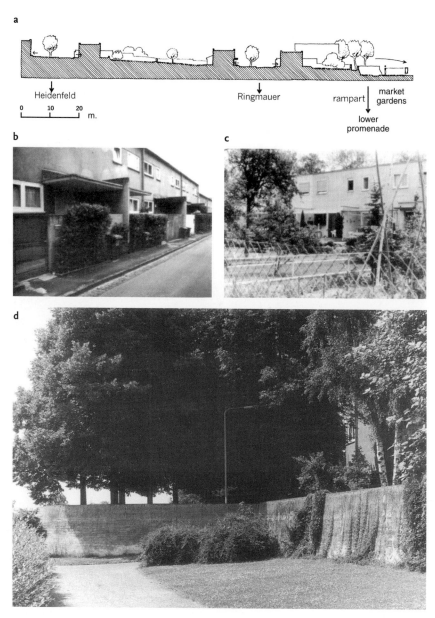

a

Heidenfeld   Ringmauer   rampart | market
                                                                                     gardens
0   10   20
⌐————⌐————⌐ m.   lower
                                                                                promenade

b

c

d

Figure 38

E. May: Siedlung Römerstadt: the rows.

a. Section across the rows of small houses showing the sloping street.

b–c. Contrast between the front façade and back gardens.

d. The fortified wall, which limits the *siedlung*, with panoramic walk and lime trees.

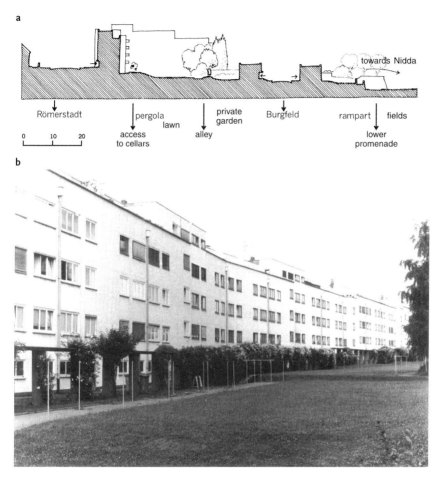

a

Römerstadt | pergola | private garden | Burgfeld | rampart | fields
lawn
0   10   20   access | alley | lower
to cellars | promenade

towards Nidda

b

Figure 39
E. May: Siedlung Römerstadt, multistorey buildings.
a. Section showing the use of a sloping site.
b. Collective use of the internal spaces of the block: the screen formed by the pergola isolates the service area of the garden (entrances of cellars, dustbins, oil spillage from scooters).

above the ramparts with the end of each row marked by a taller block of flats, which turns towards the esplanade. In addition, the access routes, which start from Hadrianstrasse, are marked by buildings, which repeat the English theme of a change of unit at the end of the row. Along the 'In der Römerstadt' route and the Hadrianstrasse, the buildings emphasize the orientation of the fronts. The access façades on the streets are matched by the rear façades, which are marked by balconies. With regard to the colour of plaster, the 'In der Römerstadt' façade is painted with red oxide with white used for the rear façade to further accentuate the differences. The internal space, although it is accessible from its extremities, contrasts with the street. It is fragmented into distinct zones, each zone governed by its own set of rules. There is a part connected with the cellars for untidy activities, which is masked by embankments and pergolas, a zone for games and promenading with lawns and lanes surrounded by groups of private gardens (for the tenants of the flats), treated like the woods of a classical park.

THE WESTHAUSEN SIEDLUNG

Intended for 1,532 dwellings,[75] Westhausen was not completed by May. Its construction (1929–31) was carried out by two companies: the Gartenstadt A. G., which we have already met at Römerstadt, and the Nassarrische Heimstatte. Although the same designers collaborated on the overall plan within the project of the Nidda valley, the design of the buildings was undertaken by a different group, E. Kaufmann, F. Krammer, and Blanck, with the participation of private architects, O. Fuster and F. Schüster. It was badly damaged by the bombing of 1944, and the damaged areas were reconstructed to the original design in 1949.

Westhausen is located alongside Ludwig Landmannstrasse (the ex-Hindenburgstrasse), which is an important north–south road with a tramline leading to the centre of Frankfurt. The development offers an accomplished demonstration of rationalist principles. Starting from the main road, two access roads lead to a regular grid of two north–south streets, Zillerstrasse and Kollwitzstrasse, and four east–west streets, Egerstrasse, G. Schollstrasse, J. Kirchnerstrasse and S. Heisestrasse.

THE HIGH BUILDINGS

The eastern edge along the main road was marked with higher buildings of four storeys arranged along footways, which were equidistant and perpendicular to the roads. The status of the spaces between the buildings was directly tied to access arrangements. There was a tidy and controlled zone on the northern side along the access lane, which was subdivided and planted with a hidden zone on the southern side appropriated by the gardens of the ground-floor dwellings. Between the gardens and the entrance zone of the adjacent building there was another series of plots for the inhabitants of the upper floors. Some rather tall hedges avoided the back–front con-

75 The dwellings subdivision in Westhausen is the following:

	Number of rooms					m²	Type of dwelling
	1	2	3	4	5		
1929			210			41	Two family house
1929			216			47	Flat
1930			754			41	Two-family house
1930			180			47	Flat
1931			190			45	Flat
				40		61	One-family house
				32		57	One-family house

The monthly rent corresponds to 1.20 marks per square metre; the areas are greatly reduced in comparison with Römerstadt, from *Das neue Frankfurt*, 2–3 February–March 1930.

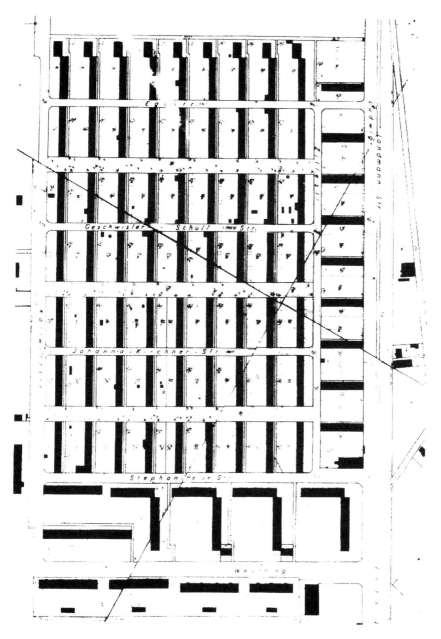

Figure 40
E. May: Siedlung Westhausen (present cadastral map).
The picturesque of Römerstadt is replaced here by a systematic organization, which anticipated the Athens
Charter.

a

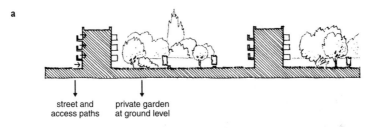

street and
access paths

private garden
at ground level

b

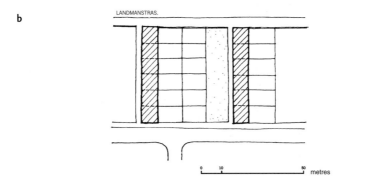

LANDMANSTRAS.

0   10   50
⌐—————┴—————————————————————┐ metres

c   d

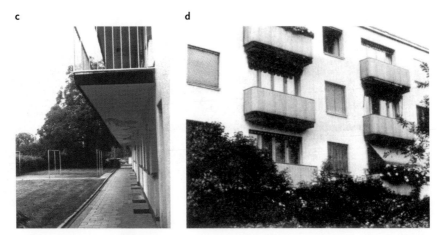

Figure 41
Siedlung Westhausen: multistorey buildings.
a. Schematic section
b. Plan showing the use of space between private and collective gardens.
c. Access façade.
d. Rear façade: the appropriation of the garden by the ground floor flats re-instates an orientation, which makes the back elevation of the building private.

a

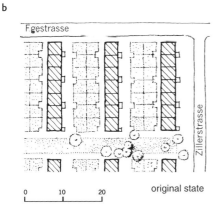

Zillerstras.

b

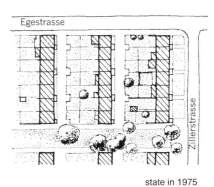

Fgestrasse

Egestrasse

Zillerstrasse

Zillerstrasse

0   10   20

original state

state in 1975

c

d

Figure 42

Siedlung Westhausen: the row houses.

a–b. These sketches show the modifications that have been introduced in the organization of the garden over fifty years of use. The tree-planted streets are kept in front of the access façades, while they disappear from the rear ones. The ground-floor inhabitants have appropriated the adjoining gardens of the rear, where they have built supplementary rooms or sheds.

c–d. Corner plots: trading and commercial activities benefit from the possibility of an extension provided by a garden connected to circulation routes.

flict that resulted from this arrangement. Equally, to the south, some buildings were to be aligned on a main road, but their late and incomplete implementation did not allow for them to be realized.

THE TERRACES

The remaining part of the Siedlung is composed of terraces of north/south-facing houses, serviced by lanes perpendicular to the street. Each house accommodates two families.[76] On the side opposite to the service lanes there are two adjacent gardens. One is a direct extension of the ground-floor dwelling, and the other is assigned to the upper floor. The sequence of service lane/ house/ground-floor garden/garden of the upper-floor dwelling, which is repeated in each unit, reproduces the arrangement we have observed in the apartment buildings. Between two streets and perpendicular to the rows there are some wide gaps, planted with trees, which cross the Siedlung. These provide a network of pedestrian paths and children's play areas separated from vehicular traffic.

Figure 43
Siedlung Westhausen: the lane servicing the dwellings.
Twin entrances are here separated by a planted hedge looked after by the inhabitants.
Cars circulate on a network of roads perpendicular to the rows of houses.

The variety that we observed in Römerstadt no longer exists here and the organization of the rows has only a very abstract relationship with the traditional block. Nevertheless, the arrangement of public fronts and private backs is continued and allows the space around the buildings to be appropriated in the same way.[77] Three problems became apparent with respect to the gardens of the high dwellings, the lanes and the corners in this layout.

Originally, a continuous lane went between the houses and the gardens of the ground floor, with the space between two rows being considered as a group of square market gardens. The ground-floor inhabitants quickly decided to prevent access in front of their windows and to connect their dwellings directly to the gardens, so that the part next to the house became part of the living space of their dwellings, and they even-

76 Housing several families under the same roof is part of the German working-class tradition. The steps taken by May to solve the housing crisis included building a large number of small dwellings very quickly so that they could be later joined together to form larger ones.
77 The recent maintenance programme has progressively suppressed all extensions, verandas and pergolas, which had happened on the back façades and could still be seen in 1973.

tually constructed extensions, which were easy to build around the original steel-framed pergolas. Vegetable plots were located towards the ends of the gardens.

The case of the gardens allocated to the upper-floor dwellings is different, because no direct extension of the living space is possible. In certain cases this space was neglected, abandoned or taken over by the ground-floor garden. Alternatively, it is used in a very utilitarian manner for growing vegetables and there is sometimes a tool shed. Where it is used as a garden with space for living, with benches, a pergola, a hammock etc., it is then oriented towards the service lane and offers a front on that side of the garden. In the first row on the Zillerstrasse, the upper-floor gardens are placed in front of the houses, into which one can exceptionally enter through lanes on the axes of doors. Very much exposed to public view, these gardens are reduced to lawns, ornamented with some decorative plants, and they play an exclusively representational role.

The status of the service lanes is ambiguous, because they run behind the gardens. The house entrances, grouped in twos and marked by small steps, define a front space, emphasized by a flower bed, which gives some privacy to the ground-floor windows. In front of each entrance, an enclosure in the gardens conceals the dustbins. This disposition is sometimes resented by the inhabitants, who like to hide this space or put the dustbins elsewhere.

Contrary to previous Siedlungen, May did not provide a different unit for the end of the row, nor a return for the low walls in the corner as he had done in the last phase of Praunheim.[78] The garden of the last plot is thus directly visible from the street. The inhabitants have overcome this problem by planting hedges or building small walls. But the corner plot, because it was easily accessible and the only one serviced by vehicles, became the ideal place for commerce. Of the six shops that opened in Westhausen, where originally none had been envisaged, five are located on corner plots and the sixth is on the Zillerstrasse, i.e. in the only row directly located on a road for car traffic.

THE BLOCK IN FRANKFURT

THE STRETCHING AND THE DISSOLUTION OF THE BLOCK CONCEPT

In order to assess the experimental character of May's proposals, and the evolution of the architectural models used in Frankfurt, it is necessary to examine the chronology of the projects and of their implementation, distinguishing in each case the ground plan and volume from one viewpoint and the formal vocabulary from another. This distinction is necessary since the passage from the garden city to rationalism happened in a piecemeal way, sometimes with respect to one aspect and sometimes to another.

78 In the ends of the rows along Messel Weg, C. Sitte Weg, H. Tessenov Weg etc., the last one or two houses are slightly bigger than the current elements, which end up protruding at the back. A concrete wall of about 2 by 2 metres extends the gable and prevents lateral views. The inhabitants have often extended the wall, thus enlarging the private zone. Elsewhere they have used it as a springing for the roof in order to gain a covered terrace, i.e. an additional room.

Equally, the Watergraafsmeer (Betondorp) city in Amsterdam, begun in 1922, shows in plan the characteristics of the traditional garden city and does not differ from the other satellite cities envisaged in Berlage's plan. Nevertheless, the buildings by J. B. van Loghem, W. Greve and, mainly, by D. Greiner already use all the vocabulary and construction techniques of modern architecture, thus deliberately breaking with the Amsterdam School.[79]

On the other hand, the Siedlung Freidorf in Basle, carried out by Hannes Meyer a little earlier (1919–21), links a very conventional formal vocabulary (similar to that of May at the same time in Breslau) to a rationalization of construction types and, primarily, of plan forms, which is in the line of the working-class cities of the Krupp factories and heralds Praunheim 3 and Westhausen. This project by Hannes Meyer signalled a rupture with the influence of the English garden city, still very much present in his preceding project the Siedlung Margarethenhohe (Essen, 1916).[80] From 1925 onwards, May proceeded in two directions at the same time. One was the clear definition of town-making principles based on which each subsequent project was a unique experience.

With one exception (Siedlung Riederwald), the first phase of implementation, which was begun in 1926, after the adoption of the overall plan, represented an intervention in keeping with the existing tissue. As with Berlage in Amsterdam, it was a case of continuing the nineteenth-century city (Niederrad, Bornheimerhang, Höhenblick), to give it a clear edge and a continuous façade. The first phase of Praunheim, located opposite the city on the right bank of the river Nidda, can, if it cannot yet be considered an urban tissue, nevertheless be considered as the start of the development of the village. In all these cases, the plan, responding to the context, connected to the existing roads and accentuated the hierarchy of spaces. The building volumes confirm the plan by some devices that recall a Dutch influence such as the treatment of corners and squares and the continuity of the street façades. The formal vocabulary, which had already been rationalized, still showed some picturesque elements such as the entrance at Bornheimerhang, the tower and corners in Niederrad and the disposition and rhythm of openings. These first experiences were an opportunity for May to test his types and to start the industrial production of building elements.

This first urban phase was followed by a group of Siedlungen, where May created a synthesis between the environment of the garden cities and the vocabulary of modern architecture. Römerstadt and Praunheim, the two most important realizations of this period, are a direct extension of Unwin's principles. In fact, the differences that characterise these first two phases derive more from the context and from the situation of the projects with regard to the city than from any change in theory. The closeness

79 This project, which is an important step in the evolution of the architecture of 1920s dwellings, may have inspired E. May: it
    was completed in time for the 1924 congress and mainly presented as the experience of the period, and so it seems hardly
    possible that he had not seen it.
80 Hannes Mayer, like E. May spent some time in England (1912–13). He was mainly interested in the problems of garden cities.
    C. Schnaidt (1965), *Hannes Meyer, Bauten, Projeckte und Schrifte* (Teufen: A. Niggli).

Figure 44
Ernst May: Siedlung Niederrad.
Plan and internal view of the block called 'Zig-zag Häuser'. In a chaotic suburban zone, the enclosure of the block creates a collective garden, away from traffic.

of the dates of the projects and the presence of the same collaborators (H. Böhm, C. H. Rudloff) showed that it was the case of two sides of the same thought. There was no contradiction, but rather complementarities between the dense blocks of Niederrad and the landscaped treatment of Römerstadt. In both cases, the reference to the context and the concern for obtaining some variety counted as much as the wish for rationalization.

If we consider only the large Siedlungen, everything changed after Riedhof-west (1927–30), which showed the transition by being rationalist in the details of its units, but which still clearly showed its urban references. With the last phase of Praunheim (1928), the rationalist principles took over from the picturesque nature of the garden city. Exceptions such as staggered blocks, the corners or ends of rows treatment, are progressively abandoned while industrialization and standardization into types developed. The large Siedlungen no more played on the grid differences in the interior of the same development, as in the previous phases, nor on the affirmation of a pre-existing urban order, but on the systematic repetition of a unit (the row) and on the affirmation of an internal logic, independent of the contextual conditions of the site. They referred to a simple combinatory logic, which suppressed all traces of the block. Westhausen (1929), Lindenbaum (Gropius, 1930) Miquelstrasse Tornow-Gelände and Bornheimergang 3 (1930) marked this evolution, whose fulfilment could be observed in the unrealized project of the Goldstein Siedlung and which signalled the plans of the Soviet period. This new tendency, which did not have the time to flourish in Frankfurt, clearly showed the growing rationalist spirit within the German Modern Movement, which succeeded the expressionist romanticism of its beginnings. Gropius, at first undecided, then joined in at around the same time (1927–8) with his realizations at Dammerstock and Torten as Hannes Meyer became the head of the Bauhaus (1 April 1928). At La Sarraz the foundation of CIAM already heralded the Athens Charter. In Frankfurt, the arrival of Mart Stam accentuated this evolution, and the Hellerhof Siedlung, which he started in 1929, is an indication of this process.

From this time onwards the relationship of the building and its surrounding space was no longer the same. In the tall buildings the subtle differentiation between the façades, which could be noticed in Römerstadt, had disappeared. In Hellerhof as well as in Miquelstrasse, the building became detached from the land, and the external space, which was no more connected with the buildings, lost its status. In the rows of small houses, the same disintegration of the tissue was less noticeable. An exception was that the central space of the block, which had been protected from sight and out of the way from the public domain, ceased to exist.

To discuss the block in these conditions would be very risky, had May not himself clearly set out his problematic in the scheme published in a 1930 article, where he made the point of his actions.[81] In four drawings, which are an explosive summary, he

---

81 *Das neue Frankfurt*, 2–3 February–March 1930.

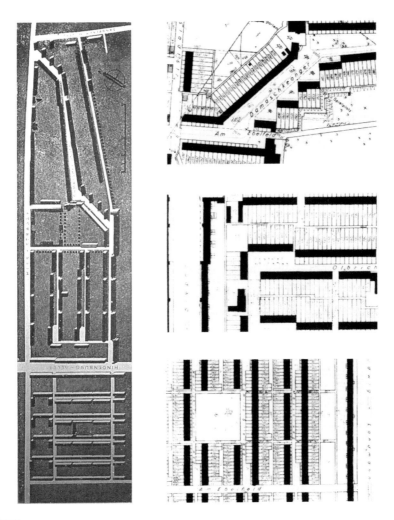

Figure 45
Ernst May: Siedlung Praunheim.
The three phases of this project, even though they are part of one concept, mark the progressive passage from 'picturesque' to 'rationalism'.

sketched out the history of the urban tissue at the beginning of the twentieth century. The series of rows, which was the collective type on which the German architects worked in the years 1927 to 1930, was presented as the logical outcome of the evolution of the block.

The starting point was the nineteenth-century block, which was dense and compact and not far removed from the form of the Haussmannian block. The second phase

Figure 46
Siedlung Praunheim.
Buildings on the Landmanstrasse.

marked the hollowing of the centre, the breaking of the grid and the reorganization of the edges. It was the block that we have seen in Amsterdam or, with some variants, in Niederrad. The third phase saw the opening up of the ends and the lowering of the density so that the block ended up being a back-to-back combination of two rows framing gardens, as in Römerstadt and Praunheim and with Gropius in Dammerstock. Thus, from the old sequence:

Street	Building	Courtyard	Courtyard	Building	Street
Public	Private			Private	Public

There was first one modification, which revealed a zone, until then hidden and private, creating a common garden:

Street	Building	Garden	Building	Street
Public	Private	Collective	Private	Public

Or some small gardens connected by a common passage:

Street	Building	Small garden	Lane	Small garden	Building	Street
Public	Private		Collective	Private		Public

Then the rows became autonomous, planned to allow for maximum sunlight, serviced by lanes perpendicular to the streets, which, suddenly, were reduced to a simple road system (Westhausen):

Lane	Building	Small garden	Lane	Building	Small garden
Public	Private		Public	Private	

Of the traditional block, two principles remain:

- There was a clear relationship between the building and its territory – a practice confirmed by the formation of some plots for use but not for ownership where they did not exist previously.

- The façades of the buildings were differentiated by defining and controlling the access façades and by allowing private initiatives on the rear façades.

On the other hand any relationship with the street and any attempt to connect with the rest of the city was abandoned.

Then the suppression of the small private gardens in favour of a common lawn was combined with a weakening of the differentiation between façades at the same time as the standardization of the block of flats produced far more uniform elevations.

Lane	Building	Lane	Lawn	Lane	Building
Public	Private		Public		Private

Private spaces were then provided only inside the dwellings and by a balcony. Public space became less and less differentiated and occupied the whole of the unbuilt terrain.

The block in Frankfurt appeared, thus, as an enlargement of the traditional concept (not forgetting the English close): an elementary grouping of buildings on a piece of land the spatial status of which was determined by the building form. Since 1929 a process of conscious experimentation led quickly to a combination of buildings and roads organized following an abstract logic, where the ground lost any connection with the reality of its use. Fascinated by tall buildings, the architects of the Modern Movement did not take long in abolishing the last differences between the façades and the different floors in the name of the series, the standard and the norm. Gropius' propositions for layered buildings (1930–1) heralded already the space of the large housing estates.

CHAPTER 5
LE CORBUSIER AND THE CITÉ RADIEUSE

The Cité Radieuse is a myth. In the same way as the ideal Renaissance cities rejected the medieval urban order, which they called *dis*order, the Cité Radieuse expressed a rejection of the city. The Cité Radieuse has no name, no place; it does not exist, it is a diagram. In choosing to discuss it we want to show the extreme point reached in the process of disintegration of the urban tissue.

Exemplary for the theoretical reduction it carried out on urban space, it is also important because of the influence it bore, as a role model for the planning thinking of postwar architects. More than the various large housing estates, which it indirectly produced, but where a compromise existed because of a given context, it remains an abstract and absolute image, the illusion of a different concept of city planning.

THE CITÉ RADIEUSE VERSUS THE CITY

H. Raymond and M. Segaud have sufficiently stressed the concepts that underpin the writings and drawings of Le Corbusier, so we do not need to develop here a critique of his ideology.[82] Le Corbusier's two favourite references regarding housing, the ship and the monastery, confirm the obsession for order and clarify the relationships he envisaged between architecture and the city and between the inhabitant and his own culture.[83] Before the Marseilles Unité d'Habitation, Le Corbusier realized, even though only partially, a long-established concept: the total control of the architect – or of architecture – of the city. We already can find this in 1922 in his project for a city of 3 million inhabitants.

From the Plan Voisin (1925), which coldly envisaged the demolition of the centre of Paris, which was reduced only to its monuments, to the many abstract projects for the Cité Radieuse,[84] the same logic was pursued. This was not only the negation of the city, but also the refusal to take into account any specific siting constraints. With the

82 H. Raymond and M. Segaud (1970), *Analyse de l'éspace architectural* (Paris: RAUC).
83 For Le Corbusier's references, see S. von Moos (1971), *L'architecte et son mythe* (Paris: Horizon de France).
84 For Le Corbusier, the isolated building is nothing more than the skyscraper office block. In the project for a contemporary city for 3 million inhabitants, dwellings are envisaged in buildings '*à redents*' or of a villa type, which take up again the principles of the block, in all other planning projects up to the war. It is only with the Clarté Building in Geneva (1930–2) that the isolated block of flats made its appearance at the same time as the Swiss Pavilion of the Cité Universitaire in Paris. This would not be systematized and the principle of the Unité d'Habitation would take its definitive form only from 1945 onwards, in the project for the city of St Dié, at the same time as the first studies for Marseilles, they continued in the projects of La Rochelle-Pallice (1946), Veyres (1947), etc. However, in the project for the university city of Rio de Janeiro one can see the first systematic application in a series of isolated blocks. In any case, this arrived after the rationalization begun by the Germans, after the contacts with CIAM and with the USSR. See Le Corbusier, *Oeuvres complètes,* Zürich, ed. d'Architecture, Vol. 8.

Figure 47
Le Corbusier: the principle of the Unité d'Habitation.

Figure 48
Le Corbusier.
a. The Cité Radieuse (the Meaux project)
b. The Marseilles Unité d'Habitation.

exception of the Venice projects, it is the domination of the 'standard' and the terrain is reduced to a plateau of representation for an object, a machine-sculpture, abstractly determined. Neither does Le Corbusier spare the country: 'If here and there some beautiful farms, some attractive barns, some recent stables are acceptable and can be conserved, the rest should be demolished and built up again bigger.'[85]

It was then necessary to produce a '*tabula rasa*', keeping only some monumental witnesses of the past, in contrast to which the Unités d'Habitations appeared as the monuments of the present. It is then a case of reducing the city to its monuments, and architecture only to its monumental aspect. Some aspects of the site are referred to by generalisations such as sunlight, green spaces, mountains and the horizon, but space is no more perceived in terms of differences, but only of absolute and enduring values. The inhabitant, called the user, is a nomad and his life is reduced to mere function-ality, calibrated as 1.13 or 2.26 metres.[86]

Among other projects, the Cité Radieuse near Meaux (1956) seems to us a good example of the application of the principles of Le Corbusier. Its publication in the volume of the '*Oeuvres completes*', at the end of the chapter dedicated to the Unités d'Habitations and in the '*Trois établissements humains*', proves that it is an example of a project judged exemplary by its author. Five 'Unités d'Habitations of conforming size', rigorously north–south-oriented, and two cylinders – the 'Singles Towers' – rise on a 'carpet', where different traffic routes (fast and slow cars, bicycles, pedestrians) interweave, connecting the Unités to their facilities and to the road to Paris, the RN3.

We will not elaborate on the segregation of different activities resulting from this zoning, or on the incapacity of the architecture to accept several functions within the same form. What interests us is the complete reversal of viewpoint that happened in such a project, not only in relation to the traditional city, but also in relation to those examples studied previously.[87] Each building is conceived in isolation in an ostentatious relationship with an abstract nature, where the overall composition is derived directly from a pictorial practice in a way that no more refers to the organi-zation of a tissue than it respects the pre-existing site. Seen from a bird's-eye view-point, the city is a model, a collection of objects that are manipulated like so many cigarette lighters on a display shelf.

THE VERTICAL URBAN BLOCK

Le Corbusier's indifference towards the site is very often veiled by his discourse, where he proposed a spectacular conception where landscape is everything. To assess the reality of these concepts, one has to begin with the ground. In the same way as the

85 Le Corbusier (1959), *Les trois établissements humains*, 1945 (Paris: Editions de Minuit).
86 Le Corbusier (1948 and 1955), *Le Modulor* (Paris: Editions de l'Architecture d'Aujourd'hui), 2 volumes.
87 This inversion of perspective has previous equivalents in the Soviet projects of communal houses (1929), from which quite clearly Le Corbusier took inspiration and, to a lesser degree, the layered buildings of Gropius (1931).

Figure 49
Uniformity.
a–b. Unités d'Habitation at Nantes and Firminy.
c–d. The pilotis at Nantes and Briey.

Cité Radieuse has neither name nor place, the Unité d'Habitation has no ground. It rejects it, withdraws from it, sits on pilotis and is literally abstracted from it. As already expressed in the Villa Savoye or in the Dom-ino projects, this negation of the ground would attain its peak in La Tourette, 'designed starting from the sky'. With regard to the pilotis, they are not only the means to lift the building, to make it more visible, but also to refute the fact that, at the level of the passers-by, there may be a possible relationship, other than pure contemplation.

From this point on, everything is connected in a remorseless logic. The pilotis go together with the rejection of the 'corridor street', the streets explode into specialized roads and in 'internal streets'. With the street no more having to be a corridor, the corridor becomes the street. The traditional elements of the block are cut up, rethought, reorganized in that new unit, which appears to us as a vertical urban block,[88] where all relationships are inverted and contradicted.

Without pretending to be comprehensive the following diagram shows the proposed schema of organisation.

	Traditional tissue	Le Corbusier
Access to dwelling	On the façade and in the open air	In the centre and the dark
Shopping	On street ground floor	Upper floor in a gallery
Facilities	On street ground floor or at end of plot	At the top (nursery) or elsewhere
Open space	Internal and hidden (the courtyards)	External and in view (under the pilotis)
The street	Outside	Inside

One is tempted to think that such an upheaval must interfere with behaviour that follows established habits. Indeed, the social project of Le Corbusier involves a complete modification in the way of life of the inhabitants. All reference to an urban life, to a traditional neighbourhood life, is abolished: no more 'corners', or 'opposites', or 'next doors'.

FROM MARSEILLES TO FIRMINY OR THE DEGRADATION OF THE FAÇADE

The inversion of space, as we have noted, shows itself at the level of the single cell and finds its culmination in the role allotted to the external screen walls. The extension of the dwelling, previously hidden (façade on a courtyard, small individual garden) is now on the façade of the building and it has to be judged on two levels: globally and from the exterior, individually and from the interior.

Globally, it is the design of the façade that counts. Le Corbusier's postwar repertory is deployed: rough concrete lightened by honeycomb walls and *brise soleil* claddings impose a strong and unifying imagery. At Marseilles the rhythmic variations of the different bays and the vertical pattern of the shopping gallery create a complexity that is that of the architect's composition. This urban block as one building takes on board a variety that previously was the result of a juxtaposition of different buildings. In Nantes (1952), design begins to be simplified as a result of the economic constraints of the building process with an elimination of the nonprofitable shopping gallery and a simplification of the textures. This simplification continues in Briey (1957) and ends in Firminy (1967), where the design of the façade is reduced to the pattern of floor slabs and cross walls crossed by the high parapets of the balconies. It is not unimportant that Firminy was built after Le Corbusier's death.

88 Sixteen hundred inhabitants on a 4-hectare piece of land is a 200 x 200 metre square urban block with a traditional urban density. This is the block that often appears in the CIAM texts.

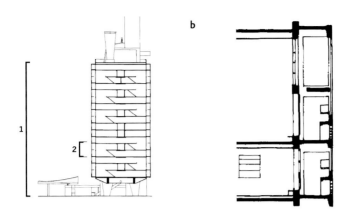

Figure 50

The Unité d'Habitation.
a. The two scales: 1. the unité; 2. the cell.
b. Section through the loggia.
c. The vertical garden city (photomontage of the façade of the Pavillon de l'Esprit Nouveau).
d. The space of the loggia (Marseilles).

The consequences of this impoverishment are not only aesthetic, but they also condition practical issues. To assess this, one has to envisage the interior of the façade, this space of the wall, which permits the transition between the dwelling and the exterior. To the overall understanding of the façade seen from outside, where it is seen by all, there must be added an individual comprehension. The balcony, which extends the dwelling, is the substitute for the garden in the same way as had already been envisaged by the Pavilion of the Esprit Nouveau and the 'vertical garden city' (1925). In Marseilles, as in Nantes, the second façade between the loggia and the dwelling is carefully designed and is susceptible to variations and modifications. The solid parapet hides from the outside the lower part of the loggia in the same way as the internal screen hides it from the living room view. The façade functions for the inhabitant as a front (which is on display) and as a back (which is hidden), but much more as a back, given the distance from the ground. It accommodates such ambivalence more or less well. We note that the dwelling's internal layout is itself disorientated[89] The *brise soleil*, accessible from the bedrooms, is used as an additional balcony, as a support for plants exposed to the sun (while the loggia is shady). The thickness of the wall and its modelling make it a space where the inhabitant can control his relation with the exterior. These are the issues that concern Le Corbusier, even though he does not see all their consequences and reduces them to some functional concerns: the 'sun-screen balcony, which has become a portico, a balcony, allows one to control one's own windows inside and outside, the cleaning of windows, the choice of curtains.[90]

The interweaving of these two scales – the building and the dwelling – is made possible by the thickness of the external wall enclosure and by the deliberate design of the façade of the building, which forms a strong enough image for the individual variations not to alter its effect. In fact, it is necessary to look very closely in order to discover the modifications the inhabitants have carried out to their space on the façades of the Unité d'Habitation of Marseilles. In Briey the more rudimentary design does not carry the individual variations as well, and, in addition, the simplification of the internal façades – the panels no longer show the subtleties of Nantes or Marseilles – does not stimulate them. Finally in Firminy, the replacement of the gridded parapet walls by metal bars makes any modification, and any use made of the balcony, visible from the outside, opening to outside view a space that until then had been protected.

If we have insisted on the role of the wall, it is not only to demonstrate the architectural qualities of Le Corbusier – qualities that are no more found in his followers and that, under the pressure of the reduced costs, become blurred in his own last works. The study of the Unité d'Habitation shows that it is now at the level of architecture that those problems once solved by the simple logic of urban tissues have to be dealt with.

89 H. Raymond and N. Haumont (1972), *Habitat et pratique de l'espace* (Paris: ISU), multig.
90 *Le Modulor*, op. cit.

Figure 51
The process of degradation of the wall.
a. Marseilles.
b. Nantes.
c. Briey.
d. Firminy.

A NECESSARY REDUCTION

The Unité d'Habitation marks a new phase, the last one in the loss of those differences that characterized urban space. The sequence – street/edge/courtyard/end of plot – that ordered old tissues and had already been reduced in Haussmann's Paris and in Amsterdam and had been compromised in London and Frankfurt, is here resolutely suppressed. The contrast of sides does not exist any more; only the vertical feature of staircase wells differentiates the east from the west façade. In this neutral space the real possibilities for growth or modification are nonexistent or are confined to the interior of the dwelling. In spite of Le Corbusier's assertions, the pilotis remained sterile, incapable of filling the role previously allocated to the ground floor. Cut off from the street, little by little, this space became a parking lot, contradicting the theory that the ground floor was given to the pedestrian. The internal street did not work as a landing – it serviced too many flats – nor as street (an absence of windows, flats facing one another, prohibition on play etc.). It was 'an obligatory passing point'.[91]

Thus the Unité d'Habitation appeared to us as the negation of the city and the last metamorphosis of the block. It is the negation of the city, because any reference to continuity and to a spatial proximity was abolished and, at the same time, the differentiated status of spaces in functional terms disappeared. The absence of articulation is cruelly perceived with the consequence that making modifications, other than the addition of new units or the limited individual appropriation within the dwelling cell, is impossible. Cut off from any context, here the image of a ship attains all its meaning and the Unité d'Habitation expects from the inhabitant a complete change in his way of life.

91 J. Ion (1975), *Productions et pratique sociale de l'espace du logement* (Saint-Etienne: CRESAL), pp. 108–10.

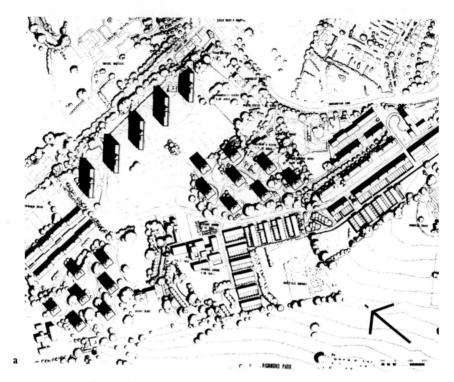

a

b

Figure 52
Le Corbusier's dream executed at Roehampton, London.
a. Site layout.
b. Like big ships in a park.

But, at the same time, the Unité d'Habitation in its abstraction exemplifies with extreme clarity the problem of the urban block, i.e. of the elementary grouping of buildings whose association creates a tissue. It is on this aspect that we would like to conclude this first part of the book, leaning on the criticism of the Unité made by the British architects of the 1950s, as noted by Reyner Banham.[92] For Banham, Le Corbusier is the first architect to break away from the conventions of modern archi-tecture, and to reject in 1945 the dogmas elaborated by the CIAM ten years earlier in a completely different economic and cultural context. The Unité at Marseilles was 'the first post-war building, which distinguished itself from the architecture of the pre 1939 years'. For the British architects, bored with half a century of garden cities, it was the revelation that audacity was possible. Their admiration derived from two sources. The first was that a change in scale with regard to urban problems cannot be satisfied by a row of cottages; and the second was an attraction to rough shuttered concrete.

Like Banham, we very well understand how the Brutalists were to start off from the Unité d'Habitation and how that starting point was necessary in order to attempt to find again a new urban space. Their criticism dealt first with the internal street. Dark and leading nowhere, it was but a vast hotel corridor. If it was moved to the façade and in the open air it could have reoriented the building: the dwellings had an entrance façade with a door and windows, from where one could see out so that the abstract duplex became again a small house. This gallery 'where children can use their bikes as they would have done elsewhere on a pavement' became a major theme in British architecture, from the Golden Lane projects of the Smithsons (1952) or the competition of Sheffield University (1953) to Stirlings flats in Runcorn (1967), via all the housing projects of the public-sector architects.

Reoriented, the Unité would have remained isolated, as in Roehampton, if the idea of extending the gallery from one building to the next – to make it into a real built-up street, integrating facilities into it, enlarging it in a square – had not made it possible to find a continuity again, which the CIAM had rejected. This tied up with the Spangen building by M. Brinkman in Rotterdam (1919) and, later on, with the first gallery housing blocks of the London County Council.[93] Housing, after Le Corbusier, rediscovered the concept of the urban tissue.

92 R. Banham (1970), *Brutalism in Architecture* (London).
93 For the origin of the gangway and the first experiences, see J. N. Tarn (1971), *Working-class Housing in 19th century Britain* (London: Lund & Humphries).

CHAPTER 6
THE METAMORPHOSIS OF THE BLOCK
AND THE PRACTICE OF SPACE

We could call the practice of space 'the space of practice' or, alternatively, 'how space is used in practice'. It is the spatial dimension of social practice that Lefebre describes as the 'gestures, journeys, body and memory, symbol and meaning'.[94] It is a practice that manifests itself through phenomena of appropriation in specific situations, where the configuration of space is significant. These can also be described as spatial-symbolic systems and are underpinned by habits or groupings of customs[95] that are typical of some forms of sociability. These, in their turn refer to social networks and to regional and national cultures. Space therefore has its own history.

Is the block, as a unit of subdivision or component of the urban tissue, a unit of spatial practice? Can it be considered an element of design practice, and has it ever been so? These questions belong to a more general set, which try to explore the extent to which an element of the city, identified through morphological analysis, covers a group of identifiable practices, and thus try to explain the possibilities that are offered for practice. It is necessary to take into account both the spatial characteristics of the block and the ways these can be linked with other possibilities at different morphological scales. In the case of the block, it is necessary to understand whether it enables, through the interplay of differences and continuities, the transition from a small space, e.g. the dwelling, to other spaces that are both adjacent to it and also part of the larger urban spatial system.

Before investigating the relevance of these questions, two warnings are necessary. First, one has to distinguish, as far as possible, between the nineteenth-century production of urban elements, which we have already considered, and that current today. They present differences and a comparison provides an opportunity to evaluate the adaptability of a space for different uses and its degree of openness to change. On the other hand only within the limits of what seems to us to be verifiable is it possible to transfer hypotheses referring to the spatial-symbolic systems of life from one culture to another.

The period of this study covers the history of the socioeconomic development of the different forms of capitalism and, more precisely, it depends on the urban transformations resulting from the Industrial Revolution and its consequences – even when it

94 Henri Lefèbre (1971), *La revolution urbaine* (Gallimard), p. 240.
95 P. Bourdieu (1972), in *Esquisse d'une théorie de la pratique* (Paris-Geneva), writes: 'The word disposition seems particularly appropriate to express what underlies the concept of habits (defined as a system of dispositions). It firstly expresses the result of an organising action, which then has a meaning very near to words such as structure; it then designates a way of being, a habitual state (especially of the body) and, in particular, a predisposition, a tendency, a propensity or an inclination.'

was the case of the effects of an industrialization programme located elsewhere. For example, in the case of Paris, the political and financial capital of France, whose economic exchanges it controlled, or Amsterdam, whose growth, certainly less than that of Rotterdam, followed the economic development of Europe and especially that of Germany. This process, with its specific characteristics and specific systems, despite some differences in time and space, tends to recompose social space and, at the same time, to separate the events of everyday life, especially with respect to the autonomy of those who are not directly involved in productive work.

This is the context of the phenomena we have considered with particular reference to their historical evolution and to the possible survival of those institutions that reproduce specific forms of social life and cultural characteristics. For example, when describing the way of life in Holland in the 1950s, B. Pingaud makes an observation that is at least worth considering as a hypothesis. He notes that Dutch people tend to the isolation of activities, that they internalise the division of work to such an extent that they do not undertake do-it-yourself jobs. This must have consequences for the use of space and in the forms of its appropriation.[96] Pingaud adds, 'Nowhere else is the sphere of private life so solid and impenetrable.' This statement should be compared with the apparently contradictory fact that Dutch houses are very transparent – they have large, often bay, windows, without curtains. Here there is no opposition between the visible and the invisible from outside, such as exists in France. Instead, we are here confronted with a different spatial-symbolic system where the interior and exterior spaces of private life are arranged in a different manner.

URBAN BLOCKS AND THE TRANSFORMATION OF SPATIAL PRACTICES

With Haussmann, as we have seen, a strategic rupture took place as the city was globally made to undergo a process of clarification, specialization and zoning. Work and productive workers were moved from the centre and social segregation was achieved by the horizontal division of urban space. However it is not possible to accept the idea that social segregation arrived only with the Haussmann type of building and that previously the rich owner of the first floor coexisted with the manual workers, dressmakers and shop assistants who inhabited the attic floor. There is an erroneous view that the social pyramid, which represented this urban society before the great rebuilding of Haussmann, was not segregated and could coexist without too strict boundaries.

This view is vigorously rebutted by A. Daumard:

Contrary to some superficial affirmations, the staircase was not a meeting point for the different social classes ... Dimensions and wealth in the apartments gradually

96 B. Pingaud (1954), *Hollande* (Paris: Le Seuil). For comparison with France, see M. G. Raymond et al. (1966), *L'Habitat pavillonaire* (Paris: CRU).

diminished towards the upper floors, especially so in those buildings that predated the Second Empire. The inhabitants of one house generally belonged to relatively homogeneous social environments. Under the July Monarchy the contrast between the two Parises had already appeared. The aristocracy deriving from wealth, position and birth settled in the west, while artisans and manual workers settled in the popular, poorer eastern districts. Nevertheless, sordid streets were located in the middle of elegant and affluent areas, residential blocks emerged in the poorer *arrondissements* and, over the whole extent of the capital city, representatives of the middle classes ensured the presence everywhere of the small and middle bourgeoisie.[97]

In fact, under Haussmann, an already existing tendency was systematically developed. Segregation, which already existed either vertically or horizontally, was organized in an ever more global way, at the scale of the whole city, by creating homogeneous districts; and, ultimately, also in a finer grain with regard to the differentiation of buildings on the same plot. In this case the social hierarchy depended on the position of accommodation in relation to the street. There was a decreasing status, from the street façade to the internal courtyards. And, even in the cases where there was a degree of horizontal social mixing, the main and service staircases ensured, together with the control of the concierges, a rigorous impermeability.

From the point of view of spatial behaviour, one can detect a phenomenon of great importance, because these reforms of the block happened at the same time as a spatial codification, quite clearly shown in architectural treatises, crystallized the way of life of the bourgeoisie.[98] This codification was the result of a slow transformation from a system where parts of the house were identified depending on the circumstances of everyday life and where differences were not fixed according to function. Thus a new style emerged: one did not talk about money in the kitchen, nor did one commit suicide in the closet.[99] Private family life happened in clearly defined places, in rooms with specific denominations as the more generic terms such as '*salle*', '*chambre*' and room were replaced by 'dining room', 'bedroom' etc. These terms also referred to the social relations that were allowed to take place in the spaces – from private to formal functions.

The dwelling itself began to function in a contrasting relationship with the exterior. These results – Ariès[100] describes the long process to achieve them, where family and

97 Adeline Daumard (1976), 'Condition de logement et position sociale', in *Le Parisien chez lui au XIXe siècle*, exhibition catalogue (Paris: Archives Nationales). See also P. Bleton (1963), *La vie sociale sous le Second Empire* (Paris: Editions Ouvrières): 'contrary to what has often been written on pre-Haussmann Paris, when reading the Countess [of Ségur], it does not seem that high bourgeois, modest employees and simple workers lived in the same buildings. This integration... can, at the most, be a reality for traders and their employees... where both have to be near the place where they work' (p. 21).
98 Adeline Daumard (1970), in *Les Bourgeois de Paris au XIXe siècle* (Paris: Flammarion), shows for Paris the extension of the concept of bourgeois at the time (from the petit bourgeois to the financier). If the process we mention deals with the diversity of the bourgeoisie, the canons of everyday life seem to have been lived in the most rigid way by the middle bourgeoisie (civil servants and members of the liberal professions). See also the chapter: 'En 1848, en France, la petite bourgeoisie, c'est la boutique', in C. Baudelot, R. Establet et Malemort (1974), *La petite bourgeoisie en France* (Paris: Maspero).
99 In this way a new symbolic and ethical universe appears in *Pot Bouille* (a novel by Zola adapted as a play [translator's note]).
100 P. Ariès (1973), *L'enfant et la vie familiale sous l'ancien régime* (Paris: Le Seuil).

childhood are 'invented' and where 'the private man' appears[101] – corresponded to the ascent of a class. The new concept of home, of *chez soi*, to which corresponded a precise formal definition, implied that the dwelling had become the terrain on which a spatial practice, which had become autonomous, was developing. The double meaning, either physical or moral, of the word '*foyer*' proved this. Daumard writes, 'The *chez soi* was *par excellence* the centre of private and family life as well as the privileged place of society life.'[102]

This separation of private life did not exist at that period for the working classes. Their dwellings were not the centre of their spatial experience; rather they had a collective, urban life, which was structured around their productive activities. The transformation, which first affected the bourgeoisie, was progressively extended to other sections of the population and became more generalized. This change was explicitly adopted in social housing policies, which, in attempting to stabilize an unstable labour force, tried to eliminate those urban and collective attitudes of the working classes that were judged to be dangerous from the point of view of hygiene, morality and social peace.

However, it would be an exaggeration to support the view that the public housing programmes saw spatial planning (and the corresponding policies) exclusively as an instrument capable of creating new forms of sociability and everyday life and also as a means of controlling the working classes. To do this would ignore the fact that in the middle of the nineteenth century social housing was still in a phase of experimentation, which in Paris was very limited. It means not taking into account the general historical conditions against which the aims of public intervention were conceived. It also isolates them from the more global process, which was to result in the definition of 'a new type of relationship with people and objects, obtained by the dissolution of previous ones, imposing on the whole of the population a new form of organization of their daily life – the closed family nucleus'.[103]

The development of large industries – and, more generally, of paid labour – led to a transformation in the relationships between work and leisure activities (the latter include consumption), between time devoted to either one or the other and between the locations where they took place (workplace/dwelling).[104] A process of subdivision and of later recomposition replaced the strongly socialized practices, continuous and superimposed, that characterize rural and artisan production. This shift, which can be found in the economic and social structures we have investigated, resulted in the general diffusion of those spatial activities specifically connected with the dwelling, which progressively became more differentiated and more hierarchically organized and controlled.

101 See W. Benjamin (1974), 'Paris, Capitale du XIXe siècle', in *L'Homme, le langage et la culture* (Paris: Denoël-Gonthier).
102 Adeline Daumard, op. cit.
103 J. Ion (1975), *Production et pratiques sociales de l'espace du logement* (CRESAL: Saint-Etienne), multig.
104 See Susanna Magri (1972), *Politique du logement et besoins en main-d'oeuvres* (Paris: CSU).

THE BLOCK AND ITS DIFFERENTIATION

Did the pre-Haussmannian block correspond to a particular set of spatial practices? We have already seen that it was the place for a range of activities including those connected with work and exchange, which were superimposed and co-existed. In Zola's book *l'Assommoir* there is a description of the working-class district of la Goutte d'Or, located at the periphery of that part of Paris that Haussmann was later to destroy, from which it appears that the centre of the block integrated different activities.

A boulevard and a street, on the edge of a district, would be the preferred locations for collective activities, especially those of the evenings of pay day. Nevertheless the block, without being the location for a specific activity, was part of a larger continuum of social life, which was characterized by its urban quality. The dwelling, without any doubt, was an element of the block, but not the most important one, if only because of the precarious nature of its tenure. There was neither a marked differentiation nor a contrast between the dwelling and the external spaces, but rather between spaces frequented by women (the washing place) and those frequented by men, such as the *Assomoir* (the tavern). There were differences within the district of la Goutte d'Or, but it was more its multifunctional character and the homogeneity of its inhabitants that were in contrast with the rest of Paris – a difference expressed by Zola.[105] This contrast depended on a morphological rupture – the boulevard – but it also represented a social distance. The Paris ladies, who lived in the Faubourg Poissonière, were not the women of the neighbourhood.

The spatial practice of the small traders in Zola's *Au Bonheur des Dames* is also characterized by the relationship between dwellings, shops, backs of shops and street, which constitutes a continuous reality in the same way as the family relationships that extend to the shop owner and his employees. The Haussmann block excluded, at least from its centre, all the diversified activities that coexisted there previously in the same way as the urbanization process excluded some activities from the centre of the city. Often only those activities connected to housing could find space within a block, whose character derives, as we have noted previously, from social needs. This did not cause great difficulties to the inhabitants, because the block became fragmented and most of the buildings were inhabited by a homogenous population.

If we take up again the distinctions made earlier between the perimeter of the block, which is in contact with the street through the façade of the buildings, and its centre, we realize that this functions only as a back space where some street activities (stables, sheds) are still located there. This arrangement ensured a distinction between the visible and the hidden parts of housing. The bourgeois building was the place of false modesty – see Zola's *Pot Bouille* and the thoughts contained in its first pages on 'the discreet ostentation' of the façade, which masks the 'internal sewer'. With regard to

105 See G. Duveau (1946), *La vie ouvrière en France au Second Empire* (Gallimard).

working-class blocks of flats, they continued, undoubtedly, to be the theatre of a more open form of sociability and activities that extended the life that took place in the dwelling – children played in the courtyard and family events spilled out from the dwelling.

There was another problem that referred to the nineteenth century as well as to our own period. Was the Haussmann block perceived by its inhabitants as an urban unit? We have no evidence that can justify such an interpretation, except in the cases where a block was used for an important function, such as a hospital, school or town-hall. This depended on the presence of facilities and local services, which can be absent from the block of houses in some urban 'deserts'. The expression referred less to the whole block than to its fronts, following the hierarchy of the surrounding roads. It is these façades that were and still are probably the defining elements for the perception of the block.

In fact, starting with the Haussmann block, which established the spatial separation of life, we begin to change our point of view. No longer should we ask ourselves if the block was the place for a specific spatial experience, which mediated between the dwelling and the city, but instead to try to observe how the block allows a connection between external and internal spaces, between private and public life,[106] to understand how it supports a spatial practice derived from differences in hierarchy and control and the extent to which it was impoverished by a process of decline and the reduction in the range of functions.

THE OPENING OF THE BLOCK

The opening up of the block first happened in England in two forms. In the first instance, it was at the corners, where, as we have seen, the inhabitants – confronted with the possibility that something symbolically experienced as hidden, at the back, could have been seen from outside – chose to close the space. On the other hand, we have observed the existence of access ways into the interior of the block from outside and independent of the houses, which gave rise to a degree of ambiguity. Nevertheless, it may be that this perceived ambiguity is created by the cultural criteria imposed by us as outside observers. There was in existence in England for a long time an arrangement, not only in the organization of mews, but also in social housing, which is characterized and defined by parallel service routes, with double access (front and back), each of a hierarchically different importance. This was a spatial practice that was rarely used in France.

The formula of the close, where the front is an extension of the street, often functions as a socialising space. From a spatial point of view, this is possible only when a back

---

106 In the way in which one clearly contrasts the front façade on the street, which is exposed, with the rear elevation on the courtyard, which is hidden, where this contrast corresponds to the internal subdivision of private and public rooms, 'clean' and 'dirty' ones (which can also correspond to ventilation arrangements). The haussmannien block allows this.

allows an individual appropriation of space. From a social point of view, this spatial organization works in some social strata (the middle classes), for which the grouping of houses constitutes a means of carrying out some forms of affiliation. In this case one can suppose that a consensus may exist about those spatial symbols that express a system of affinities. In this respect, Willmott and Young's comments on the most popular dwellings at Welwyn Garden City seem applicable. In spite of the lack of services and institutions favouring different modes of socialising, these forms, in the most favourable cases, find a way to affirm the relationships within homogenous age groups. This sociability is reinforced by a tendency to a matriarchal dominance of space that parallels the development of the main social relationships[107].

The process of opening up – i.e. from the point of view of the use of space and the possible mixing of the fronts and backs – can also be observed in Amsterdam. Here the centre of the block – instead of being the place of individual appropriation, as happened in the case of a garden connected with a ground-floor dwelling (there is no functional connection with the upper floors) – becomes a passing place, accessible from outside. There was also an opening up when the block contained common zones or when it integrated collective facilities. In all these cases one has to accept the existence of collective activities at the scale of the block or, as in the last case, at a larger scale, that of the neighbourhood.

The same happens in Frankfurt, when the block, formed by two parallel buildings, is not closed at its ends, but a difference remains between the front and the central zone, which is the back, even though this is by now almost devoid of meaning. This confusion between the front and the back does not derive from the complete abolition of differences, but only from the effacement of some of them. This ambiguous situation poses a question that is implicitly contained in the ways the block is used and can be observed through the signs these uses leave in the spaces. Can the central space of the block, in the most favourable cases, be considered as a socialising space, the theatre of a collective appropriation in which forms of individual experience are also possible? Can it play a role, comparable to the role of the collective, public zone of the English close? From the visible manifestations of its use, it appears as a collective facility (a green zone for living and children's play) or as a purely representational space, which inhibits individual expression, or as an ambiguous space, in which active and personal appropriation coexists with that more associated with representational criteria. Either internal uses or external representational criteria prevail.

An even greater ambiguity results when, as in Frankfurt (Westhausen), the upper-floor dwellings are related, without a direct connection, to small gardens. Here, one has to distinguish, between two types of building. On the one hand, there are the low buildings, which were intended by May initially to be inhabited by one family only, with the top floor served by an internal staircase and inhabited by people considered

---

107 See the works of the 'Institute of Community Studies', and R. Hoggart, *La lecture du pauvre*, Paris, Editions de Minuit, 1970,

as their lodgers. Once the housing crisis was over, these were to become one-family houses and the garden plots were to be amalgamated. On the other hand, there are buildings where the distribution system showed that they were, once and for all, conceived as separate superimposed dwellings. In this case, and depending on the owner, the gardens, as we have seen, could be either purely ornamental or serve as storage or kitchen gardens. This was in accord with May's initial project, which followed the ideas of the theoreticians of garden cities and, more specifically, those of the gardening propagandist Dr Schreber, the father of the *Schreber-garten*. The garden provided not only the opportunity for healthy leisure and a source of complementary income, but also, for May, an expedient in times of economic crisis. The inhabitants would always have some carrots to eat. Is it a question of ambiguities or one of contradictions that lead to conflict? Since we are here only to observe facts, we are not able to formulate a final judgement.[108]

THE BLOCK ABANDONED AND THE DISORIENTATION OF PRACTICE

The cases we examine now do not only demonstrate the morphological degradation of the block, whose centre emerges as an ambiguous place with regard to the use of space and where spatial differentiation is not precisely expressed. There is a real transformation, i.e. a deep modification not only of the block as a formal, abstract unit, but also of the block as a place for the location of activities with a clear and hierarchical articulation between interior and exterior space.

We can observe this, when the block shrinks and when the buildings, or each row of buildings, have the same orientation. In fact one can say that it has lost its sense of orientation, because the back of each building or row faces onto the front of the next one. This front exists only in relation to itself and is defined in practice by the presence of the main entrance. It is only by starting from the interior of the dwelling that we can understand the way the space is used. Outside the buildings this is limited by the extent to which the forms can absorb change. That which in the traditional block remains hidden can be in evidence, in the same way as that which it is deliberately intended to expose. The contradiction is so great that not even the interventions of the users are capable of resolving the situation. The 'block' in this case is a unit that is separated from its more global relationships and makes sense only through the proximity of other similar units. Spatial experience is reduced to neutrality with the negation of all those elements that normally constitute the spatial/symbolic system of housing.

---

108 Without any doubt, the answer would depend in part on the homogeneity of the population and on the density of the block. It seems possible to us to compare these comments with those of Jean Remy and Liliane Voyé, with regard to the removal, in some Dutch schemes, of hedges and walls between private gardens, which had previously resulted in an individual enclosure and not a collective appropriation. See *La ville et l'urbanization* (1974) (Gembloux: Duculot), p. 102.

The Cité Radieuse is indifferent – like an ocean liner it can sail and find its orientation by following the sun. This dramatic reversal has been described above – the street is now in the centre and the back is now on the perimeter, but this back presents such a monumental character that it also seems to be a front.

As we have seen, the decrease of differences, their neutralization and even their inversion, can be described in spatial terms. But patterns of use often oppose this state of affairs and, wherever possible, seek to reaffirm the logic of earlier arrangements.

In fact uses are defined not only by the way in which they adapt to the built environment, but also by the way in which they produce and define places, which may not be those designated by the planners. But their power to do so may be extremely limited because different forces are competing for the use of these external spaces. These are social forces, which exercise control, impose rules and even lead to the rejection of undesirable situations, which could pro-

Figure 53

The interior of the block in Amsterdam. A place of individual appropriation in a collective building.

duce negative reactions among the inhabitants. This risk is avoided by a withdrawal from these spaces.

We started off from an analysis of the Haussmann block, which consecrated and codified a new practice of space, where the dwelling became the preferred centre of life, which became progressively more private and more important. Then we observed that, little by little over the period we examine, this practice of space became more generalized and more constrained within the limits of solutions, which almost totally negate those differences that characterise and define the block. In an apparently paradoxical way, the multiplication of functional, social and spatial entities – i.e. of separate units from a morphological point of view, where the exterior, as well the interior, is abstractly conceived (and whose social utility is doubtful) – contradicts a practice whose origin we have tried to reconstruct. We seem to have witnessed the deepening of the initial rupture and the exacerbation of its main premise, i.e. a process of the reduction of spatial experience exclusively to the dwelling itself, which was finally conceived as a distinct unit. Where is the street, the city, the urban space? Where do we start from? Do places exist for the inhabitants, where, at least symbolically, they could be guaranteed a gradual transition between different spatial scales?[109] These questions provoke another: has a new spatial practice taken shape?

As we have seen, the study of the block, from the point of view of the use of space, has led us not to consider it in isolation, but in relation to those elements adjacent to it in the range of spatial scales – the dwelling and the urban space. Neutrality, with regard to the urban situation and the indifference of the latest forms, to which the block has given rise, seems to suggest an analysis with regard to both location and to substitution where space has an exchange value (an exchangeable and interchangeable good). This, following Raymond and Segaud, could be called the dominant space in our economic and social system.[110] This viewpoint comes close to the comments of C. Aymonino[111] on the quantitative requirements for construction and their impact on everyday buildings, which has resulted in the isolation of buildings in the contemporary city. Here 'the means of building development have been reduced to quantitative values expressed in numbers, indexes, regulations, functions given through the private subdivision of a constructible piece of land' (where the notion of 'lot' not only signifies a plot or a parcel of land but also the process of taking part in a lottery).

In this way the block does not escape the logic of production of our society, and not only because it seems to be a projection of the productive forces and a reflection of the technical conditions of its realization – although one cannot see why the limits imposed by the path of a crane should necessarily produce what we have called a 'loss of orientation' of a building. The block also raises issues of social function and the instruments of design; i.e. the issues regarding the role of architects in the production of built space and the resolution of architectural problems. This is the representational role, which Aymonino questions, as well as the relationships between these issues and the use of space.

109 See H. Raymond (1975), *Espace urbain et image de la ville* (ISU).
110 H. Raymond and M. Segaud (1973), 'L'espace architecturale: approche sociologique', in *Une nouvelle civilization* (Paris: Gallimard).
111 C. Aymonino et al. (1970), *La città di Padova, saggio di analisi urbana* (Roma, Officina), p.57.

CHAPTER 7
THE DEVELOPMENT AND DIFFUSION OF ARCHITECTURAL MODELS

HISTORY OF ARCHITECTURAL MODELS

In the five examples we have studied it is possible to see how the more or less successful answer to a social question had been translated into a new spatial concept. Progressively abandoning any reference to the city, ordinary buildings such as houses were treated as a monument or a single object. This evolution, which developed in parallel with important transformations in the European economy, was simultaneously a consequence of these changes and one of the factors that promote them, to the extent that architecture, in conditioning the inhabitant's everyday life, accentuates and accelerates social transformations.

In the course of this evolution, which embraced almost a century of the history of architecture, the work of the architect changed, his social role was modified and his ways of working were transformed. It is true that the history of architecture cannot be understood outside social history, because architecture, understood as production, relates to the history of work. As Manfredo Tafuri sees it,[112] we are now dealing with part of this work and we are going to analyse it from a specific point of view. In each of the realizations considered, forms and operations are expressed that structure their composition. These forms refer to specific concepts and techniques, from which the project is managed. These are referred to as architectural models. The history of architectures must include the history of these models, the study of their creation, their transmission and of their alterations.

In adopting this viewpoint, it appears clear that, in a global reading of architecture, we operate a double reduction. First, with regard to the whole of the work of architecture, we consider only the work of the architect alone and, within this, only the conceptual issues. We have to take into account the risk of mystification that such an attitude can lead to, which is the danger involved in going back to an abstract vision of architecture, similar to that of traditional art history. The history of modern architecture and of its builders, building sites, offices and techniques has only just started. Within this history – which is not the history of buildings but of the processes that make them possible – we cannot avoid taking an interest in architectural models.

Their study presents some difficulties, because they do not result in the demonstration, when this happens, of the theories explicitly supported by the architects or their doctrines. The architectural models represent often subconscious or implicit

---

112 M. Tafuri (1976), *Théories et Histoire de l'architecture* (Paris: SADG).

schemes, which are at the base of the architect's thinking. They can be common to a group of architects, to a 'school' or, on the contrary, be the product of an isolated individual. They are certainly related to the general conditions of the period (development of industries, with its consequences for urban planning, environment and ways of life), but, with regard to economic conditions, they are in a relatively autonomous position.

Their transmission happens in different ways:

- through direct contact among people and, from this viewpoint, it is important to reconstruct the circumstances of these meetings: teaching, working together, conferences, participation in events (exhibitions, congresses) and personal relationships;
- through publication, books, magazines and exhibitions, which are the means of communicating the theories of the architects and the images of their realizations; to study this, references, dedications to works, notes of thanks and other references are sometimes as precious as explicit quotations;
- through the observation of the built work; in this case, one has to be particularly careful in picking up references to foreign journeys and work periods abroad;
- finally, one can discover the role played by some individuals, who were the real means of transmission of information – Muthesius, Wijdeveld, Mart Stam.

This vast field of research is too often neglected in the classical texts of architectural history. In order to study it, we have carried out a sample analysis, without claiming always to go back to prime documentation or to get involved in the deep historical research, which would require tools and methods we do not have at our disposal such as visits to archives and analysis of personal letters. On the other hand, having shown analogies or affinities between some spatial configurations, we have tried to justify the comparisons we propose, by basing our assumptions on the existence of a relationship or an effective meeting between the designers. In this way we hope to be able to demonstrate not only that there were relationships of common interest, but also to demonstrate the specific elements on which it was based. When we have not been able to establish clearly a relationship, even though chronology did not specifically refute its existence, we have continued using hypotheses, opening in this way a field of historiographically correct research.

The study of these meetings and relationships constitutes a chapter of the history of the movement of ideas and it reveals two apparently contradictory phenomena. From one side this movement is conditioned by economic and political factors – the stays in England of Ernst May correspond to the efforts of German industrialists of the period in trying to assimilate the English experience. These efforts officially took place in the missions of Muthesius and were crowned by the successful achievement of the creation of the Deutscher Werkbund. From another side, one has to take into account the existence of specific problems within the world of architecture and urban design, which go beyond the general tendencies of society. This fact, which can often be found when the development of a scientific subject is studied, takes on a special significance here, because of the purely visual role of the tools of transmission, which go beyond language barriers: Ebenezer Howard's diagrammatic schemes, Camillo Sitte's drawings or Le Corbusier's sketches.

These aspects illustrate a degree of autonomy, mentioned earlier, but the existence of several modes of transmission goes back to the status of architecture – a status that starts in the Renaissance period – which consecrates the division between intellectual activity (of the architects) and the technical one, of the actual realization of the project. The elaboration and transmission of architectural models, even though they may be sometimes autonomous in relation to economic conditions, always reside in a given economic structure.

THE CLASSICAL TRADITION

We have already briefly shown the influences on Haussmann, especially his references to seventeenth- and eighteenth-century France.[113] Between the prefect, the employees of the technical services (Alphand, Barillet, Belgrand and Deschamps) and the architects who collaborated in different projects, there seems to have been such a deep agreement as to justify the temptation to define globally as 'haussmannien' the transformation of the capital.[114] This agreement is revealing of the characteristics of French society in the second half of the nineteenth century. Napoléon III and Haussmann represented the mobile bourgeoisie, the business bourgeoisie, which obtained great economic advantages from the modernization of Paris. The architects were part of the class in power, even though their belonging to a liberal profession tended to mask this condition. Their aims and their cultural models tended to be the same as those of their clients, and this situation continued until the end of the century. French city planning and urban architecture were worked out following haussmannien schemes in Paris, as well as in the main provincial cities, until the time when Art Nouveau produced a rupture in this state of affairs.

Such homogeneity could make one think that haussmannien planning, which was so tightly connected to a specific political situation, had an influence only on those cities whose problems were similar. However, we must not forget that spatial models convey information that goes beyond the social content of realizations and that in

113 Haussmann, prefect of Bordeaux in 1851 and familiar with the city since his wedding (1838), could not help but be touched by the improvements carried out in the previous century under the initiative of the Intendent Tourny (1690–1760). 'It is a capital' is what the president prince had said at the time of his October 1852 trip, impressed by the width of the avenues decorated by Alphand for the occasion. Haussmann himself, in his speech in the Sénat of 6 June 1861, established a parallel in Paris to Tourny's activities in Bordeaux.
114 If the initiatives of Napoléon III are important – he, in fact, decided the main layout and priorities – it was Haussmann who decided how one had to intervene in the city. Napoléon III was mainly a pragmatic individual. On top of this, he did not know Paris well. He had been impressed by what he had seen in England and he criticized the prefect for his inclination towards orderly layouts and perspective views, while, for Haussmann 'the three principles of classical town planning – rectilinear layouts, order, perspective – were sacred'. From P. Lavedan (1960), Les villes françaises (Paris: Vincent and Freal).

Haussmann's interventions there were criteria that concerned the administration of a large city as well as morphological problems, and these could be used in different circumstances for very different and even opposite aims.

Through what mediation were Haussmann's models transmitted? Mainly through the direct observation of the capital. Paris, in fact, was one of the most important cities in Europe, frequently visited by heads of state, political persons and foreign delegates. Universal exhibitions started from 1855 onwards (1867, 1878, 1889 and 1900); Berlage visited the 1889 exhibition.

Teaching and publications also played an important role. The official teaching of the École des Beaux-Arts was perfectly in tune with the Haussmann vision, while Viollet-le-Duc, Choisy and Anatole de Baudot were rather marginal in their time, and their influence was only to be felt later. On the contrary, César Daly, Charles Garnier and Julien Guadet [115] were the codifiers of official architecture and transmitted principles of classical composition and respect for conventions.

Besides, the influence of the haussmannien model was beginning to be felt from one municipality to the other, because Haussmann's organization of the City of Paris's technical services was a significant example for many large cities, which wanted to acquire the necessary technical means in order to be able to control their planning process. In order to concretely measure Haussmann's influence on the examples we have analysed, we will first refer to Raymond Unwin's criticism. [116]

Unwin began with the historical development of cities, but was less concerned with historical reconstruction than with the intention of drawing references from them. Haussmann appeared to be continuing baroque planning, opposed to the English landscape planning practices as well as to the more recent picturesque pan-German initiatives (Camillo Sitte, Schultze-Naumburg). Unwin retained from Haussmann the principles of a global, readable, monumental and hierarchical composition, based on the presence of axes, of straight lines and crossroads, which all favoured the rational functioning of the city. This standpoint was sufficiently close to that of German theoreticians and practitioners, who constituted Haussmann's legacy, such as Otto Wagner or H. J. Stübben. [117] For Unwin the monotony of details, the inappropriate isolating of monuments, the incapacity of layouts to engender real spaces – 'there are no closed spaces in Haussmann's plans' – were to be criticized. He absolutely rejected the Haussmann block, which was for him tied to a French urban culture that was too different from the English tradition and too far away from the ideals of the garden city.

115 See C. Daly, op. cit.; C. Garnier (1889), *L'habitation humaine* (Paris: Amman Hachette); J. Guadet, op. cit.
116 R. Unwin, op. cit.
117 Unwin was in contact with Stübben, who was the author of the plans for Köln, Antwerpen... whose theories had been published (*Der Städtebau*, 1890) and were later divulgated in the planning seminar created in 1907 at the Polytechnic of Berlin.

The influence of Haussmann, as an examination of his achievements confirms, happens at a precise level, which is that of the general structure of interventions, even though one has to observe the considerable difference in scale between the large Haussmannian layouts and Unwin's monumental attempts, which have the dimension of a village.

Unwin also stressed that Haussmann was not the only one to conduct a global operation of reorganization of an urban territory. Without going as far back as the Rome of Sixtus V, significant precedents of Haussmann were to be found at Karlsruhe, Nancy and, above all, the plan of London by Christopher Wren. One cannot but be impressed by the fact that for Haussmann, as for Wren, it was the case of proposing an immediate solution to a problem that could not be solved by partial interventions.

Thus, we can note how, already from the beginning of one of the movements, which had mostly influenced the planning of the twentieth century, the persistence of classical tradition was recognized and accepted, especially by those who, going back to the principles of the Art and Crafts Movement, would have been presumed to move away from it. This classical tradition, which is discretely present in Unwin, is much more so in Lutyens as the central square of Hampstead Garden Suburb demonstrates; and it becomes more emphatic in his later projects (New Delhi).

The compromise proposed by Unwin and disseminated through his writings and his lectures found its natural conclusion in Welwyn Garden City. The architect Louis de Soissons, author of a plan whose perspectives directly evoked French garden layouts, combined in his personality a Beaux-Arts education and English traditions. Welwyn, more than Hampstead Garden Suburb, better illustrated Unwin's principles: a monumental and classical composition of the whole and a picturesque rendering of details.

In its turn, Holland, which was closely connected to England, could not but take up part of these theories – the more so because the nineteenth century had been marked by P. J. H. Cuyper's attempts at monumental urban compositions, of which the Rijksmuseum is the most accomplished example. Contrary to what had happened in Paris, where Haussmann was, in his own way, continuing the general principles of Louis XIV city planning, such compositions were new in Holland, where the eminently commercial activities of the seventeenth century had led to a bourgeois city planning (the plan of the three canals), where any form of pomposity was excluded.

Influenced by Ruskin and Viollet-le-Duc's books, Berlage was seduced by the garden city, as can be seen in his first project for south Amsterdam (1903) and in the plan of the Vreewijk district in Rotterdam (1914). In the latter, carried out by the architect Granpré-Molière, Unwin's principles clearly appear again and the central radiating pattern inserts itself in the classical tradition. In Amsterdam the eminently urban conditions that had finally been imposed did not fit with Unwin's compromise and Berlage went back to Haussmann's principles. He knew about Haussmann's Paris, of

a

b

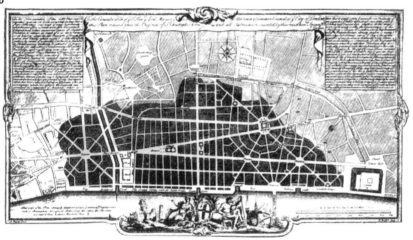

Figure 54
Berlage and Wren.
a. H. P. Berlage: plan for the southern extension of Amsterdam.
b. Sir Christopher Wren: plan for the reconstruction of London after the Great Fire of 1666.

which, in 1883, he had written that it was 'the most beautiful modern city', and the 1889 exhibition had given him the opportunity to visit it again. Finally, he was familiar with Otto Wagner's and H. J. Stübben's theories, which essentially went back to the technical devices that had been tried out in Paris. South Amsterdam, with its avenues and high-density buildings, can appear to be the last intervention to be inspired by Haussmann, as Giedion suggested, although he mildly regretted that in this intervention the architecture was not 'more modern.'[118]

Among the classical precedents for the plan of Berlage, one has finally to give special place to the plan of Christopher Wren for the reconstruction of London after the Great Fire of 1666. Both Rasmussen and Summerson insist on the significance of this plan,[119] which proposed to carry out in one phase and over an extended area a number of operations, which, until then, had remained isolated or unique like the Piazza del Popolo in Rome, the Bernini square in front of St Peter's and the access projects of Paris; or landscape projects like those of Le Nôtre. Wren, as well his contemporary John Evelyn, who was the author of another project for the reconstruction of London, designed a road layout based on two superimposed grids, one common and rectangular and the other monumental and depending on some 'geometrical figures', characterized by the urban classical-baroque culture: symmetry, perspective effects, radiating street systems. These types of proposal were to be found in Berlage's extension plan for the Hague of 1908 and in the plan for south Amsterdam, where the resemblances were not just limited to the principles. In Amsterdam as well as in London the composition started from a bridge over the Amstel and over the River Fleet, which entered the Thames at Blackfriars. The part located behind the bridge is slightly autonomous in relation to the whole. The system originating from an octagon in London recalls the garden city of Watergraafsmeer in Amsterdam. In Berlage then, as in Wren, one finds a principal monumental sequence: bridge/avenue/square/monument/doubling of the avenue. The tower of J. E. Staal plays the same role as St Paul's Cathedral as the generating point of the system of perspective views. This principal sequence is combined with a secondary one, perpendicular to the principal one, whose origin is another access point – the Minerva Station, the bridge over the Thames. Finally, some elements, like the classical gardens, form autonomous geometrical figures.

These characteristics of the Wren plan demonstrate the existence of a classical planning trend, different from the French tradition inherited by Haussmann, which, while being less pompous, used more complex geometrical figures. The garden cities show the signs of this trend and, if Unwin in his treatise quotes Haussmann, it is, however, to Wren that he referred in practice.

In Unwin as in Berlage, the classical tradition and the Haussmann influence appeared together and also underlie the principles used – an overall, clearly ordered composition achieved by means of monumentality, symmetry, convergence and axiality. But, while Haussmann's project was carried out rapidly under the pressure of speculative impulses, using the same procedure (and the same forms) at all levels, Unwin and Berlage thought that the composition's logic with regard to the smaller scale of development related to different rules. From this point of view, they con-

118 S. Giedion, *Space, time and architecture*, op. cit.
119 Steen Eilen Rasmussen (1967), *London, the Unique City* (1934) (Cambridge, MA: MIT Press).

nected to the less academic classicism of the seventeenth century, where the overall organization did not imply a similarity of the parts and where several systems were superimposed. The plan of Versailles is a clear demonstration of this flexible way of planning, which did not happen in Haussmann's projects – the autonomy of the geometrical form of the small woods, which are connected to the monumental layout only by their location and by some perspective views. In Amsterdam this was used to achieve changes of scale and made the division of work between the different architects easy, and in England it allowed for picturesque detailing.

The influence of haussmannien models was evident in the town planning at the beginning of the century. In Le Corbusier, for example, we can find, although more abstractly, an aspiration for order that recalls Haussmann's strategic preoccupations. In the proposals like that for a city of more than 3 million inhabitants or the Plan Voisin, illustrating the first large urban plans, there was a reinterpretation of an axial monumentality, which might not have displeased Napoléon III's prefect, but this direct reference did not go any further. The Modern Movement was influenced only in an indirect way, mediated through the experiences we have discussed or through a process of historical change.

THE TEMPTATION OF THE PICTURESQUE

The nineteenth century was marked by experiences that moved in the opposite direction from the classical tradition, aiming rather towards a spatial reinterpretation of the spontaneous picturesque of vernacular architecture or medieval cities. Initially inspired by theories from the field of literature and art history and supported by painters, a movement strongly established itself in England that referred to the naturalistic experiences of the eighteenth century, to the first garden cities of John Nash and to the working-class cottages of the beginning of the century. In 1859 the Red House, by William Morris and Philip Webb, opened the way for the Arts and Crafts Movement. Godwin, Norman Shaw, Lethaby, Ashby, Voysey, Baillie Scott and Lutyens perpetuated the new ideas and dominated English architecture until the end of the century. Their work was published in Germany by Muthesius[120] and had a decisive influence on Germany, Scandinavia and Holland and, to a lesser degree, on France.

This movement, notable for having produced buildings, furniture and everyday objects, dealt with the city only on a theoretical level. In the production of spatial models, its influence can curiously be associated with that of Camillo Sitte.[121] While British architects usually made reference to rural architecture, Sitte, in his book,

120 The role of the architect Hermann Muthesius (1861–1927) is important with regard to his work in the definition of models for German architecture. After a stay in Japan, he was sent to London as technical attaché to the German Embassy (1896–1903) and entrusted by the Prussian government with industrial espionage in the field of construction, architecture and design. This mission was followed by the publication in Berlin of three works: *Die englische Baukunst der Gegenwart*, 1900–1902; *Die neue kirchliche Baukunst in England*, 1902; *Das englische Haus*, 1904. Muthesius, with P. Behrens, T. Fischer and others, was the founder of the Deutscher Werkbund in 1907.

121 C. Sitte (1843–1903), architect and director of the Vienna Imperial School of Industrial Arts (1889), *Der Städtebau nach seinen Kunstlerischen Grundsatzen* (Vienna); French translation (1902), *L'art de bâtir les villes* (Paris); new edition (1996) (Paris: Le Seuil).

a

b

c

Figure 55

'Picturesque' and urban landscape.
a. Camillo Sitte: illustration for 'Der Städtebau...'
b. Raymond Unwin: illustration for *Town Planning in Practice*.
c. Ernst May: the main street in Siedlung Praunheim. The way of drawing of Sitte is directly taken up by Unwin as well as the principles for the organization of the urban landscape: perspectives centred on a monument, widening and narrowing of the visual field. In Amsterdam in a direct way and in Frankfurt after reinterpretation, the treatment of urban spaces expresses the same attitude.

published in 1889, gives as examples 'urban illustrations', from medieval and Renaissance cities. The British architects and Sitte both rejected the nineteenth-century industrial city, but, while the British saw a solution outside the city, in rural simplicity, which then led to the theory of garden cities, Sitte proposed a reinterpretation of old cities, even if he denied it, by positioning himself outside history. In spite of this, he had a great influence on Unwin and Berlage, even though both of them were aware of the real problems that town planning was facing during that period.

This influence was felt in two ways: on a formal level, through the fascination exercised by the sketches contained in Sitte's book – picturesque illustrations, drawings of squares and monumental layouts – and on a theoretical level, by the observation of picturesque solutions, carried out systematically; thus implying the possibility of basing planning activities on systematic research.

FROM CAMILLO SITTE TO UNWIN

Twenty years after the publication of Sitte's work, Unwin evaluated his first experiences. His dependence on Sitte clearly showed itself in his plans. The spatial definition of corners and crossroads and the limits of perspectives literally recalled Sitte's principles, even though the low density of garden cities made this less obvious. This dependence appeared even in the illustrations, which sometimes reproduced the same graphic devices of *Der Städtebau...*, even if this similarity was partly due to the type of reproduction. And, finally, it appeared in Unwin's talks, which demonstrated the limits to the extent he intended to use the proposals of the German theoreticians, which he considered inadequate when attempting to define an overall structure for the interventions: 'an outsider would lose himself in such a labyrinth'.

These proposals, though, allowed variety in details and diversification in neighbourhoods etc. The divergences appeared quite clearly in the references to the medieval city. Sitte isolated squares, streets and monuments in a long inventory, which, really, were a catalogue of solutions to adopt and a collection of examples to reinterpret. When Unwin studied Rothenburg, he tried to show the structure and understand the underlying principles, such as the differentiation of districts within a global organization, the emphasis on the most important spaces and the hierarchy of parts, in order to make continuity and contrast legible.

It is necessary to evaluate carefully the important role played by Unwin in the development of this picturesque tendency. If he took up again principles previously formulated by others, he transcribed them into a homogeneous and personal vocabulary, integrating the contribution of the Arts and Crafts Movement and adopting the English tradition of landscape design. Since its beginning he was placed at the very heart of the garden city movement. He did not stop at imagining an urban landscape, but also attempted to solve the social problem of housing. From here originated his interest in domestic architecture, for which he codified some elements,

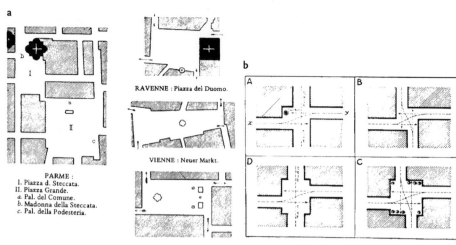

PARME :
I. Piazza d. Steccata.
II. Piazza Grande.
a. Pal. del Comune.
b. Madonna della Steccata.
c. Pal. della Podesteria.

RAVENNE : Piazza del Duomo.

VIENNE : Neuer Markt.

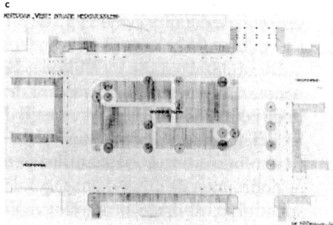

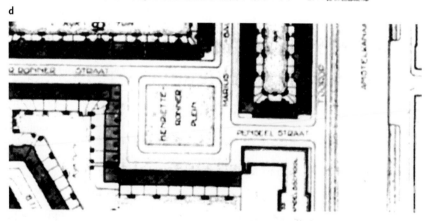

Figure 56

The role of the square in an urban composition.
a. Camillo Sitte: grouping of squares and theoretical scheme for an urban square (Der Städtebau...).
b. Raymond Unwin: sketch of different types of crossroads and treatment of a square in Hampstead Garden Suburb (*Town Planning in Practice*).
c. H. P. Berlage: Mercator Plein (Mercator Square) in Amsterdam.
d. Michel de Klerk: Henriette Ronner Plein in Amsterdam.

helped in this by a typically English tradition of classifying residential buildings. In England, in fact, not only the principles but also the aspect of buildings were to practically remain the same for the next forty years. He introduced elements that are not to be found in Sitte, such as vegetation, which, with the exception of decorative plants, Sitte allowed only if it was out of sight. But his main contribution was to have made an inventory of possible house groupings, particularly the close, this collective space surrounded by houses and separated from traffic, which reinterpreted the traditional courtyard of the farm or manor house.

Unwin criticized the picturesque of the German theoreticians, which he considered to be 'a very artificial imitation' and he concluded that 'the real issue is not to attempt to plagiarise the old'. This position is particularly sensitive to proposals for the reinterpretation of the old boundaries of traditional cities. It was not the case of rebuilding ramparts following the example of the boulevard, which 'conserves the limit formed by the old wall', or to 'create, in an interesting way, a line up to which both the city and the countryside could each extend and clearly stop'. Parks and gardens as well as buildings contribute to mark spatial differences. The division between the housing areas and the extension of Hampstead Heath, with its simple brick wall, interrupted by the verandas of houses and doubled by a planted avenue with its entrance marked by a small slightly raised esplanade, clearly show the distance of the garden city movement from the German picturesque. And it is this lesson that will be transferred to Amsterdam and Frankfurt.

BERLAGE AND THE DUTCH EXPERIENCE

Berlage[122] knew Sitte's theories, because his training in Zurich put him in contact with the German environment. He visited Germany and Italy between 1879 and 1881. He stayed in Florence, where he directly acquired a knowledge of the Middle Ages and of the first Renaissance. The picturesque of Flemish cities was part of Dutch culture, whose inheritance Berlage appropriated in saying, 'we must conserve old Holland's artistic tradition'. He, then, carefully followed the experience of the garden cities and took up again in his own way some of their principles. On the other hand we can find in Berlage's planning ideas the same references found in Unwin, Sitte, Schulze–Naumburg, Stübben and Henrici.

From this point of view two projects are of great interest. One, the extension plan of Purmerend (1911), clearly shows a relationship with the old city, which is not only a theoretical and intellectual relationship, but a clear morphological relationship between the two parts of the city. We do not know whether Berlage, when he worked on this plan, had already read Unwin's book, which was published in 1909, but it is clear that he applies the same principles as in Unwin. The conservation of the old city limits was ensured; the extension presented itself as an area whose shape (a clear square) was defined by an enclosure, formed by a boulevard

122 P. Singelenberg, M. Bock, K. Broos (1975), *H. P. Berlage, bouwmeester, 1856–1934*, catalogue of the exhibition, The Hague, Municipal Museum.

Figure 57
a. Parker & Unwin: entrance of Hampstead Garden Suburb in London (1909). The 'gate' marked by two arcaded buildings is the place where shops are located.
b. G. Rutgers: small shops under arcades where the Gerrit van der Veenstraat meets the Minervalaan in Amsterdam (1926–8).

146

with planting on three sides, while the fourth side was the conserved enclosure of the old town. The main entrance to the town consisted of the station, which was connected to the old town by a diagonal road, marked by a monument, which fixed the centre of the new area. The central square followed Sitte's principles, with the shifting of the axis of the diagonal road in order to limit the perspective views, one closed with a monument (entrance perspective) and the other with a small planted square (exit perspective).

The other project, the Hague extension plan of 1908, was more ambitious. Its layout essentially took up again De Bazel's project, carried out in 1905 for the World Capital Foundation of Internationalism competition and recalled some parts of the London plan by Christopher Wren. In fact, if we examine it we will notice that the role of the park was here a division between the town and its extension and the role of the station was to be a new pole, located opposite the old town (as in Purmerend and as Berlage would have wished it to be for south Amsterdam). There was also a marked difference between the densely built centre and a periphery based on the principles of garden cities. The station as a new entrance to the city and the boulevard separating the centre from the periphery took their inspiration from the layout of the ramparts of old Dutch seventeenth-century fortified cities and from Renaissance ideal cities. The railway itself was used as a circular barrier to define the limits of the garden city and the idea itself of the station as the 'new gate to the city' indicates the similarity existing between the Dutch and English theoreticians.

Generally speaking, Berlage's architectural models were similar to those of Unwin, not only in the principles, but also in the concrete solutions. Only in the details are some differences noticeable. The specific technical conditions that are typical of Holland, such as the problem of stabilising the ground, resulted in a higher density than in England. Besides, the limited land surface available produced a reduction in the area available for occupation, which could not be achieved by just applying the rules of the garden cities. It is known, in fact, that the first project for the extension of Amsterdam was not accepted, because of its too low density. When intervening in a tissue with strong urban characteristics, Berlage, however, applied many picturesque details, even though this implied important changes of scale.

The architects working with him in Amsterdam all, more or less, belonged to the Amsterdam School, which was dominated from 1915 to 1925 by Michel de Klerk and P. L. Kramer. They all had in common a preference for a picturesque romanticism, in which expressionist reminiscences and Scandinavian influences were present. Once one moved away from the large monumental avenues, the wish to interrupt perspective views and to create new closed squares became evident and often the layouts followed Sitte's and Unwin's principles. The 'Dageraad' development, which was one of the first initiatives in the south Amsterdam plan, clearly showed this, even though density and the Dutch tradition of the block provided it with an urban character not found in the garden cities.

In the above examples, the role played by the architects who designed the buildings was as important as that of Berlage, but the treatment of Mercatorplein, where Berlage intervened, clearly showed his reference to Sitte (e.g. the shifting of the axes of the main street, leaving some zones available for use away from the main circulation routes). At the same time, the grouping of arcades and shopping areas, which can be found in several places in the south Amsterdam plan (corner of Minervalaan/Garrit van der Veenstraat, crossing Tijnstraat/Victorieplein) took up again Unwin's proposals for Hampstead Garden Suburb's commercial entrance.

Finally, although strictly connected to the logic of the block, which continued in Holland until 1934 (the date of the early work of J. J. Oud in Rotterdam), Berlage and the architects of the Amsterdam School tried out variations on the *hof*, a type of grouping similar to the English close, which took up again the Flemish tradition of the *béguinage* and introduced, with a common enclosed space, those modifications that will be applied in the future in the urban tissue.

THE PROBLEMS OF THE INDUSTRIAL CITY: ERNST MAY AND NEW FRANKFURT

Among the architectural models of the Modern Movement, Frankfurt and Ernst May's intervention represent a fundamental aspect that is too often neglected. May's training happened at a time when art criticism in Germany was at its peak in those universities that were dominated by Wölfflin's influence. He followed the teaching of Theodor Fischer in the classical line of architectural theoreticians and a great number of his collaborators shared this background. At the same time, before World War One, he felt close to those modern architects who were grouped around the Deutscher Werkbund and he was in touch with Peter Behrens and Bruno Paul, who were advocates of industrialization. In addition, he had been to England twice, where he attended courses, but, most importantly, he worked for two years in Unwin's office in Hampstead Garden Suburb. He knew and appreciated London.

More than Berlage, he was aware of the unstoppable explosion of urban centres. Germany's forced industrialization at the beginning of the twentieth century led him to conceive of extension schemes that recalled Howard's principles – discontinuous urban growth, agricultural belts etc. When, in 1925, he was put in charge of the planning of Frankfurt, he had behind him his experience of Breslau, his knowledge of London and of garden cities. He had also participated in the international congress for city building in Amsterdam (1924) and in the international conference of town planning in New York (1925). Both of these were opportunities for meeting the main theoreticians and practitioners of the time.

His socialist convictions and Germany's situation after the first monetary crisis of the Weimar Republic led him to consider planning issues from a different angle than the picturesque one of Sitte and his disciples. Nonetheless, if we observe Frankfurt's Siedlungen, at least up to 1928, we will notice that the architectural models used were not simply reduced to the 'rationalist' principles, that can be seen applied in other works of the same period, such as the Siedlung Dammerstock by Gropius in Karlsruhe or the Siedlung Hellerhof by Mart Stam in Frankfurt itself. May, above all, was concerned with problems of overall urban form, the city as a whole.

Giorgio Grassi[123] has underlined the relationship between the new Frankfurt and 'the European historical city ... of which neither any of the phases in its development nor any moment of the specific circumstances that contribute to its definition is ignored'. He also referred to the issue of parks and to the treatment of their edges, which connected with 'the beautifying idea of the classical city', and cited May's project for the improvements of the banks of the River Main. He compared this project to de Cotte's project for the Place Bellecourt in Lyons and to Gabriel's project for the Place Royale of Bordeaux and to the improvement project for the Nidda valley, which he compared to the relationship between the palaces and villas of the classical city (the Belvedere in Vienna, the Borghese or Farnese villas in Rome). Grassi makes further, similar comparisons between plans:

- Frankfurt in 1925/Bordeaux and Lyons in the eighteenth century – May attempted to establish again a morphological relationship between the city and the river following the classical tradition. Frankfurt in the twentieth century was 'the European historical city' as Bordeaux was so to the eighteenth century.
- Römerstadt, Praunheim/Belvedere, Villa Farnese ... The twentieth-century public green space structures the relationships with the city in the same way as once did the classical garden.
- Main/Nidda – the valley, in both cases, creates a conceptual relationship between the areas that lie on the opposite river banks. This relationship is an architectural one since 'the river bank is an architectural element in the same way as a building or a public square'.

Without any doubt, we are in agreement with the view that Frankfurt's layouts recall classical city planning[124] and that the reorganization of the twentieth-century city set a similar problem, with regard to the nineteenth-century city, as the extensions and planning improvements of the classical city posed for the medieval city. We can also accept that the general category of the 'European historical city' can help to clarify the issue of the evolution of urban form. However, in his enthusiasm, Grassi too easily eliminates the matter of the English influence, when he too quickly says that 'the problem of green spaces with regard to the new Frankfurt has no relation to the issue of the garden city'.

123 G. Grassi (1973), 'Das neue Frankfurt et l'architecture du nouveau Francfort', in *Neue Bauen in Deutschland* (Zurich: ETH).
124 In the commentary on the Breslau project (1921) the councillor Behrendt noted the perfect agreement between the thinking of the planner and the formal proposals, which recalled the ideal cities of the Renaissance.

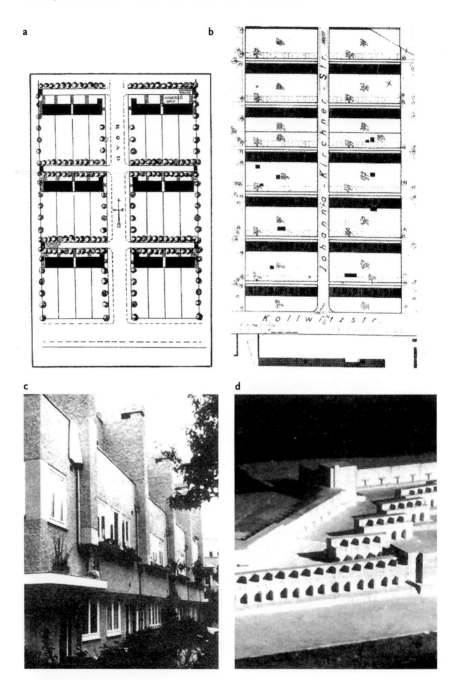

Figure 58

Borrowing from 'rationalism'.

a. Raymond Unwin: theoretical scheme for the distribution of row houses (*Town Planning in Practice*), 1909.
b. Ernst May: organization of row houses in the Siedlung Westhausen (1929).
c. Greiner: Central Square of the garden city of Watergraafsmeer in Amsterdam (1922–4).
d. Ernst May: Siedlung Praunheim in Frankfurt (1926–30).

In May, the overall idea of the city, based on an awareness of its explosion (*Trabantenprinzip*) shows the links between the garden city and the planning of Frankfurt. We propose the hypothesis that these links, besides May's direct knowledge and practical experience in Unwin's office,[125] go through specific steps that illustrate English influence on the Germany of the beginning of the century.

With regard to direct influences in the period 1890–1910, the English architects connected with the Arts and Crafts Movement were invited to Germany and Austria as consultants. There they designed buildings, worked as planners and designed furniture and objects for artisan groups that were organized like the English Guilds (Deutsche Werkbund, Wiener Werkstädte). C. R. Ashbee, for example, was often in touch with Germany, where, in 1911, he presented Frank Lloyd Wright's work in the second Wasmuth edition. He had been invited after Baillie Scott as an adviser by Ernst Ludwig of Hesse to establish the colony of artists of Darmstadt, which had been designed by J. M. Olbrich and which impressed May; in 1908 'I used to spend all my free time in the colony at Mathildenhöhe'. It is possible that the terraced garden overlooking the city, which constitutes the ordering element of the different buildings, had inspired part of the solution of the Nidda Valley project.

The indirect influences of English culture are shown in publications and exhibitions and in the reports of Hermann Muthesius, which were published in a rapid sequence in the years 1900, 1902 and 1904 and on which are based the theories of the Deutscher Werkbund. The garden city of Hellerau, built by Heinrich Tessenov in 1908 under the initiative of the Deutscher Werkbund, is a concrete proof of this wish to experiment with English solutions. Baillie Scott, at the time when he worked on Hampstead Garden Suburb, designed in 1909 some buildings for the Hellerau garden city, which was an important point of reference among the modern architects of the time (Le Corbusier visited it soon after). Franz Schüster, who worked in the Siedlung Westhausen, Römerstadt etc., was a pupil of Tessenov.[126] This return to the picturesque applied to the garden city, and filtered through the English experience, found in Germany a direct echo of Sitte's ideas. These had been translated by his pupils in projects such as the garden suburbs of Darmstadt, built from 1904 onwards by the architect E. Pützer, one of Sitte's draughtsmen at the time of *Der Städtebau* ...

Finally, the Breslau period (1919–25) was rich in lessons for this type of project. Having been under the influence of Fritz Schumacher, the planner from Hamburg,

---

125 May is extremely open with regard to his experience in England: 'In 1910 I went to England again and this time it was to deepen my superficial knowledge of English architecture through practical work in a large architect's office. I was taken on by Sir Raymond Unwin in Hampstead. At that time they were working on the Hampstead Garden Suburb garden city. I became acquainted with the plan and the realization of a project which, from that time onward, had a decisive influence on European architecture and which one has to consider still as a milestone for the evolution of the contemporary city.' Related by Justus Bueckschmitt (1963), *Ernst May*, with a foreword by Walter Gropius (Stuttgart: Alexander Koch).
126 Heinrich Tessenov (1876-1950), after having studied in Munich, was an assistant to professor Schultze-Naumburg, one of the theoreticians of the pan-Germanic picturesque, whose influence can be found in Unwin and Berlage.

who believed in the idea of a city progressing from its administrative and commercial centre to a residential periphery of individual houses, May connected himself again with the garden city theories in the context of the competition for the extension plan of the city of Breslau (1921). This competition, in which he obtained only a commendation, marked the beginning of the application of the principle of satellite cities and the refusal to continue the radioconcentric development of the city. In his articles from the *Schlesiche Heim*, he insisted on the importance of the publication in 1921 of the works of Unwin and Lethaby: *Theorie und Praxis im Städtebau*.[127] With the development plan of Breslau (1924) he stressed even more the necessity of planning urban growth within a regional framework, which would go beyond the traditional city boundaries, through satellite cities connected by rapid urban transport.

May's reference to the English garden city, though, was not only as a theoretical and global model of growth, but was directly inspired by his practical experience in the Hampstead Garden Suburb project. The Siedlungen were not considered as independent cities, but they had a specific relationship with the old city. As in Berlage's projects, the urban park connected as much as it divided, which means that its role must be further compared to the role of the London parks, and the Hampstead Garden Suburb comes to mind rather than the 'agricultural belt of Howard'. We have seen how the development plan of the Nidda Valley to the west and the completed project of Bornheimerhang to the east clearly show the dialogue between the new areas and the old city.

In Römerstadt the bastioned wall that dominates the Nidda corresponds to the fortifications of the city centre, and the underlying allotments refer to the external gardens of medieval cities, adjoining the ramparts as in Rothenburg, which is one of Unwin's favourite examples. More than the terraces of Villa Medici, Römerstadt recalls the brick wall that encloses the houses of the Hampstead Garden Suburb extension.

Considering the park as the connection between the city and its extensions has its consequences. For May the explosion of the city does not mean a loss of urban form. On the contrary, in his projects he attempted to abolish the uncontrolled sprawl of suburbs that was typical of the nineteenth century by replacing a mononuclear structure – which no longer suited the conditions of twentieth-century planning – with a multinuclear structure organized around parks, as in London. In order to achieve this May gave the old city a clear edge with respect to the new nuclei. This meant that, at the time when the large Siedlungen, together with old villages enclosed in the development, created the peripheral units, a new intervention in the nine-

---

127 The close relationship between Unwin and May, which started again after World War One, can be easily demonstrated. In giving a series of lectures in Berlin in 1922 on the theme of 'the construction of the modern city', Unwin chose to illustrate his theories with the example of May's project for the development of Breslau. We must remember that, while in Hampstead, May had translated Unwin's book: *Town Planning in Practice*, having in mind to get it published in Germany.

teenth-century city created small Siedlungen, inserted into the urban tissue so as to give the old city a definite edge.

This type of intervention, which could not be completed in the time available at Frankfurt, can be compared to Berlage's intervention in Amsterdam. Here the Old-South (Oud-Zuid) to the north of the Noorder Amstelkanaal was completed, before the building of the new areas (Niew-Zuid), even though in Amsterdam the separation between new extensions and old centre was reduced to the dimensions of the Amstelkanaal, because of the particular problems of ground consolidation.

Finally, the idea of a very large industrial city with several poles – subject to a degree of zoning and had gone over its natural boundaries, which had been transformed into urban parks – recalled Berlin (Frankfurt, the old imperial capital, had to accept a secondary position). It also recalls London, which May discovered during his first stay there, when he was twenty: 'The English metropolis first makes you feel dizzy because of its huge size, its enormous traffic... For the first time in my life I felt carried away by the rhythm of a gigantic city.'[128]

This concept of a modern city structured by a system of parks, where the different strategic points were expressed spatially, had Unwin's imprint, which also appeared in the treatment of details, especially in his first works. The principles experimented with in Hampstead Garden Suburb and collected in *Town Planning in Practice*[129] can be found in the Nidda projects or in Niederrad. They included the differentiation of areas through the use of distinct grids, the morphological treatment of centres through taller buildings (Römerstadt), squares (Praunheim) or the combination of the two (Niederrad), the creation of small woods recalling the theme of the orchard by grouping individual gardens (Römerstadt) and the use of the centre of blocks for play areas or collective facilities (Niederrad, Praunheim). These interventions show how May used in his own way all the solutions suggested by Unwin. The same can be said about the already mentioned wall and bastions of Römerstadt, the planted esplanades that decorate secondary streets and the hierarchical definition of roads.

From England he also inherited the grouping idea, where the housing unit is no more the isolated house, but the row of houses, a topic of systematic research. Due to the German economic situation of the 1920s, he developed the private garden, directly connected, when possible, to the dwellings, in a way recalling the terraces and cottages, but also the German working-class cities of the beginning of the century.

But the similarities end here. If in Breslau the form of buildings and the general housing layout recalled the rustic picturesque of the garden city, this did not occur in Frankfurt. The reasons for this are to be found in the economic history of the Weimar Republic. The reference to a rustic architecture is frequent in a period of

128 Related by J. Bueckschmitt, op. cit.
129 R. Unwin, op cit.

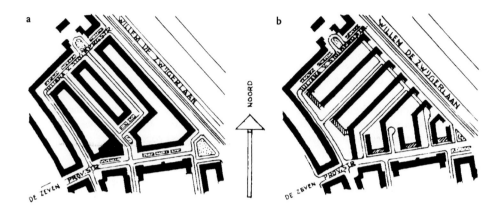

Figure 59
Landlust Quarter, Bos en Lommer, Amsterdam.
a. Project by Berlage (detail from the overall plan of the western extension, 1925–6).
b. Executed project by the architects Karsten and Merkelbach (1932–6). Giedion, a faithful witness of the CIAMs, takes this project as the point of 'progress' in the planning of Amsterdam.
c. The internal space: the beginning of large housing estates.

154

monetary crisis. It is the period when Gropius built Sommerfeldhaus in wood, when industrial techniques were not possible and when German architecture seemed to have regressed when compared with the 1910s, that is when it did not escape into utopia. With prosperity a new hope in a modern, scientific and rational architecture reappeared and, at the same time, a more pressing need for a mass architecture.

We will deal later with this rationalization and will further discuss here formal references. May's change was not an isolated fact. In Germany it corresponded to a clear shift in the theoretical and ideological standpoint of modern architects, which was the consequence of the improvement in the economic and political situation. It was also influenced by the progress in foreign countries of the Modern Movement, especially in Holland and Switzerland, which had not been directly touched by the war.[130]

The planning of Frankfurt was influenced by these changes. It was conceived with the global transformation of an agglomeration following new planning principles so as to adapt Frankfurt to the conditions of a large industrial city. All the formal repertory of modern architecture was made available for this project. The magazine *Das neue Frankfurt* bears witness that May was aware of all the experiments carried out during that period and the presence in Frankfurt of Adolf Meyer, F. Roeckle, Mart Stam and E. Kaufmann confirms the connection with all the most important centres of theoretical experimentation (the Bauhaus, ABC etc.). The particular conditions of May's activity in Frankfurt allowed him there, better than elsewhere, to pursue the unity of architecture and town planning. He was practically the only architect who was able to carry out on a large scale this synthesis, which represented, as Le Corbusier's writings show, the main objective of the architects of the 1920s.

May's dependence with regard to the English garden city is clearly expressed in an article in *Das neue Frankfurt*, which came out in 1928 at the time of Howard's death.[131] This was not only an occasion for remembering the founder of the garden cities, but also an opportunity to locate his contribution within the whole evolution of the Modern Movement. For May and the editors of *Das neue Frankfurt*, Adolf Loos, Camillo Sitte and Ebenezer Howard were the most important personalities of the years 1890–1900, those who 'had set out the basis for town planning and rational construction'. The following three issues, his project to combine architecture, urban design and the control of urban development, best synthesize May's aims.

---

130 One can judge the collective awareness of the connection architecture/town planning among the architects of the Modern Movement when observing the evolution of the themes of the CIAM congresses The first one at La Sarraz (1928) consisted of a meeting of modern architects reacting against the decision regarding the competition for the Geneva Palais des Nations; this grouping happened from an aesthetic/ethical position with regard to issues of form. From the second congress in Frankfurt (1929), which was devoted to social housing (*Das Wohnung für das Existenzminimum*), the CIAMs progressively became interested in town planning: CIAM 3 – house groupings in Brussels (1930); CIAM 4 – town planning principles in Athens (1933). May and Frankfurt were not unaware of this evolution.
131 *Das neue Frankfurt*, 7–8 July–August 1928.

THE RATIONALIZATION OF THE BLOCK AND RATIONALIST ARCHITECTURE

The epithet 'functionalist' is today regarded as pejorative but the rediscovery of the architecture of the twenties and thirties went together with a return to fashion of the word 'rationalism'. Suddenly, all types of architecture that did not comply with the canons of CIAM were implicitly designated as irrational. While all architecture, which today reuses its formal vocabulary, even though the theoretical, economic and technical conditions are no more the same as fifty years ago, is protected from any criticism by the fact of having belonged to that heroic period. This can lead to confusion. Those who have analysed Le Corbusier's houses at Pessac, especially those called 'the skyscrapers', found it difficult to find there a rational and logical answer to the problems of the workers of Bordeaux in 1925 or to the problem of mass production of dwellings, apart from the charm and interest of the project. When we deal with the issue of the rationalization of the block, we do not look in the first instance for a 'rational architecture'.

An emerging rationality within an urban order usually appears when the following two factors converge. First the necessity or opportunity to rapidly construct a large number of buildings and an agency that can assume this responsibility. Without going back to Roman cities or to the *bastides* of Guyenne, the problem existed and was generally solved since the seventeenth century in France and England, to cite only two examples. In France this happened in the case of limited speculative operations such as the Place des Vosges and later the plot subdivision of the Palais Royal, which only rarely achieved the rationalization of the urban tissue as was the case of the city of Richelieu. In England an urban order on a large scale was achieved at the time of the reconstruction of London after the Great Fire of 1666 and also the systematic plot subdivision of the estates, where one can clearly see the acquired awareness of the block as a basic unit for the construction of a city.

Since it starts with the Paris of Haussmann, this investigation does not really attempt to find the origins of the rationalization of the block. Paradoxically, the English example had not been taken up by Haussmann in spite of the attraction Napoléon III had for London. Except in some rare cases, the Parisian block remains a collection of independent parts, built by different developers. Its rationalization, which happened in the quest for maximum possible rent obtainable from the buildable volume, shows itself in the loss of autonomy of the plot – the courtyards are joined together in order to occupy the least possible area – and also through the homogeneity of the types used and the uniformity of façades.

In the garden city, which ignored the city, the close is experimented with in a further attempt to turn the space inside out. The Dutch, especially in Amsterdam and Rotterdam, renewed the tradition of the urban block and gave a last spectacular demonstration of its possibilities. During a period of 21 years, from 1913 to 1934, Holland gave the most accomplished interpretation of the rationalization of the block.

With a strict and legible hierarchy of roads – which did not prevent façades from having a monumental or picturesque composition, corner treatments and the development of internal spaces – the block in Amsterdam showed a particular sensitivity with regard to the relationship of architecture and the city.

The rationalist architecture that developed in Germany started from a completely different analysis and it established a more abstract and fragile relationship with the form of the old city. The block was only an accidental element and was soon abandoned; even though a clear relationship of the building and its associated ground space remained, as was shown in the terraces that inherited the traditional tissue.

From 1928 onwards the CIAMs did away with these remaining ties and attempted to bring back to the scale of the city the principles carried out in the avant-garde experiments. The block was dissolved and the formal vocabulary continued to be further simplified. The abolition of differences between back and front façades and between floors, a consequence of homogenising space, led to a uniform treatment of façades, to a modular repetition of a typical cell, where openings were determined once and for all and no more expressed a dialogue between the dwellings and urban space. Buildings became objects, leading to the complete explosion of the urban tissue of which the Unité d'Habitation is the most complete manifestation.

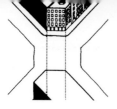

CHAPTER 8
BUILDING THE CITY: 1975–95

Because of successive crises, the issue of having to build the city remains at the top of the list of architects' preoccupations and so regularly provides a motive for them to explore new ground in their projects. It is no more the case that developers or public agencies deny a desire to be concerned with the urban environment. But this passage to an urban society does not happen without pain. If, between the difficulties that contemporary cities and their peripheries are faced with, some are without doubt the direct consequences of an economic crisis that mostly goes beyond the domain of architecture and deeply destabilizes society, while others are due to planning errors, from which it is difficult to avoid blaming the profession. Often, these errors have even accentuated and exaggerated the effects of the crisis, creating, locally, some situations that are unsustainable. To understand this state of affairs we have to keep reminding ourselves at regular intervals of Brixton, Venissieux or Mantes. Today the issue of the city remains a challenge and so we believe that at the conclusion of our study it is useful to identify some future directions.

THE PROBLEM OF THE URBAN TISSUE

This study has dealt little with the bigger scale of projects. Without denying their importance, it chose to concentrate on an intermediate scale, which is essential for understanding an urban project and which we can call the urban tissue. The concept of tissue, in fact, with the double textile and biological connotations, evokes ideas of interweaving and of connections between parts, together with a capacity for adaptation. It is in contrast to the completed or fixed work and, instead, implies a process of transformations. It can provide a critical response to those problems that we have inherited from recent developments.

The urban tissue, which is the superimposition of several structures acting at different scales, but which appears as a system with linkages in each part of the city, can be defined as the culminating point of three logical systems:

- the logic of roads in their double roles of movement and distribution;
- the logic of plot subdivisions, where land holdings are built up and where private and public initiatives take place; and
- the logic of buildings that contain different activities.

The old cities, in their own way and each with different modes, ensure the coherence of the tissue. The street does not exist without the buildings that define it, and the buildings are built on plots that form the framework of their evolution. Spaces have a status, which determines legal responsibilities as well as possible uses. Systems of reference, orientation are generally legible; activities are mixed and modifications are easy.

It is necessary to come back to this forgotten lesson of the old cities and to the ease of everyday life that they enabled. This can take on the nature of a word puzzle so that we have to observe the rules:

- remember that, generally, in the old system, the number 7 of a street is located between numbers 5 and 9 – obviously with the exception of the *bis* numbers; but, what lies next door to number 56 of the Rue Salvador Allende of Nanterre? or try to find where on a plan is Collina D-26 in Brasilia;
- notice that the entrance of a building opens onto a pavement, and notice how easy it is to park the car, to walk on the pavement and to ring a bell, or the more recent fashion to compose a code and to enter a hallway;
- appreciate how the everyday types of shop occupy the ground floors of busy streets and that, from the exit of the underground or bus stop to one's home, one can buy one's favourite frozen dishes or bread or batteries for quartz watches or writing paper, a child's shirt or a bunch of flowers;
- note that a computer-repair firm has replaced, without any problems, an umbrella store and that the old cabinetmaker at the end of the courtyard has become a busy graphics and communications office;
- read again *Au bonheur des Dames* (novel by Dumas) and then return to the basement of the BHV (a Parisian department store);
- go to see again *Rear Window* (Hitchcock film);
- sit on the terrace of a café looking at passers-by.

The topic of the urban tissue cannot be dissociated from the everyday and ordinary experience of the city, because, even if one prefers Venice to La Grande Motte or Rodez to Cergy-Pontoise, aesthetics are here secondary and it is on the grounds of qualities for the user that we have become interested in the old city and in the analysis of its tissues. Building the city today could mean the wish to find again, perhaps with different forms, the qualities of proximity, mixture and the unexpected, i.e. a public space accessible to all, a variety of mixed activities, a built-up area that keeps adapting and transforming itself in unplanned neighbourhoods.

By dealing with the urban tissue we return to an ability to think once again of the city in other than the functional categories we have inherited. The application of these categories, in spite of any denials has, as an inescapable consequence, produced our cities. Two examples taken from different aspects of our lives can illustrate this subject: our relationship with the car and the programming of activities.

The relationships we have with the car are schizophrenic. Cars are omnipresent and we seem to be incapable of accommodating this presence in new neighbourhoods, or rather we only pretend to take them into account. Paradoxically, this seems easier in old cities, where, once some measures have been taken to moderate speed and control parking, the presence of the car does not conflict with normal urban activities. But, in recent urban planning, any attempt to make cars coexist with pedestrians becomes

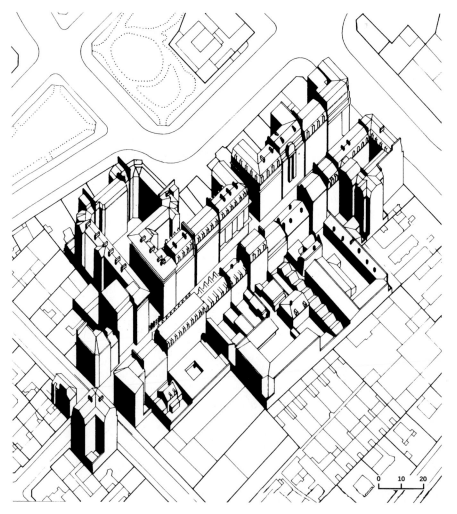

Figure 60
The street as the basic element of the urban tissue.
Rue Daguerre, Paris, beginning of the nineteenth century.

impossible, like combining transit with residential routes, a simple crossing point, delivering goods from a public road and so forth. And, the more density decreases, the more things become complicated. Urban space becomes diluted into primary roads, lined by embankments, which go from one roundabout to another, and you do not get the time to find out where you are before you end up in some service cul-de-sac or parking place. Retracing the route becomes an obstacle race and going

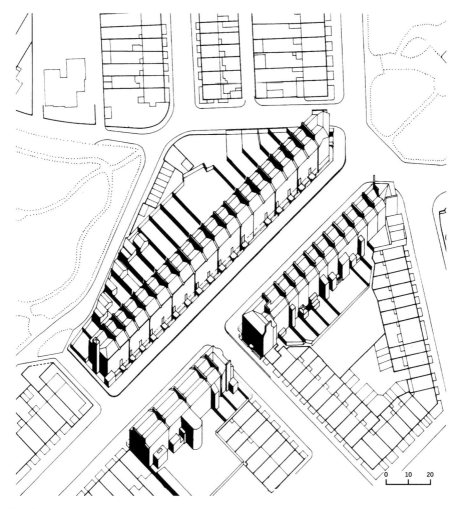

Figure 61
Row housing as an element producing tissues.
Bath, row houses, beginning of the nineteenth century.

anywhere else is an adventure. Our own urban experience, which makes us appreciate the open-air cafés of the Boulevard Saint-Germain or the Ramblas of Barcelona or Rome's Spanish Steps, seems irrelevant beyond the ring road. In considering new towns, a solution such as the Place de la République is unthinkable.

The functional categories that we apply to activities also appear archaic and unsuitable, because they describe a stable world and a work organization that does not correspond to the reality of the city. Thus, putting into the same category 'retail' as hypermarkets and corner shops of 50 square metres will not enable one to imagine, from the beginning of a project design the implications and transformations possible. The same area of between 100 and 200 square metres can consecutively house a shop, a small public facility, medical or paramedical services, a small firm, an artist's studio or dwellings – sculptors (in the 'artists' category) work with the same tools as coppersmiths (in the 'artisans' or 'industrial' category). The gym hall (in the 'sports and leisure' category) is not very different from the rehabilitation space (in the 'medical facilities' category), but can be easily transformed into lofts (in the 'dwellings' category). Any large villa can become a local library, a community centre or a police station. An important daily newspaper has moved into a garage, shopping arcades become theatres and abattoirs museums.

Rather than concern itself excessively with functional changes, which need drastic modifications, the urban project should endeavour to define a set of ground rules with regard to those divisions and simple morphological rules, which constitute a stable basis on which tissues can then be progressively built.

OPEN BLOCKS AND CLOSED BLOCKS

The analysis of the five cases that, from Haussmann to Le Corbusier, mark out the tearing apart of the tissue, which has given rise to different interpretations, the most frequent of which has consisted of linking a desire for urbanity with the taking up again of the so-called traditional block structure. There is here a source of confusion and we therefore need to reiterate some points.

The block (in French, îlot, which etymologically means small island) is a part of the urban area 'isolated' from the neighbouring parts of the territory by streets. Thus, the block is not an architectural form, but a group of interdependent building plots. It has a proper meaning only when it is in a dialectical relationship with the road network. If we put aside the special cases of facilities or monumental blocks, which consist of only one plot, like just one building, the block of the traditional city is rarely homogeneous and the buildings on its perimeter obey some rules, especially those of that economic logic that has shaped the surrounding streets. Interdependent, but distinctive, the plots provide the construction processes with a fixed legal and real estate framework, which conditions the evolution of buildings

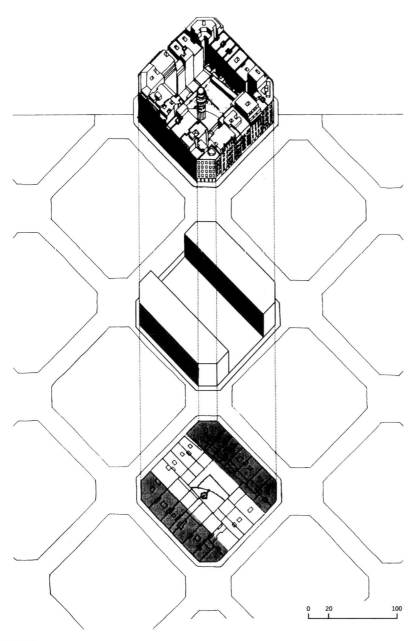

Figure 62
The block as a large-scale structuring element.
Barcelona, the plan by Cerda.

0   20   100

and the types of use by the inhabitants. This definition does not influence at all the continuity of the enclosure and the homogeneity of perimeter buildings. Indeed, the old tissues demonstrate a great number of incomplete alignments and heterogeneous fronts, where one can see a large number of buildings of different heights along the streets – and some even recessed – gaps and walls, which shelter courtyards or gardens and allow for planting to be seen. It is often only in the central areas, and as a result of several centuries of progressive densification, that one can find compact built-up blocks and a degree of continuous enclosure.

To think of the block as a whole would be missing the point, and reducing it to a continuous and homogeneous built-up area surrounding an empty centre would be a caricature of reality, where complexity and depth of tissue is ignored to the advantage of a central area of uncertain status or function. The examples discussed, for that matter, show how the general adoption of this global way of thinking has brought about the explosion of the tissue. To take up this generalization today, without questioning the issue of internal subdivisions, risks showing the outward appearance of urbanity without ensuring the conditions to allow it to happen. It brings to urban planning an attitude comparable to that of architectural post-modernism which replaces history with references and uses by symbols. Post-modern planning, which developed in response to the urban crisis, ends up in a proliferation of signs, as if these would be sufficient to ward off reality.

It is not by adding pediments to social housing (the French HLMs), that one will solve the problem of large housing estates, nor by redesigning the paving in the small pedestrian squares created in town centres. The closed block does not guarantee urbanity a priori more than the open block and the post-neoclassical 'European city' resembles Disneyland.

STREETS AND SUBDIVISIONS

It is convenient to talk about the block. The block can be read in the plan of the city as the negative of the road layout and the drawing of the roads itself isolates it. But this leads to confusion and the strength of the image of the block risks, as we saw previously, arriving at a reductive reading. In this way a caricatured image appears, where the block becomes a sort of Viennese *Hof* or a Parisian HBM (*habitations à bon marché*) whose interior is reduced to a large more or less controlled courtyard, a distant memory of the courtyard of Florentine Renaissance palaces.

To understand the block, not as an a priori form but as a resulting system, capable of organising parts of the urban territory, implies forgetting for a moment the great regular layouts that, from the chequerboard of Hippodamus to the super blocks of Brasilia, marked the history of spontaneous city planning. It also means abandoning the haunting image of the Roman city, the bastides and Spanish colonial cities, and

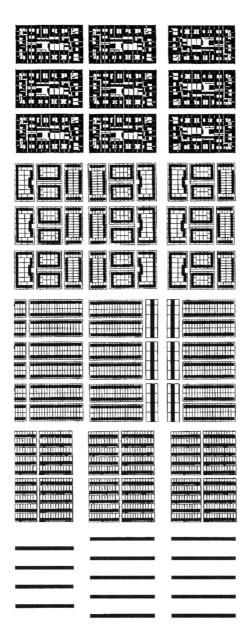

Figure 63
Hommage to Ernst May.

forgetting Jefferson's chequerboard pattern and Cerda's plan. Or to consider at least that these projects marked the periodic return in history of a global way of thinking, where the logic of the block and that of the road network are fused together in a rationalization of previous experiences. It is only necessary to look at the plans of the very first bastides or the first Spanish attempts at city planning in Latin America, to appreciate the necessary trial and error and vicissitudes, before the codified plans were achieved, which we regard as canonical.

Without negating these interesting proposals or their relevance to the debate on the contemporary city, it is essential to start again from a different viewpoint, in order to rediscover the elementary logic of the urban tissue. Whether it is pre-existing or originates from a new layout, it is the street that distributes, feeds and orders development. The dialectical relationship between street and built plots creates the tissue and it is in the continuation of this relationship – capable of modification, extension and the substitution of buildings – where reside the capacity of the city to adapt to the demographic, economic and cultural changes that mark its evolution. The street layout determines the relationship with site, centre and capacity for extension. The width of plots (their opening on the street) and their depth condition (and are conditioned by) the type of buildings used. To a narrow plot correspond the row house and the small building (the Gothic plot); to larger plots correspond villas and detached houses, houses with courtyards, and apartment buildings. The regrouping of small plots or the subdivision of larger ones, when historical conditions require it, allows for the integration of new types of building. The same block can accommodate different buildings and densities. Courtyards and gardens can coexist with stores and small factories and several functions can be located next to one another.

MODERN URBAN ARCHITECTURE

Questioning the city, the urban tissue and plot subdivisions will have some consequences for architectural design. The first of these implies that one will have to locate all programmes and projects in their right place, in the interlocking scales typical of each city, and capture in this way the urban values (often little or badly specified in the briefs), that are connected to the site and the location. Urban planning can no more be reduced to the production of stereotyped solutions, but will have to involve the design of new buildings in an overall concern for the territory and its future transformation. This also means to take on board the inheritance of the Modern Movement, even if it means to have to correct its effects in urban terms.

The second consequence implies a debate on the relative importance of style and to go beyond the contradicting tendencies in professional discussions. Urban architecture is mainly involved in solving problems concerning the city, respecting its logic, whatever its formal aspect. This should lead us to a double rereading. First, of those works of the Modern Movement, which have been able to connect the urban aspect with modernity, and, second, of one exploring older architecture, which has experienced solutions or dispositions that may now respond to our present concerns. The Mazarin district of Aix-en-Provence (1643) then appears to us to be close to a Siedlung and the Clarté building in Geneva (1927) to be a small cousin of a Georgian terrace.

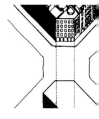

CHAPTER 9
AN ANGLO-AMERICAN POSTSCRIPT

INTRODUCTION

This chapter is intended as a supplement to the latest French edition of *Formes urbaines*. In it we will try to bring the narrative of this book forward by considering recent developments in the US and UK that, in a sense, bring the story told by the original three authors full circle. This additional material will deal in detail with four exemplary projects accomplished over the last fifteen years in these two countries and discuss the changing role of the block as an element of urban composition. In order to set the context for this it is necessary to discuss the urban design culture of both the US and the UK together with some of the aspects of the wider planning contexts that have had and continue to have a bearing on the form of towns, especially with regard to new housing developments, whether in town, on the urban periphery or in new settlements.

While the earlier chapters of the book emphasise the cross-European fertilization of ideas, this one extends the discussion to a transatlantic exchange that has been and continues to be close because of the shared language and historical and cultural links. For example, in relation to the themes of this book, Ebenezer Howard, father of the garden city, which has been such a seminal idea in the previous chapters, spent some years of his early adulthood in the United States, while Clarence Stein, one of the designers of Radburn, knew Howard and Unwin, visited Letchworth and Welwyn and worked as a consultant on Stevenage, the first of the New Towns[132].

A further intention of this contribution is to fill in some of the byways that lie off the path of the original version. Some of these, for instance the Radburn superblock, have arguably been as destructive to the urban tissue as the Ville Radieuse. This focus on the urban block (it is part of the title of the French edition) does not imply that we regard it as the primary element in the production of urban form. From a morphological point of view, as explained in Chapter 8, this role is played by the street as that element of the public space system that structures settlements. The block is the space between the streets occupied by the private space of plots, semiprivate space and sometimes public space and buildings. This space is generally private, but, as has been explored in previous chapters, the balance between public and private has shifted over the period discussed. This chapter takes further this exploration of the use and appropriation of the space between the streets and, in particular, how this practice has been modified to accommodate the motor vehicle. The chapter concludes with a discussion comparing the use of space in the examples described.

132 K.C. Parsons (ed.) (1998), *The Writings of Clarence S. Stein: Architect of the Planned Community* (Baltimore, MD: Johns Hopkins University Press).

It may be considered presumptuous to write of events that are so relatively close in time, since it could be objected that we have not had the time to absorb them and identify their true significance. However, we suggest that such a discussion is justified for a number of reasons. First, these projects have their origins in tendencies started at the time of the projects discussed in the previous editions of this work and their consequences. Second, we will discuss projects that have been built and have already had a manifest impact on practice. We are able to observe them on the ground and note how they work. Third, some of these projects are no closer to us in time then the last of Le Corbusier's Unités was to the writing of the first French edition of the book. Finally, this postscript should be regarded as a hypothesis, a sketch to be updated as the projects are revisited and the transformations, which time will bring to them as to all our towns, can be observed.

THE CULTURE OF URBAN DESIGN IN THE UK AND THE US

There are many similarities between the urban design cultures of the United Kingdom and United States, especially with respect to the evolution of the suburb[133]. Both countries have been and continue to be distinguished by a high degree of home ownership and a propensity to live in single houses with gardens, whether these are detached, semidetached or terraced (row houses in the US). The cities in both countries lost the constraining effect of systems of fortification long before their European counterparts.

Both countries have evolved financial institutions and tax regimes that favoured house purchase over renting as a preferred form of tenure. Unlike the case in many European countries, renting in the UK and US is usually confined to those who cannot afford house purchase. The housing market represents a much more important factor in the economies of the United States and the United Kingdom than those of Continental Europe and as a consequence housing design may have been more affected by market considerations.

There are also considerable differences between the two countries in a number of respects. In the spatial field, for instance, and in the use and character of the public and private realms. The most obvious of these are the much bigger houses and more extensive road space of the United States, where car ownership has long been much higher with a commensurate decline in the provision and use of public transport and a consequent dispersal of activities. The average price a US house sells for is only 10 per cent more than that of the average UK house, yet it is 66 per cent bigger in floor area[134].

There are also major differences in the planning control systems. The United States system is based on a written constitution and precise local ordinances, which are capable of controlling the layout and design of urban areas to a considerable degree

---

133 R.A.M. Stern (1981), *The Anglo American Suburb* (London: Architectural Design).
134 *The Economist*, 21 May 2003.

of detail, especially where questions are involved concerning protecting the rights and property of the individual. It has many parallels with the Roman law-based systems of most of Continental Europe. In contrast, under a system of common law, British planning takes many factors into account when a local authority makes a decision to allow development. Legally adopted plans are only one of these factors and, in any case, they are usually much less specific about detail than either the US plans or the plans produced in Continental Europe. The British system is also much more centralized, so there is a plethora of guidance that comes in the form of planning advice from central government and has a bearing on local decision making.

In both countries the importance of the private sector in urban development means that the examples considered in detail below are cases of plans prepared by private developers or, in the case of Hulme, a public/private company. They are not prepared by the local authority, which was the case in Amsterdam or Frankfurt in Chapters 3 and 4 and the public housing projects and British new towns of the 1950s and 1960s. This private-sector-led process represents the continuation of a tradition that produced Bath and the new town of Edinburgh in the eighteenth century and Letchworth and Welwyn, built by nonprofit companies, or Coral Gables and Forest Hills Gardens in the United States.

PATTERNS OF RECONSTRUCTION AFTER WORLD WAR TWO

In the postwar United Kingdom there were two models for the reconstruction of the bomb-damaged towns and those (e.g. Glasgow) that were both damaged and were subject to large-scale clearance in the quest for better living conditions. The first of these was in the image of the Ville Radieuse, for example the rebuilding of the Glasgow Gorbals, the Hulme district of Manchester with gallery-access flats, or the Roehampton Estate in south London (see Chapter 7). It is a great irony that in both the former cases, as in many others of their contemporaries, these blocks are now being systematically demolished to make way for new houses constructed according to a system of streets and urban blocks closely resembling that which was demolished thirty years earlier. Hulme, described below, is an example of this process.

The second model was typically used in the construction of the new towns. Their planning was based on two innovatory concepts: the Radburn superblock and the neighbourhood unit. Although both were imported from the US, the latter, as a technique for subdividing large areas of housing, had its origins in the work of Ebenezer Howard, whose garden city of 30,000 inhabitants was subdivided by roads into wards of 5,000. Even though he gave no reasons for this dimension, it proved to be a prescient choice since that size has continued to be used in further interpretations of the neighbourhood unit concept. The use of the road network to divide the urban area into neighbourhoods with a school at the centre of each one was also in advance of its period. At the time that Howard was writing the car was not in common use and Howard never mentioned it in his book, but the whole issue of accommodating motor vehicles has proved to be a major factor in town design ever since.

THE NEIGHBOURHOOD UNIT

The first complete formulation of the neighbourhood concept came in 1929, when, in a volume of the regional Survey of New York, Clarence Perry proposed a unit based on a population of between 5,000 and 9,000 people that was needed to support local facilities[135]. Again, it was to be separated from adjoining neighbourhoods by arterial roads. An important feature of this project was the location of the shops at one corner of the neighbourhood at a point of maximum accessibility, not in the centre, as recommended in the British Dudley Report[136]. This document legitimized the use of the neighbourhood unit as a tool for postwar reconstruction, including in the new towns programme, and the concept has continued to be interpreted and applied with variations up until the present day, especially by the New Urbanists in the United States and the Urban Villages Forum in the United Kingdom[137].

THE RADBURN SUPERBLOCK

With the exception of the radical response of the Ville Radieuse, previous chapters hardly needed to discuss the way the accommodation of moving and parked cars influenced the form of the projects described. The motor vehicle was not a sufficiently important factor impinging on the design of the urban tissue. It will be a major factor in this chapter, starting in 1929, when the superblock was conceived for the new town of Radburn in the US by Clarence Stein at a time when car ownership was at levels that were not to be reached for another 25 years in the UK[138]. This layout set out to completely separate pedestrians from vehicles while, unlike the Ville Radieuse, still using conventional single-family houses. It excluded all through movement from a two-square-mile block of development that was surrounded by a 350-foot-wide (100-metre-wide) wide reservation accommodating arterial roads with a limited number of access roads into each superblock.

At a first glance the layout of the houses within the superblock bears a striking resemblance to the closes of Welwyn discussed in Chapter 2. A more careful examination reveals that the houses have two public 'fronts'. One faces the car-access cul-de-sac and the other faces a linear park that accommodates a network of pedestrian routes. These link all the houses to facilities such as schools using bridges or underpasses where it is necessary to cross a road. The role of official policy in influencing the form of the urban tissue has been noted in previous chapters. This applied to the Radburn superblock, which was adopted in the 1930s by the United States Federal Housing Authority as its preferred form. This was important because, as the agency that approved government-insured mortgages, it was able to encourage lenders to favour loans to houses on culs-de-sac rather than to those on the traditional layout of a grid of connected streets.

135 C.A.Perry (1929), 'The Neighbourhood Unit', in *Regional Survey of New York and its Environs* (Vol. VII) (New York, NY: Regional Plan of New York).
136 Ministry of Health (1944), *The Design of Dwellings (the Dudley Report)* (London: HMSO).
137 M. Biddulph (2000), 'Villages don't make a city', in *Journal of Urban Design*, 5 (1), pp. 65–82.
138 C.S. Stein (1958), *Towards new towns for America* (Liverpool: Liverpool University Press).

a

Figure 64 (Clarence Stein, *"Towards New Towns for America"*)

a. Clarence Stein and Henry Wright. The 1929 plan of the residential districts of Radburn, NJ. The horizontal separation of vehicle and pedestrian routes is clear.
b. The plan of a cul-de-sac at Radburn. There is a superficial resemblance to the closes at Welwyn Garden City discussed in Chapter 2.
c. Four alternative ways of developing a block, from Clarence Stein, *Toward New Towns for America* (1950). They are intended to show a progressive reduction in the importance of the lot as 'the controlling factor in design'. The lowest plan is that of the blocks as built at Sunnyside in 1924. There are interesting comparisons to be made with May's work discussed in Chapter 4.

b

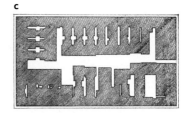

c

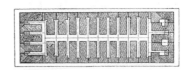

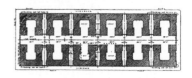

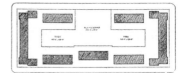

a

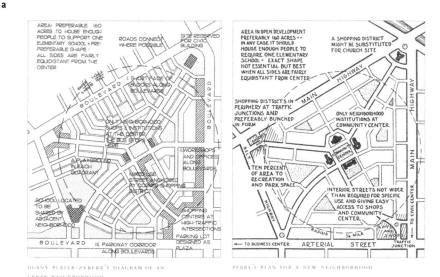

DUANY PLATER-ZYBERK'S DIAGRAM OF AN
URBAN NEIGHBORHOOD

PERRY'S PLAN FOR A NEW NEIGHBORHOOD

b

c

SUBURBAN SPRAWL

TRADITIONAL NEIGHBORHOOD

Figure 65
a. The neighbourhood unit as conceived (right) by Clarence Perry in 1929 and (left) by Duany Plater-Zyberk, from *Charter of the New Urbanism* (1999). The latter differs in that the school is on the edge of the unit, there are road links to adjoining neighbourhoods and office buildings and open spaces flank the arterial roads to act as sound barriers.
b. A figure ground plan of the new town of Milton Keynes (Martin Davies (2002), unpublished urban design project, Oxford Brookes University).
c. A comparison between sprawl (above), which eliminates pedestrian connections and focuses all traffic on to a single road, and the traditional neighbourhood (below) (Duany Plater-Zyberk and Speck (2000), *Suburban Nation: the Rise of Sprawl and the Decline of the American Dream*).

In Britain the apotheosis of the combined paradigms of Radburn layout and the neighbourhood unit was achieved with the 1km-square blocks of Milton Keynes, the last new town, which was designated in 1966 and is still growing. But, even in places where the concept was less rigorously applied, the growth of traffic volumes made the exclusion of through traffic from residential areas seem ever more desirable. But the means adopted for this exclusion also served to isolate neighbourhoods from one another and from the rest of the town. The horizontal separation of vehicles and pedestrians and the way motor car movement was privileged over other forms of mobility, including walking and public transport, was to set the mould for development over the rest of the century.

Accommodating the motor car was to be the determining factor in the design of housing areas for the latter half of the twentieth century. It impacted in two ways. The first was through the layout of dendritic or treelike road systems, which were intended to facilitate fluid vehicle movement by reducing the number of junctions, eliminating crossroads and, wherever possible, shifting pedestrians onto separate route systems. The second impact came from the need to accommodate a continually growing number of parked cars in housing areas – and in the other parts of our towns for that matter.

THE PLANNING CONTEXT IN THE UNITED KINGDOM

The major planning questions in Britain over the last decade have been the quantity of new housing that will be needed, where it is going to be built and what form it will take. The consequent debate has once again focused on the question, 'The people: where will they go?' posed by Howard in that most iconic of town planning diagrams, The Three Magnets. The government advocates the intensification of existing settlements to take the 3.5 million new homes that it is claimed will be needed by 2011[139] (Breheny and Hall, 1996) with a target of 50 per cent of all new housing to be built on reused urban sites by 2005[140].

The challenge for urban design is the form this new housing will take in relation to existing settlements – how it is connected and how it will deal with issues of a policy shift towards increased density while car ownership continues to rise. A further consideration that impacts on the design of these new housing areas is that they are all being built by private developers. The public sector has all but withdrawn from the design and construction of housing and the new housing is being built by the private sector, which brings a concern for market issues to the problems of urban design.

Not that the public sector had a monopoly of design virtue. The housing programmes of the postwar reconstruction had been mainly public-sector projects and it was the

139 M. Breheny and P Hall (eds.) (1996), *The People – Where Will They Go? National report of the TCPA Regional Inquiry into Housing Need and Provision in England* (London: TCPA).
140 UK Government (1994), *Sustainable development: the UK Strategy*, Cmnd 2426 (London: HMSO).

results of these that were the targets of so much criticism from a design point of view. This critique started in the 1960s with Jane Jacobs and Kevin Lynch, both American writers who quickly found an echo in Britain. In relation to the theme of this book, it should be noted that the only illustration in Jacob's graphically austere, but never-theless immensely influential work[141] demonstrates the advantages of a street network with small urban blocks. It is an indication of the close transatlantic cultural ties that these authors were so influential in promoting a British critique of the Modernist planning tradition. This is exemplified by the English Townscape School as codified by Gordon Cullen in his book *Townscape* of 1963 and the Outrage campaign waged by the *Architectural Review* around the same time against the low quality of the urban environments produced since World War Two.

DESIGN GUIDANCE IN THE UK: THE FIRST GENERATION

Punter[142] has traced the role of American authors in influencing a number of works that were published in the 1980s in response to the growing public criticism of the lack of quality in new urban environments. The Prince of Wales has a place in this list. Punter points out that his book[143], which put forward Ten Commandments of archi-tecture, topped the hardback bestseller lists for Christmas 1989. Prince Charles emphasized the qualities of place derived from a respect for place, harmony and a hierarchy of relationships between buildings and their different elements, local mate-rials and craftsmanship, enclosure and human scale. These were later to be put into practice in his development at Poundbury, Dorchester.

Many of these qualities were familiar to the Townscape School and had formed the basis of the influential *Essex Design Guide*, which was published in 1973 as a response to the poor quality of the new housing estates that had been built in the London com-muter belt. The *Guide* and its many emulators have in common a concern with the picturesque qualities of the historic town and seek to achieve these qualities in new developments. But from our viewpoint they often miss the point by neglecting the importance of connected street networks and the use of the urban block in achieving these qualities. The first edition of *The Essex Design Guide*[144] accepted the road engi-neers' concept of a treelike street network that resulted in unconnected, illegible and often unsurveilled street networks and an ambiguous relation between the public and private realm. This has been modified in the latest edition (1997), which is radically different from the first in its concern to achieve connected street networks and accep-tance of the urban block.

Firmly based in the English Picturesque tradition, this generation of guidance was primarily concerned with façades and saw the urban landscape as a sort of stage set to

---

141 J. Jacobs (1981), *The Death and Life of the Great American Cities* (New York, NY: Vintage Books).
142 J. Punter, 'The ten commandments of urban design', *The Planner*, 5 October, 1990, pp. 10–14.
143 HRH the Prince of Wales (1989), *A Vision of Britain* (London: Doubleday).
144 Essex County Council (1973), *A design guide for residential areas* (London: Anchor Press).

be tastefully composed. It was only with the publication of *Responsive Environments*[145] that the importance of the perimeter block was emphasized as the key to achieving the qualities of the traditional town. It is worth noting that, because of this championing of the importance of the urban block, this book has often been accused of being reactionary. In spite of this, it has been reprinted ten times.

URBAN VILLAGES

A later protagonist for designing better places, with an explicit social agenda that has contributed to changing policy was the British Urban Villages Forum, launched in 1993. As a lobbying group it has promoted its view of development to local authorities, development agencies and house builders. It proposed that new developments should be characterized by a diverse architecture, a legible layout, a variety of uses, sustained by an appropriate density of development, a choice of tenures, a strong sense of place and a high level of involvement by local residents in planning and managing the development. The urban village is intended to be small enough to allow a degree of familiarity with other inhabitants of the village and big enough to make the provision of commercial and social functions feasible[146]. In place of the urban monoculture, which was held responsible for the absence of these qualities in new development, the campaign proposed a notional area of 40 hectares with a population of 3–5,000 people, all of whom can reach the centre in ten minutes by foot – the neighbourhood unit again.

The term 'urban village' has been applied to various projects of very different characteristics and of various sizes (from 1 to 300 hectares), which are claimed to meet the criteria defined by the group. They include both Hulme and Poundbury described below. The flexibility of the concept – some have described it as vagueness[147] – has led to its usefulness in legitimising developments, however varied their formulation, and its inclusion in government policy guidance.

DESIGN GUIDANCE IN THE UK: THE SECOND GENERATION

The two British projects discussed in detail below were emerging from the scaffolding at a time when the critiques of the residential environment described above had permeated into a new generation of Government Planning Guidance[148]. It could be argued that their emerging success in demonstrating that it was possible to produce places that responded to this critique led the public authorities to give their official

---

145 I. Bentley et al. (1985), *Responsive Environments: A design manual* (London: Architectural Press).

146 M. Thompson Fawcett, 'The Contribution of the Urban Villages to Sustainable Development', in Williams et al. (eds) (2000), *Achieving Sustainable Urban Form* (London: E. & F. N. Spon).

147 M. Biddulph, M. Tait, and B. Franklin, 'The Urban Village: an obituary', in *Urban Design Quarterly (81)*, Winter, 2002.

148 Department of the Environment, Transport and the Regions (DETR) (1998), *'Places, Streets and Movement: A Companion Guide to Design Bulletin 32 Residential Roads and Footpaths'* (London: Department of the Environment, Transport and the Regions).

DETR (2000), *'Planning Policy Guidance Note 3: Housing*, (London, DETR).

DETR/ Commission for Architecture and the Built Environment, (DETR/CABE) (2000), *'By Design: Urban Design in the Planning System: Towards Better Practice'*, (London: DETR).

blessing to the principles that underpinned them. In contrast to the Congress for the New Urbanism (CNU) charter discussed below, this guidance is part of an established planning system[149] and its recommendations have to be taken into account in any proposals for planning consent. The implication is that if developers demonstrably follow the guidance they are more likely to get a project approved by the planning authority.

In these documents there is a generally increased concern with design than in previous planning guidance, combined with a willingness to learn from good practice that is historical as well as contemporary. In summary, these publications seek to move away from the dominance of layouts by road engineering standards towards a concern with the quality of both public and private spaces and recognition of the importance of designing for pedestrian movement. Car dependence is to be reduced by these measures together with the provision of a mix of uses and improved public transport connections. A range of housing types and tenure at higher densities than have hitherto been achieved is recommended in order to save land, allow convenient access to facilities and make public transport systems more viable.

Most significant in relation to our theme is the observation in 'Better Places to Live' that 'a block structure defined by a network of interconnected roads has been the predominant form of housing layout for centuries. Only recently have structures created primarily for the car resulted in formless residential environments characterized by a dead end system of "loops and lollipops"' and that '... some of the most attractive housing has the simplest of structures, houses face the street, gardens run end to end'[150].

The virtues of the urban perimeter block have been rediscovered.

THE UNITED STATES CONTEXT

We have seen how the superblock was introduced to the UK from the US, where it was to become the desired norm by the end of World War Two. Open space was regarded as desirable and congested streets were to be avoided. Much speculative development, however, was to drop the communal open space provision of the original Radburn concept (it used too much land that could otherwise be used to build houses for sale, it had to be maintained and by giving access to houses on two sides it posed security problems) but the traffic network aspects of the concept were retained. Blocks or pods of activity were created, which were surrounded by major arterial roads. While there was no through traffic inside the blocks, a subsequent high volume of traffic was directed onto these roads, which were functionally suited only to vehicle movement – pedestrians and cycles ventured on or across them at their peril. There

149 S. Tiesdall, 'The New Urbanism and English Residential Design Guidance: A Review', in *Urban Design Journal* vol. 7 no.3. 2002, pp. 353–376.
150 DETR/CABE (2001), '*By Design: Better Places to Live: A Design Companion to PPG3*', (London: DETR/CABE), pp. 40–41.

was no continuity of streets as in the traditional town grid or city and land uses were zoned by their functions into apartment complexes, shopping centres, office parks, resort hotels, housing condominiums etc. The zoning regime is so assiduous in the US that there is not only zoning of uses but also a separation within use zones so that low-density housing is separated from medium-density housing, which, in turn, is separated from high-density housing. These different zones are separated by landscaped areas or, more likely, by car parks, since each activity had to have its own dedicated lot and there was no question of sharing parking space.

The blocks or pods of development are held together by a dendritic street pattern. This protects residents from through traffic but this isolation from traffic results in isolation from everything else. Visiting friends or facilities that may be a few yards a way demands long and circuitous journeys through the hierarchy and often onto a major highway. In summary, to paraphrase Duany et al.[151], we have adjacency without accessibility and the street has been as effectively killed as in the Ville Radieuse.

IN SEARCH OF DEFENSIBLE SPACE

Oscar Newman's idea of 'defensible space' fits in very well with the hierarchical road system described above[152]. His book (1972) has been and continues to be very influential in both the US and the UK. In the search for security, as the crime problems, which had been confined to the inner city, spread out to the suburbs, he proposes different levels of territorial surveillance between the main roads and the personal space of the house and the cul-de-sac. Only people living in or with legitimate business in the cul-de-sac should be in that space. The argument as to whether this makes for greater security than a connected street system, where people passing by make for informal policing, is still being hotly debated.

From the defensible space of the cul-de-sac it is only a short step to the gated community, where the public space of the street is closed to public access by a gate. In 1997 the number of gated communities in the United States was put at 20,000[153] with 8 million people living in them, and eight out of ten new urban projects are gated. The majority are middle- to upper-middle-class enclaves and they are becoming increasingly extensive in the search for economies of scale in providing the enclosing structures and the security staff for the guard houses.

THE NEW URBANISM CRITIQUE

The New Urbanists point out that the patterns of development described above are leading to an atomization of American society as people increasingly come into con-

151 A. Duany, E. Plater-Zyberk and J. Speck (2000), *Suburban Nation: The Rise of Sprawl and the Decline of the American Dream* (New York, NY: North Point Press).
152 O. Newman (1972), *Defensible Space: People and Design in the Violent City* (New York, NY: Macmillan).
153 E.J. Blakely and M. G. Snyder (1997), 'Divided we fall. Gated and Walled Communities in the United States', in Ellin, N (ed.), *Architecture of Fear* (New York, NY: Princeton Architectural Press).

tact only with those of a similar background and income level. It is against this background that the real innovation of the New Urbanists has to be seen. In fact, while the language of their buildings in some cases might be regarded as pastiche or passéiste (but see below in relation to the architecture of Seaside), their project is very much part of the Modern Movement in its quest to do no less than transform the conditions of life to the same degree, but not in the same way, as a Le Corbusier or, more relevantly, an Ebenezer Howard.

In contrast to the gated community, the New Urbanists seek to replace the physical barriers with socially based mechanisms. It has been argued that there 'is little urbanity in the New Urbanism... [They] speak of community and neighbourhood as physical rather than social entities, as if community resulted from the built form rather than from the people who inhabit it'[154]. On the other hand, the evidence confirms that smaller is better from a social-capital point of view – i.e. getting involved is easier 'where the scale of everyday life is smaller and more intimate'[155]. The same authority asserts that a pattern of homogeneous suburbs and an increase in commuting times work against the formation of social capital.

In a country where the car has to be used to fulfil the most basic of daily needs outside the home, the New Urbanists advocate a return to the possibility of satisfying them within easy walking distance. They also advocate a traditional open street pattern that provides security and privacy without barriers, based on the assumption that face-to-face contact and interaction are necessary to make a community and that the physical pattern of development, while it cannot ensure that this communication will occur, at least makes it possible, unlike the gated community and the hierarchical street network with its culs-de-sac, which render it impossible.

THE CONGRESS FOR THE NEW URBANISM

If the recent story of the rediscovery of traditional urbanism in the UK is character-ized by several strands, this is also true of the United States. But in the latter the reaction to the new environments being produced by the public and private sectors has been much more focused by the establishment in 1992 of the Congress for the New Urbanism (CNU). This has brought a number of different tendencies together and served to concentrate the individual efforts. Through congresses, institutes, publica-tions and websites, they expertly market both the movement and their separate firms. The New Urbanists are consummate publicists for their cause. In 1995 they reached the cover of *Newsweek* magazine, which devoted eleven pages to criticising suburban sprawl and explaining the New Urbanist remedies (Fulton, 1996)

It is no accident that the name of this organization is resonant of the Congrès International d'Architecture Moderne (CIAM), which was so instrumental in pro-

---

154 M. Southworth, 'Walkable suburbs? An evaluation of neotraditional communities at the urban edge', *Journal of the American Planning Association,* 63 (1), 1997, pp. 9–34.
155 R. Putnam (2001), *Bowling Alone: the Collapse and Revival of American Community* (New York, NY: Touchstone), p. 205.

moting the very approach that the CNU is criticising. The original suggestion for this title came from Leon Krier[156], the Masterplanner of Poundbury, yet another example of the transatlantic connection.

The New Urbanism has taken much of its inspiration from the small American town and the nineteenth-century tradition of the city beautiful. It also revived an interest in the qualities of the first American suburbs conceived in the spirit of the garden city. Robert Stern was one of the few prominent architects of his generation to acknowledge the significance and the relevance of these traditions hitherto ignored or maligned by architects of a modernist persuasion[157]. Mainly known for his private houses, he was one of the planners of Celebration[158], and Andres Duany, one of the CNU's founders, worked in his office. Of Stern and his 'fellow nostalgists' it has been said that 'they were trying to reconnect with architectural forms that most Americans understood instinctively rather than intellectually ... A house by Stern looked like a house, not a construction site or an artistic manifesto in built form'[159].

The New Urbanists' work in general has been accused of being directed at the affluent, and the same accusation has been made of Poundbury, but their policies have been adopted for subsidized housing by the US Federal Department of Housing and Urban Development, and CNU principles have been applied in renewal schemes in the less favoured parts of US cities. But the fact is that the experimental schemes were 'done for citizens with strong incomes, and that it is, ultimately, far more socially advanced to experiment with living patterns for the affluent, as opposed to an earlier planning and architecture practice of imposing experiments on the poor'[160].

According to Peter Katz[161] and Ray Gindroz[162] the most important of the strands of the CNU were a West Coast group exemplified by Calthorpe and the 'Pedestrian Pocket', focusing on issues of regionalism and ecology; an East Coast group represented by Andres Duany and Elisabeth Platter Zyberk (DPZ) and their work, especially at Seaside, which connects to European town planning (notably the work of Unwin), the United States tradition of eighteenth- and nineteenth-century metropolitan projects, of which Battery Park City in New York is a contemporary example; and a group concerned with small-scale urban infill projects, which include Urban Design Associates.

Battery Park City is important because the original 1969 master plan for this extension of downtown Manhattan on 92 acres of reclaimed land was typical of its period. It envisaged superblocks and megastructures with upper-level walkways and linked 40-, 50- and 60-storey office towers. After a long saga of vicissitudes, the project that

156 P. Katz (2002), 'Notes on the History of the New Urbanism', in T. Bressi (ed.), *The Seaside Debates* (New York, NY: Rizzoli).
157 R.A.M. Stern, op.cit.
158 J.A.Gause (2002), *Great Planned Communities* (Washington, DC: Urban Land Institute).
159 C. Wiseman (1998), *Shaping a Nation: Twentieth Century American Architecture and its Makers*, New York, NY: Norton), p. 294.
160 R.Gastil in J.A. Dutton (2000), *New American Urbanism. Reforming the Suburban Metropolis* (Milan: Skira), p. 10.
161 P.Katz, op.cit.
162 R. Gindroz, Lecture given at the Prince's Foundation, London, 8 November, 2002.

finally emerged in 1979, designed by Cooper Eckstut, was based on an extension of the streets of the Manhattan grid[163]. Instead of the superblocks and megastructures that implied one designer and a single investor for a few very large and expensive projects, these streets defined moderately sized urban blocks that were capable of accommodating buildings designed by a variety of architects using different developers according to design guidelines drawn from the characteristic New York domestic architecture of the 1920s and 1930s.

The project as realized demonstrates, a decade before Seaside, most of the traits of the New Urbanism. It is based on connected streets and a mix of uses; it refers to the local traditions and is implemented through a master plan and a typological code for the different buildings within which a number of architects were obliged to work. The project rejects the idea of one mind designing everything 'from the city to the spoon' and acknowledges that the most successful places are where many have contributed within an agreed framework.

THE CHARTER OF THE NEW URBANISM

The parallels between CIAM and CNU have been discussed at some length by Dutton[164]. They were both established to influence both public policy and professional practice and among the similarities is the way the former inscribed its principles in the Charter of Athens and the latter in the Charter for the New Urbanism. This was first proposed in 1998 and then elaborated in a book with essays on each of 27 principles by different authors who draw on historical precedents, current schemes and proposed projects to argue the case[165]. The principles are discussed under three headings:

- The Region, Metropolis, City and Town
- The Neighbourhood, District and the Corridor
- The Block, the Street and the Building

The Charter thus ranges widely. The first nine principles deal with regional planning to avoid sprawl, tax-allocation policies and transport planning and the next nine cover the importance of pedestrian-accessible neighbourhoods and sufficiently high building densities to support mixed-use districts, with the final section most closely relating to our theme and therefore worth considering in more detail.

The last nine principles emphasise the importance of safe public spaces for a variety of users. They should accommodate cars yet respect the pedestrian. Safety is to be achieved, not by exclusion, but by providing surveillance and an environment that encourages walking and enables neighbours to get to know one another and protect

163 A. Garvin (2002), *The American City: What Works and What Doesn't* (New York, NY: McGraw-Hill).
164 J.A. Dutton, op.cit.
165 Congress for the New Urbanism (CNU) (2000), *Charter of the New Urbanism* (New York, NY: McGraw-Hill).

their communities. Public streets and squares should be defined by an urban architecture that respects local diversity, including climate and history, with public buildings being distinctive by their design and location on important sites. 'Individual architectural projects should be seamlessly linked to their surroundings' and contribute to 'providing their inhabitants with a clear sense of location'[166]. The application of these principles can be seen below in the discussion of Seaside and King Farm.

The Charter was ratified at the annual Congress held in Charleston in 1996. It was significant also because it was the occasion for the then secretary of the United States Department of Housing and Urban Development (HUD) to announce his department's adoption of the principles in the building and revitalization of public housing. This has had an impact on the form of American public housing through the HUD HOPE VI and Home Ownership Zone programmes. Belmont Heights, Tampa, Florida, by Torti Gallas and Partners, and Diggs Town, Norfolk, Virginia, by Urban Design Associates, are examples of the application of the Charter principles to low-cost housing.

THE BLOCK IN DETAIL

The following section discusses the structure of the urban block as used in four exemplary schemes: Hulme (Manchester) and Poundbury (Dorchester) in the UK and Seaside (Florida) and King Farm (Maryland) in the US. Hulme has been chosen as an example of urban regeneration where clearance took place in the 1960s and large blocks of flats inspired by the Ville Radieuse had been built only to be demolished thirty years later and replaced by developments that sought to return to a street pattern that predated the demolition.

Poundbury is important because it pioneered the connected street network at a time when most guidance was still advocating treelike networks with culs-de-sac. It is also remarkable for its attention to detail and the quality of its execution. Seaside is an early realization of the characteristics advocated by the New Urbanists and has been very influential on many later developments, including that at King Farm, a more recent and much larger project, which shows how the application has evolved.

HULME

This part of Manchester was the site of the now infamous crescent blocks built in the 1960s, which were claimed to be a reincarnation of the neoclassical crescents of Bath or Edinburgh. These replaced streets of nineteenth-century, two-storey, terraced slum housing, which had been condemned as early as 1934[167] and were part of a development that included tower blocks and six- to eight-storey maisonette blocks. All these building types were clearly progeny of the Ville Radieuse. They proved to be

166 T.W.Bressi (ed) (2002), *The Seaside Debates: A Critique of the New Urbanism* (New York: NY: Rizzoli).
167 D.N. Rudlin and N. Falk (1999), *Building the 21st Century Home* (London: Architectural Press).

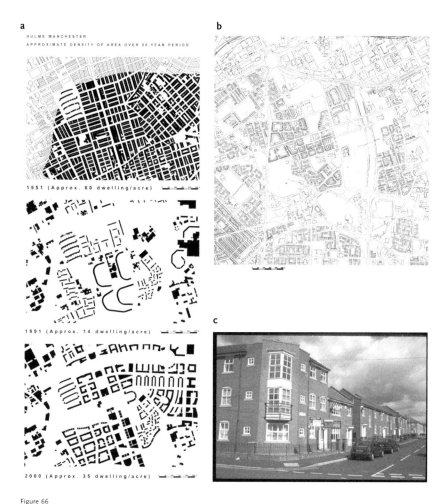

Figure 66
Hulme.
a. Figure ground plans of Hulme in 1951 (top) before renewal, in 1991 (centre) with the notorious crescent blocks and (bottom) according to the current plan (MBLC Architects and Urbanists).
b. The master plan for Hulme (MBLC Architects and Urbanists).
c. A street of speculatively built private housing at Hulme. It has been implemented according to the design guide principles with three-storey flats as a landmark at the corner of the block. (All photographs in Chapter 9 are by the author).

functionally and socially disastrous and were demolished. Since 1991 the whole area has undergone a regeneration process implemented by a partnership between Manchester City Council and a private developer through a joint company, Hulme Regeneration Ltd. Part of the development has been built by housing associations and later schemes have been constructed by private house-building firms.

Figure 67

Hulme.

a. Plan of part of Hulme as built. There are a variety of block sizes, some of which include existing non-residential buildings. Parking is incorporated in the centre of each block (MBLC Architects and Urbanists).

b. The gated entrance to a parking area in the centre of a block.

c. The parking areas in the centre of the blocks are surrounded by the opaque fences of the house back gardens.

The master plan was prepared by a local practice – Mills Beaumont Leavey Channon (MBLC) Architects and Urbanists.. With a housing density of 75–85 houses per hectare, it proposed a grid pattern that was claimed to reflect the original grain of the area and re-establishes some of the streets that existed in the nineteenth century. The plan was implemented through an urban design guide that was adopted by Manchester City Council to coordinate the work of the different private- and public-sector developers. It emphasized aspects such as buildings fronting onto streets, a relatively high average density, a variety of uses and street design to reduce vehicle speed rather than increase traffic flow[168]. These are all directly comparable to the

168 D.N. Rudlin and N. Falk, op.cit.

principles laid down in the Charter of the New Urbanism and the design guidance emanating from the UK government.

The rebuilt Hulme is based on a layout of streets with traditional perimeter blocks. The size of the elements comprising this layout is determined by rules of thumb that are widely applied in contemporary British housing and inevitably lead to certain homogeneity of all layouts. The minimum dimension of the street grids is 60 metres, which is determined by the highway engineer's minimum distance between roads carrying vehicles. The minimum internal dimensions between houses across the back of the block is usually 18–21 metres, which is considered to be the dimension that ensures the occupants a sufficient degree of privacy. Although there does not seem to be any empirical evidence for the efficacy of this distance, it is rigorously enforced throughout the UK and departures are rare.

Perhaps the most striking innovation at Hulme has been the incorporation of cross-roads. This may seem a modest achievement but it runs in direct contradiction to British highway engineering practice and guidance as recommended in various government publications. In the United States the four-way junction with no one route having priority is common and makes a very effective traffic-calming tool. British drivers are not trusted to negotiate this type of junction without accident.

In order to accommodate parked cars with a minimum of on-street parking, most of the blocks have been enlarged at Hulme beyond the minimum size so as to allow car parking at the rear. There are small rear gardens to the houses but otherwise all the space in the centre of the blocks is devoted to car parking. For reasons of security this is accessible only via a single controlled gated access from the street where visitors have to park. While this arrangement keeps the street relatively free from cars, it does mean that the houses have two entrances, one for those arriving by car via the parking court and the private back garden and the other for people arriving from the street. There is a subsequent loss of activity and vitality on the street frontage of the blocks.

There are small front gardens opening on the street side of the blocks, which vary from one to three metres in depth and are enclosed by walls or railings. These serve as an interface between the street and the private space of the house but are usually too small to allow much activity in front of the house such as sitting out-doors. Unlike the case in the United States, this may not be a common practice in Britain, but the size and arrangement of the front space certainly does not encourage it.

Although some of the earlier blocks, built by housing associations, manage to integrate different types of dwelling in the same block, the later developments by private builders restrict the blocks to one or two types. The earlier blocks also took great care to create focal points on corners by the use of higher buildings, a feature that is lost in some of the later private housing.

The application of the code has been remarkably successful in avoiding the normal cul-de-sac maze characteristic of most private house building. It has been criticized for the lack of unity it has produced in the street scene – especially where there are two developers on either side of the same street. The logic of the development process, whereby an attempt is made to share as much of the infrastructure among as many protagonists as possible, results in the boundaries of the development parcels running down the middle of streets and not across the backs of blocks as in south Amsterdam (see Chapter 3).

There are some shops under apartments on the Stretford Road, which runs through the area and functions as its main street, but there are few uses other than housing. It may be possible to return to a resemblance of the former block structure but it is much more difficult to achieve the range of uses that the area had accommodated in the past. There is a supermarket on the edge of the area. The intention had been to wrap it with housing but in practice it has turned out to be just another large container typical of urban-edge development. The satisfactory integration of large containers such as supermarkets and the large areas of parking associated with them into a block structure remains one of the most intractable of design problems in new housing developments both in the UK and the US.

Another problem that needs resolution is that of the temporary treatment of sites that will be needed for development in the future but, because of programming, may remain empty over many years. In the fecund natural environment of semitropical Florida luxurious vegetation quickly takes over, but in the climatically less favourable ambience of northwest England the air of dereliction and neglect they convey has a negative impact on the image of the whole area.

POUNDBURY

Begun in 1993, this was intended to be a twenty-year staged development for 5,000 inhabitants on a site of 158 hectares with four mixed-use quarters each of between 500 and 800 houses. The first of the quarters has been largely completed and the second has been started. On the edge of Dorchester, a historic market town of 15,000 inhabitants, it is on land of the Duchy of Cornwall and has been an opportunity for the Prince of Wales to oversee the implementation of some of his ideas. In this he was advised by Leon Krier with Alan Baxter & Associates, who prepared the master plan and has been able to exert a continuing influence on the implementation of the project, with several architects and building firms, mostly local, being responsible for different parts of the project. It has been argued that its illustrious patronage and unusual funding arrangements make Poundbury a special place of doubtful relevance elsewhere. While these aspects may be impossible to replicate, its influence has been very strong on subsequent housing design in Britain.

From a design point of view it was intended that the development should reinterpret the traditional forms of the local Dorset vernacular by defining clear urban bound-

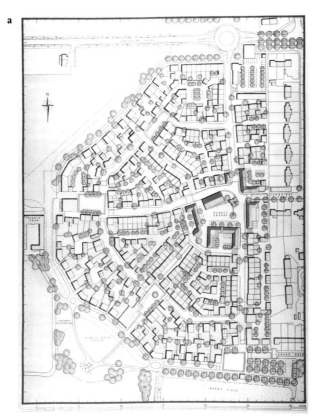

Figure 68
Poundbury.
a. Master plan for Phase 1 (Leon Krier with Alan Baxter & Associates).
b–c. Streets at Poundbury. A variety of house types and tenures are incorporated in each street.

aries and a legible and harmonious variety of buildings and spaces, which are achieved by the use of local materials and building forms. There is a clear street structure with all but a few of the houses having their front doors opening directly off the street. Car parking is at the rear of the blocks and the narrow streets discourage cars from parking in front of the houses. There is a network of alleys, which links the rear car-parking areas, and the consequences of this for the vitality of the public realm are discussed below. This block structure with its rear access and alleyway arrangements has been very influential and has been emulated in many later developments. This is somewhat surprising given that the dual vehicle access to the major-

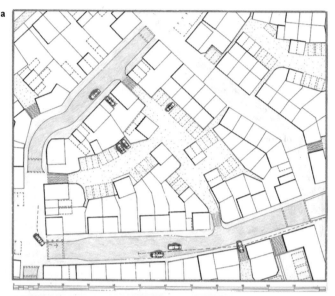

Figure 69
Poundbury.
a. Plan of a typical block at Poundbury. Note the houses overlooking the parking court with their back gardens facing the street. (Leon Krier with Alan Baxter & Associates).
b–c. The internal space of the blocks with car parking and surrounded by the back walls to gardens and the fronts of one or two houses.

ity of houses implies a greater infrastructure investment on the part of the developer than a single-sided arrangement.

As in the New Urbanist projects discussed below, there is an explicit agenda of building a community by providing local facilities. These are located in the centre of the quarter with landmark buildings such as the tower of a retirement home marking the entry. In this way it repeats the British interpretation of the neighbour-hood unit by locating the commercial facilities away from the edge and it must be questioned whether this has not hindered the early establishment of essential everyday facilities locally.

The size of each quarter is limited and various house types and tenures are located in close juxtaposition. In this way it intended to promote interaction on the public street network between a diversity of people. While the encouragement of a sense of community seems to be succeeding, the extent of the social mix that is being achieved remains debatable[169]. Nevertheless, it has been a financial success and shows how the close integration of social housing with unsubsidized open-market housing can be achieved.

Poundbury has been criticized for its lack of connection to the adjoining housing estate. Links are made where possible, so this is not the fault of the Poundbury plan but rather that of the design of the earlier estate, where no possibility was allowed for connections to be made. This is an issue in most edge-of-town developments and we will also come across this problem in New Urbanist schemes in the United States.

SEASIDE

This holiday village has become the archetype of the New Urbanist planned community. It was a speculative venture by an unusually enlightened developer, Robert Davies, who appointed the architects, Andrew Duany and Elizabeth Plater-Zyberk (DPZ), in 1980 to prepare a plan for a holiday settlement that would also function as a small town. In spite of its small size (8 acres, with a target population of 2,000 people) and remote location on the coast of the Florida panhandle, an area of sprawling urbanization, its return to the qualities of the small town and its connected system of streets – which keep pedestrians and traffic together but privilege the former – were a radical departure at that time from the paradigms then current for planned developments. The master plan has been implemented by a code that specifies such details as plot sizes, setbacks and landscape regulation as these affect the streetscape of the different parts of the settlement. DPZ were careful to investigate and understand the local vernacular before reinterpreting it in their construction of this code.

The other three developments discussed here are entirely speculative but most of the houses at Seaside were built to order by a number of architects. This process explains why the individual buildings are criticized as being *passéiste*. There are modern-style buildings there, not many, but this is presumably because the clients didn't want them, not that they were prevented from being built. The Walt Disney Enterprises town of Celebration is an interesting contrast because it is much more restrictive with respect to the architecture. Here a Pattern Book (prepared by Urban Design Associates) identifies six styles, or 'languages', that are permitted: Mediterranean, Colonial, Coastal, Victorian, French and Classical. This eclectic practice seems to

169 M. Thompson Fawcett, op.cit.

Figure 70
Seaside.
a. The plan of Seaside showing blocks streets and pedestrian alleys (Duany Plater-Zyberk).
b. Seaside as built. Note the roads connecting to the adjacent development of Watercolour (DPZ).
c. A street at Seaside with resident parking only.
d. A pedestrian alley running between and clearly overlooked by the gardens.

throw into doubt the whole question of local distinctiveness, which has been one of the fundamentals of the reaction against the universal solutions of the Modern Movement.

Seaside has been greeted by some with scorn because of both its size and, as a holiday village, its special character. Deyan Sudjic is typical in observing that 'as a summer retreat it is hardly a real test of the power of Duany and Plater-Zyberk's approach, yet on this slender basis they have been declared urban geniuses and have been deluged with work'[170]. Larsen[171] points out that Seaside is 'first, based on the exclusion of the automobile; second, is a small private project for the upper middle class; and, third, is a frankly nostalgic mixture of an American small town and English village that has nothing to say to the large cities' (1993, p. 126). DPZ are very capable

170 D. Sudjic (1992), *The 100 Mile City* (London: Andre Deutsch), p. 29.
171 M.S.Larsen (1993), *Behind the Post-Modern Facade: Architectural Change in the Late Twentieth Century* (Berkeley: University of California Press), p. 126.

a

b

c

d

Figure 71
Seaside.
a. The offices, shops and houses surrounding Ruskin
Place show the variety of architecture that can be achieved
within rules of the Code for Seaside.
b–c. The servicing and parking at the rear of the Central
Square are very public and require careful control.
d. The edge of the Central Square, which is the main entrance to Seaside. This view shows the problem posed
by reserve sites and blank gables.

of defending their own projects, but this criticism seems unfounded when we consider
that cars are not excluded from Seaside but their speed and parking are controlled.
This is not unusual: traffic calming and residents' parking schemes are also found in
every British city. As we have noted, New Urbanist concepts have been applied in
other, less favoured, contexts. Finally, there is no evidence at Seaside of the social
hierarchy that can be clearly read into the built form of every English village.

Seaside, although small, demonstrated that it was possible to make at least a piece of
town with joined-up roads and a mix of house types and even of uses. One reason for
its success may be that it has triggered a latent demand for this type of place. In so far
as it is not a normal settlement, Gindroz[172] has suggested that one of the reasons for its
great influence is that, because it is a holiday community with accommodation available to rent for short periods, many more people have been able to experience it than

172 R. Gindroz, op.cit.

would normally be possible in a residential community. It has also been featured widely in the media and it has served as a movie location.

It is important because it demonstrated a suburban environment where pedestrians are more important than cars and it manages to integrate different uses and different types of house into the same street network while avoiding the illegible and circuitous routes normally arising from the imposition of a hierarchical vehicle network. In other words, it does what traditional towns do and demonstrated that traditional neighbourhood development (TND) is possible. From the point of view of our interest in the urban block it is assembled from blocks of plots with houses facing the streets and vehicle access on only one side of the plot. In this respect it differs from the later more extensive schemes built by either the same designers, such as Kentlands, or other members of the CNU, such as Cooper Robertson at I'On or Torti Gallas at King Farm, which will be examined in more detail below. Peculiar to Seaside is a network of very narrow alleyways, about one metre wide, providing public routes though the centre of the blocks. It has been suggested that the reason for these is to enable barefoot holidaymakers to reach the ocean beach by walking over sand.

The street system focuses on the central area or the beach across the main coast road, which links Seaside to the other communities on the coast. The shops are located at right angles to the coast road in an arrangement that makes them easily accessible to outside clients, not just the denizens of Seaside. This arrangement also pertains at the adjoining development of Watercolour, planned by Cooper Robertson, which has shops in the same relationship to the main road. This is very important because a community of only 2,000 could support a very limited range of shops and the more specialized outlets depend on outside custom to make them viable. This is particularly relevant at Celebration, where the town-centre facilities, including a hotel and cinema, are far beyond what could be supported by its target population of 12,000.

The issue of connecting to neighbouring areas urbanized at a later date has been resolved at Seaside by enabling the adjoining Watercolour scheme to link its streets to those of the earlier development even though at present these allow only pedestrian and cycle movement. The situation is less satisfactory at another nearby DPZ project at Rosemary Beach, where there is no possibility of a connection between this scheme and the adjoining housing area. Rosemary Beach is worthy of note because of its very large detached houses and the introduction of a variation on the Radburn layout with a network of pedestrian routes running parallel to and duplicating the streets leading down to the beach.

KING FARM

There is a considerable body of CNU housing that can be studied. We have chosen King Farm, planned by Torti Gallas and Partners, whom one might classify as 'second-generation' New Urbanists, in order to show that the principles of this

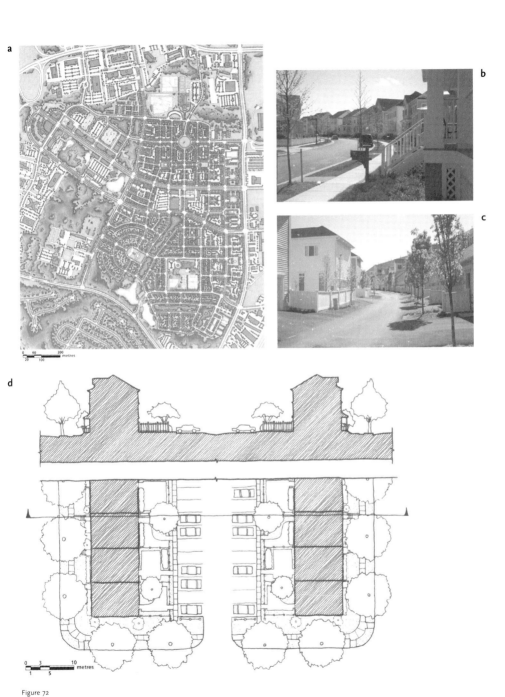

Figure 72
King Farm.
a. The master plan for King Farm (Torti Gallas & Partners, CHK).
b–c–d. (Torti Gallas). Two-storey row houses with on-street parking and a rear-access alley to garages, small gardens and, in some cases, house extensions.

movement are widely diffused and not just the private trade tools of a few cognos-centi. It is also of interest because it is a large scheme that offers some very clearly differentiated examples of the way the urban block has been modified to accommodate the motor car. King Farm is a 440-acre parcel of land in the City of Rockville to the north of the Greater Washington, DC, area. It will accommodate 3,200 residential units, 3.17 million square feet of office space and 125,000 square feet of retail facilities. It is located at the end of one of the lines of the Washington Metro system and is at the point where a proposed light rail will connect to run north and west. A central boulevard to carry the light rail system runs though the centre of the site and links the metro system to Highway 1270. A large supermarket and some smaller shops and restaurants are directly linked perpendicularly to this boulevard. The development extends in a grid street pattern from this spine. The scheme is organized into neighbourhoods with a mix of housing types and tenures and three examples illustrate clearly how the New Urbanist principles have been interpreted at block level.

The lowest-density block is typical of the US in that it has an alleyway down the centre, which gives access to car-parking spaces or garages and in some cases small apartments over the garage looking onto the lane (Figure 72). This is similar to an English mews arrangement. The platting of the earliest US towns did not include alleyways and they were inserted into blocks around the middle of the nineteenth century in much the same way as they were used in English bylaw housing. As the location of cheap housing in many cities, they became synonymous with all the problems of crime and unsanitary living conditions and were subject to clearance. They therefore fell out of fashion until they were revived in the early years of the twentieth century as a way of accommodating cars. The alley with garages opening onto them became a common feature of American towns, especially where there was no room for a side access drive in detached or semidetached houses.

In streets with access from one side only, the garage was progressively shifted towards the street façade of the house. In the 1960s, as car ownership increased and the cars themselves became bigger, large double garages began to dominate the street façade, especially where the plots were narrow, so that garages began to occupy up to 80 per cent of the frontage (Ford, 2000).

The second type of block at King Farm is surrounded by large, three-storey, terraced town houses. These back onto a shared parking court with garages taking up most of the rear of each house at ground level. There is a private deck at first-floor level, which acts as roof to the car port. There are no private rear gardens and only a small space in the front. In some examples there is a small shared garden inserted into the centre of the block.

The third type of block has been devised in response to the parking problem posed by apartment blocks that are often quite simply set in the middle of a car park. At King Farm the solution to the car-parking problem has led to the complete transformation

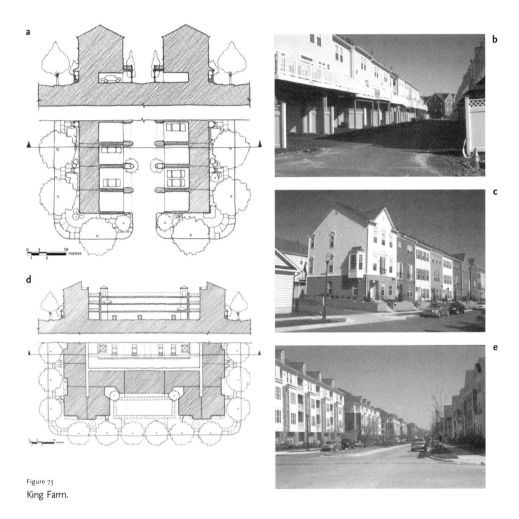

Figure 73
King Farm.

of the interior of the block into a car-parking garage. There is a three-metre gap between the rear of the single-aspect apartments and the parking garage. This is inaccessible and is used to accommodate air-conditioning plant. But its real function is to make the parking structure a separate building and therefore avoids the need for mechanical ventilation. The parking garage, built of precast concrete, links to all floors of the apartment, which are of timber-frame construction.

An arrangement such as this at King Farm can be achieved only where the costs of the parking structure are justified by the values generated by the resulting development. A similar solution would be out of the question in a British suburban

f

g

h

Figure 73
King Farm.
a. (Torti Gallas), **b–c**. Three-storey row houses with on-street parking and rear access to garages at ground level. Each house has a rear deck at first-floor level but no ground-level private open space other than car parking.
d. Part plan and section of four-storey apartment block with four-storey car park occupying the whole of the centre of the block.
e–f. Street views of the apartments showing the entrance to the multistorey car park in the centre of the block.
g. The top floor of the car park structure.
h. The space between the car park (left) and the apartments (right). There are access galleries between the two structures at each level.

situation, possibly because purchasers are not prepared to pay as much for a car-parking space as in the US. The number of housing units that can be achieved on a site is often determined by car-parking arrangements, so that all attempts to reach a local population threshold capable of supporting public transport or other facilities can be frustrated by the need to accommodate parked cars in a cost-realistic manner.

CONCLUSION

This attempt to draw together some of the salient points arising from the previous discussion starts with those issues pertaining to the neighbourhood, for all of the examples use some sort of residential subdivision larger than the block, even though they may have different labels. It then goes on to consider the relationship between the street defining the block and the way the space has been used inside the block, including the subdivision between the public and private realms and access arrangements.

There is a fundamental criticism that has been levelled against the neighbourhood unit for the last half-century and, that is that it does not work, since it has no significance for its inhabitants. More important, it atomises the city, a criticism to which the New Urbanists would respond by claiming that their principles include the need to conceive the city at a bigger scale. The lack of connections between new developments as we have seen above is a common problem in recent urban expansions. It may be that this idea of separation is fundamental to the very concept of the Anglo-American suburb, which evolved as a way of separating people from the temptations of urban life in accordance with a view that people should be kept apart from certain activities. One suspects also that it might be inherent in some of the strands of the CNU thinking. In any case, it is much easier to make good small places but much harder to join them up.

The all-pervading issue that distinguishes these last four cases from the rest of the book is the way space has had to be configured to accommodate the motor car. This has had an impact on all aspects of the urban tissue, from the dimensions and arrangement of the streets defining the blocks to the semiprivate area at the rear of the dwellings. With the exception of Seaside, car parking has been inserted into this space, which, in the cases examined in previous chapters, was used for private or semiprivate gardens linked to the dwellings or uses not connected with the housing function of the buildings defining the block perimeter.

When we examine the distribution of uses across the blocks of a neighbourhood, we notice the difficulty of combining different uses in the same block. The integration of units, whether schools or supermarkets, with housing units has become difficult in the past fifty years. The arrangement we saw in south Amsterdam of inserting a school into the back of a housing block is now much more difficult because of playing-field standards and the need to accommodate cars in this space. Because of the hours they operate and the heavy trucks that are used, it is also difficult to wrap large retail units with dwellings. In most of the cases where a shopping street has been planned, the backs of the shops face onto car-parking areas. At King Farm the problem has been resolved by a using one block to accommodate a large supermarket and a row of shops. The backs of both are hidden from the public realm but the supermarket presents long stretches of blank façade to the street. Also, there are fewer small shops and other businesses to fit under apartments, as was possible with the haussmannien block.

Unlike the cases in the three last chapters of the original edition of this book, but like the first example in this edition, the majority of the projects described are private speculative developments. This harks back to another Anglo-American tradition, that of the high-quality speculative development. However, the more extensive of the schemes we have discussed are beyond the scope of single house builders,

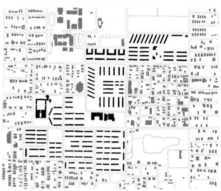

Figure 74

a. The porch is an essential element of the American way of life.

b–c. Large detached houses at I'On have back gardens that are completely open to view from the rear access alley.

d–e. Figure ground plans of Belmont Heights, Tampa, Florida (Torti Gallas), before and after regeneration. The parallel building blocks of the public housing project have been replaced by perimeter blocks of houses and apartments.

f. Belmont Heights is a development of subsidized and market rental and, at a later stage, home-ownership housing. The common space around the rental housing is managed by a private company.

however large they are. There is a need for them to be subdivided into development parcels. The marketing logic of the master developer implies an offloading of the maximum possible of infrastructure development costs onto the individual builders, together with ease of management while maintaining the quality of the design and therefore the value of the investment. This leads to an interesting comparison with south Amsterdam, where, as we have seen, the development parcels cross over the streets. In Britain the development parcel usually coincides with the street blocks so that the builders on either side each contribute half the cost of the road that they share.

The choice of the block defined by streets as the unit of construction also derives from the difficulty of managing a property boundary through the centre of a block. This is easy to manage where the boundary runs along the backs of gardens but it is more complicated where there is car parking in the rear. In this case access ways have to be shared by two developers who may choose to build at different stages in the project's implementation, and it is very difficult to manage a property boundary through the middle of a car park.

In detail, when compared with their transatlantic counterparts, the English blocks are distinguished by the very small yet private front gardens, often too small to plant yet walled or fenced off from the street. The streets are overlooked by the houses, which satisfies the demands of security but the amount of street activity is reduced by the presence of car parks and rear access to the houses from the interiors of the blocks. This is also true of the US, where usually there is alley access to each dwelling. During most of the day there is little enough street activity in residential areas and, if this is dispersed between the front and the back of the block, then inevitably the streets will appear deserted for much of the time.

At Poundbury the interiors of the blocks are not private as at Hulme and they can be freely entered from the street. Indeed it is possible to traverse the neighbourhood using the garage courts and connecting alleyways. This route system also serves to run underground services, which enable a narrower street section to be achieved. The interiors of the blocks are not overlooked from the houses facing the streets, since, without exception, the back gardens are enclosed by opaque wooden boarded fences. The issue of security at Poundbury has been resolved by locating one or two houses in the interior of the block facing inwards and overlooking the car-parking space. In any case, the socioeconomic profile of Poundbury makes security less of a problem than at Hulme.

This British lack of transparency is in direct contrast with all the US developments, where the back gardens are enclosed by an open and transparent barrier, which is usually white picket fencing with a rural or country-cottage feeling. This enables the garden activity to be seen from the street, which helps surveillance in both directions. Both streets and rear alleys can be seen from the garden or the house – especially as the back gardens are often surprisingly small for such large houses.

Houses with front lawns became the norm in the United States after about 1900 as a result of fire codes, the introduction of the street car and of course the invention of the lawnmower. The absence of fences to the front gardens of US houses has also been associated with a desire for extensive grass reminiscent of the eighteenth-century English landscape[173]. It may also have to do with the difficulty of controlling the untidy appearance of a variety of fencing. It is much easier not to allow any at all than to try to control its appearance. In Britain this problem is solved by the house builder's providing a substantial wall or metal railing at the front a wall or close boarded fence at the back.

The American porch is perhaps a unique contribution to the design problem of providing an interface between the public and private realms in residential buildings. With the raising of the ground floor to allow a daylit basement – also found in eighteenth-century houses in Britain – front steps up to the main door became necessary and the landing space developed into an intermediate space between the street and the inside of the house. In America, this building element evolved, via the vernacular of the subtropical colonies, from a climatic imperative into an essential element of the American way of life. In 1952 the journal *House and Garden* asserted that 'the front porch is an American institution of high civic and moral value. It is a sign that the people who sit on it are ready and willing to share the community life of their block with their neighbours'[174]. Its reinstatement is regarded by the New Urbanists as fundamental to restoring a sense of community involvement and local pride. For example, Urban Design Associates in their proposals for Diggs Town in Norfolk, Virginia, have fixed front porches onto the dwellings of this public housing estate as a first stage in their regeneration strategy.

There is a surprising absence of private space in the United States examples. Of the three King Farm blocks described above, two have no private open space at ground level. The apartment blocks have no private open space at all and there is only a small communal space at ground level. The town houses have decks at first-floor level above the double garages, which occupy the whole of the rear ground floor. These decks overlook the car-parking area, which takes up the whole of the interior of the block. The only houses that have back gardens or yards are those that also have a rear access alley running down the centre of the block.

All towns change in response to shifts in economic and social conditions. A characteristic is the robustness or the mutability of the first four cases discussed in the early chapters of this book. The haussmannien block has proved itself able to accommodate change over time and one could argue that there is a reducing degree of mutability through the other examples, which culminate in the Ville Radieuse model, which is incapable of being adapted to changing circumstance. It has either to be protected as a monument – this has happened to the Park Hill flats in Sheffield – or demolished, as

173 L.R. Ford (2000), *The Spaces Between Buildings* (Baltimore, MD: Johns Hopkins University Press).
174 Quoted in L.R.Ford, op.cit.

we saw in Hulme. There is no doubt that these Anglo-American cases will adapt more easily than the single block of flats of Le Corbusier, because the different sets of elements can mutate independently of one another: buildings can change on plots without affecting the overall plot arrangement, plots can be subdivided or amalgamated without affecting the form of the block and blocks can be modified without affecting the road network.

In summary, when transferring experience from one culture to another, even cultures that may seem superficially very similar, account has to be taken of the local habits, customs, regulatory regimes and development processes. As designers we have to be prepared to modify our values and even be prepared to abandon some of those we cherish most.

REFERENCES

Bentley, I., et al. (1985), *Responsive Environments: A design manual* (London: Architectural Press).

Biddulph, M. (2000), 'Villages don't make a city', in *Journal of Urban Design*, 5 (1), pp. 65–82.

Biddulph, M., M. Tait, and B. Franklin (2002) 'The Urban Village: an obituary', in *Urban Design Quarterly* (81), Winter.

Blakely, E. J., and M. G. Snyder (1997) 'Divided we fall. Gated and Walled Communities in the United States', in Ellin, N (ed.), *Architecture of Fear* (New York, NY: Princeton Architectural Press).

Breheny, M., and P. Hall (eds) (1996), *The People – Where Will They Go? National report of the TCPA Regional Inquiry into Housing Need and Provision in England* (London: Town and Country Planning Association).

Bressi, T. W. (ed.) (2002), *The Seaside Debates: A Critique of the New Urbanism* (New York, NY: Rizzoli).

CNU (Congress for the New Urbanism) (2000), *Charter of the New Urbanism* (New York, NY: McGraw-Hill).

DETR (Department of the Environment, Transport and the Regions) (1998) '*Places, Streets and Movement: A Companion Guide to Design Bulletin 32 Residential Roads and Footpaths*' (London: Department of the Environment, Transport and the Regions).

DETR (Department of the Environment, Transport and the Regions) (2000), 'Planning Policy Guidance Note 3: Housing (London: Department of the Environment, Transport and the Regions).

DETR/CABE (Department of the Environment, Transport and the Regions/ Commission for Architecture and the Built Environment) (2000a), 'By Design: Better Places to Live: A Design Companion to PPG3' (London: Department of the Environment, Transport and the Regions).

DETR/CABE (Department of the Environment, Transport and the Regions/ Commission for Architecture and the Built Environment) (2000b), '*By Design: Urban Design in the Planning System: Towards Better Practice*' (London: Department of the Environment, Transport and the Regions).

Duany, A., E. Plater-Zyberk and J. Speck (2000), *Suburban Nation: The Rise of Sprawl and the Decline of the American Dream* (New York, NY: North Point Press).

Dutton, J. A. (2000), *New American Urbanism. Reforming the Suburban Metropolis* (Milan: Skira).

Faucet P. G. (2000), 'The Hulme Estate and the "Homes for Change Development"', in Williams et al. (eds), *Achieving Sustainable Urban Form* (London: E. & F. N. Spon).

Ford, L. R. (2000), *The Spaces Between Buildings* (Baltimore, MD: Johns Hopkins University Press).

Garvin, A. (2002), *The American City: What Works and What Doesn't* (New York, NY: McGraw-Hill).

Gause, J. A. (2002), *Great Planned Communities* (Washington, DC: Urban Land Institute).

Gindroz, R. (2002), lecture given at the Prince's Foundation, London, 8 November.

Jacobs, J. (1961), *The Death and Life of the Great American Cities* (New York, NY: Vintage Books).

Katz, P. (2002), 'Notes on the History of the New Urbanism', in T. Bressi (ed.), *The Seaside Debates* (New York, NY: Rizzoli).

Larsen, M. S. (1993), *Behind the Post-Modern Façade: Architectural Change in the Late Twentieth Century* (Berkeley: University of California Press).

Ministry of Health (1944), *The Design of Dwellings* (the Dudley Report) (London: HMSO).

Newman, O. (1972), *Defensible Space: People and Design in the Violent City* (New York, NY: Macmillan).

Parsons, K. C. (ed.) (1998), *The Writings of Clarence S. Stein: Architect of the Planned Community* (Baltimore, MD: Johns Hopkins University Press).

Perry, C. A. (1929), 'The Neighbourhood Unit', in *Regional Survey of New York and its Environs* (Vol. VII) (New York, NY: Regional Plan of New York).

Punter, J. (1990), 'The ten commandments of urban design', *The Planner*, pp. 10–14, 5 October.

Putnam, R. (2001) *Bowling Alone: the Collapse and Revival of American Community* (New York, NY: Touchstone).

Rudlin, D. N. and N. Falk (1999), *Building the 21st Century Home* (London: Architectural Press).

Southworth, M. (1997), 'Walkable suburbs? An evaluation of neotraditional communities at the urban edge', *Journal of the American Planning Association*, 63 (1), pp. 9–34.

Stern, R. A. M. (ed.) (1981), *The Anglo American Suburb* (London: Architectural Design).

Sudjic, D. (1992), *The 100 Mile City* (London: André Deutsch).

Thompson Fawcett, M. (2000), 'The Contribution of the Urban Villages to Sustainable Development', in Williams et al. (eds), *Achieving Sustainable Urban Form* (London: E. & F. N. Spon).

Tiesdall, S. (2002), 'The New Urbanism and English Residential Design Guidance: A Review', in *Urban Design Journal* vol.

UK government (1994), *Sustainable development: the UK Strategy*, Cmnd 2426 (London: HMSO).

Wiseman, C. (1998), *Shaping a Nation: Twentieth Century American Architecture and its Makers* (New York, NY: Norton).

ILLUSTRATION CREDITS

CHAPTERS 1-8 INCLUSIVE

Unless otherwise noted below all illustrations are the property of ADROS, School of Architecture, Versailles.

Raymond UNWIN: *L Etude pratique des plans de ville*, Paris, 1922 (Librairie Centrale des Beaux-Arts); Figures: 9, 10a, 12, 13, 49 b, 50b, 51a, 52a

Ordnance Survey plan of London; Figures: 10 b, 11

C.B. PURDOM: *The building of satellite towns*, London, 1925 (Dent & Sons Ltd); Figures: 14, 15, 16b, 18 a, 18b

Municipality of Amsterdam.; Figures: 24b, 25b, 26

Das neue Frankfurt, Frankfurt, 1925-31; Figures : 30a, 31, 32, 52d

J. BUECKSCHMITT: *Ernst May*, Stuttgart, 1963 (A. Koch); Figure: 33c

City of Frankfurt Cadastral plan; Figures: 36, 40a, 41, 52b

LE CORBUSIER: *Oeuvres completes*, Zurich (Les Editions d'architecture); Figures: 44a, 46c.

Siegfried GIEDION: *Espace, temps. Architecture*, Bruxelles, 1968 (La Connaissance); Figures: 48, 53a, 53b

Camillo SITTE: *L art de batir les villes*, Paris-Lausanne, 1922 (Atar); Figures: 49a, 50a

CHAPTER 9

Unless otherwise noted below the illustrations are the property of the author of the chapter.

C.S. STEIN, *Towards new towns for America*, Liverpool, 1958 (Liverpool University Press); Figures: 64a, 64b, 64c

DUANY, PLATER ZYBERK, Figures 65a (left), 70a, 70b

C.A. PERRY, *The neighbourhood unit*, New York, 1929 (Regional survey of new York and its environs, Vol VII); Figure 65a (right)

DUANY, PLATER ZYBERK,AND SPECK; *Suburban nation; the rise of sprawl and the decline of the American dream*, New York, 2000 (New Point Press); Figure: 65c

M. DAVIES, Unpublished MA dissertation, 2002 (Joint Centre for Urban Design); Figure 65b

MBLC ARCHITECTS AND URBANISTS, Figures 66a, 66b, 67a

L. KRIER with ALAN BAXTER & ASSOCIATES, Figure 68a, 69b

TORTI GALLAS & PARTNERS, CHK, Figures 72a, 72d, 73a, 73d, 74d, 74e

BIOGRAPHICAL NOTES AND
BIBLIOGRAPHY – CHAPTERS ONE–EIGHT

Without pretending to have exhausted the whole field, we have collected here some biographical and bibliographic information as well as some indications as to where the works quoted are located. Haussmannien Paris and the works of Le Corbusier, which are sufficiently well known, have been left out.[175]

RAYMOND UNWIN, 1863–1940

BIOGRAPHY

2 November 1863: Born in Whiston, near Rotherham (Yorkshire), he spent part of his youth in Oxford.

1882–3: Worked as an engineer at the Staveley Coal & Iron Company, Chesterfield, where he was noticed for his work on baths/showers for the changing rooms of mines and for his projects for working-class cottages. Little by little he moved towards architecture.

1893: Married Ethel Parker, sister of the architect Barry Parker (1867–1947).

1896: Went into partnership with Barry Parker in Buxton (Derbyshire), where the latter had worked as an architect since 1895. He became interested in socialism and joined the Fabian Society.

1901: Designed New Earswick for Rowntree.

1903: Designed Letchworth Garden City.

1905: Hampstead Garden Suburb for Henrietta Barnett, founder of the Hampstead Garden Suburb Trust; moved to Wyldes in the Garden Suburb.

1907: Ealing Tenants Estate; Leicester Anchor Tenants Estate.

1909: Published *Town Planning in Practice* shortly before the Housing and Town Planning Act.

1910: Organized the conference on 'Town Planning' sponsored by the RIBA jointly with the international exhibition of city plans, organized by Sir John Simpson.

1911–14: Lecturer at Birmingham University on Town Planning.

1913: A founder of the Town Planning Institute.

1914: Split up from his partnership with Barry Parker and abandoned architectural supervision of Hampstead Garden Suburb. Parker left for Portugal and later for Brazil. Unwin became chief town planning inspector for the Local Government Board.

1915: Took part in the competition for the plan of the United Nations building in Geneva.

1915–16: President of the Town Planning Institute.

1916–18: Director of housing in the War Ministry; three rehousing projects were carried out: Gretna, Mancol Village and Queensferry.

1918: Chief architect in the Health Ministry; in contact with Lewis Munford; presented a report to the RIBA on the issue of skyscrapers.

1920: Welwyn Garden City was founded on Unwin's principles.

1922: Travelled to Germany for the conference in Berlin on the theme of 'Construction of modern cities', where he explained his ideas following the example of the Breslau plan by Ernst May.

1923: In contact with the Regional Planning Association of America (Henry Wright).

1925: International Congress on Regional and Urban Planning and on Garden Cities (New York).

1927: Barry Parker designed Wythenshave satellite city, near Manchester.

1928–31: Took over from Ebenezer Howard as president of the International Federation for Housing and Urban Planning.

1929–33: Chief technical adviser to the Greater London Regional Planning Committee, headed by Sir Banister Fletcher.

1931–3: President of the RIBA.

1932: Knighted.

1932–5: President of the Building Industries National Council.

1933–4: Administrator of the British Building Research Board.

1934: Participated in the study trip organized by the National Association of Housing Officials (NAHO), to study low-cost housing in the United States. Presented his report in Baltimore at the NAHO, early enough for this to have an influence on the New Deal (1935).

1936–40: Professor of Town Planning and Housing at Columbia University. Lecturer at Cornell and at MIT.

1937: Awarded RIBA Gold Medal.

1938: Awarded medal by the Howard Memorial Association (for garden cities and urban planning).

1939: Chief British delegate to the Washington International Congress of Architects.

1940: Died 28 June at his daughter's house in Old Lyme, Connecticut, USA.

BIBLIOGRAPHY

UNWIN'S WRITINGS

1886: *The Dawn of a Happier Day*.

1897: *Gladdening v. Shortening the Hours of Labour*.

1901 (with Barry Parker): *The Art of Building a Home* (Longman: London).

1902: *Town Planning in Practice, An Introduction to the Art of Designing Cities and Suburbs* (London: Fisher Unwin).

1912: *Nothing Gained by Overcrowding: How the Garden-City Type of Development May Benefit Both Owner and Occupier*.

1924: *Higher Building in Relation to Town Planning*.

1930: *Regional Planning with Special Reference to the Greater London Regional Plan*.

1936–7/1938–9: *Housing and Town Planning Lectures at Columbia University*.

1940: *Land values in Relation to Planning and Housing in the United States*.

WRITINGS ON UNWIN

Walter Creese: *The Legacy of Raymond Unwin*, Cambridge, MIT Press, 1967.

BIBLIOGRAPHY FOR GARDEN CITIES

J. Aymard (1936), 'Le logement populaire en Angleterre', in *Le Musée social*, February.

Benoit-Levy (1904), *La cité-jardin* (Paris, Editions des Cités-Jardins).

Benoit-Levy (1923), 'Les cités-jardins de Letchworth et de Welwyn près de Londres', in *Le Génie civil* (Paris), 10 November.

C. Chaline (1868), *Londres* (Paris: Armand Colin).

C. Chaline (1968), *L'urbanisme en Grande-Bretagne* (Paris: Armand Colin).

Walter L. Creese (1992), *The Search for environment: the garden city: before and after* (Baltimore and London: Johns Hopkins University Press)

Peter Hall and Colin Ward (1998), *Sociable Cities: the legacy of Ebenezer Howard* (Chichester: John Wiley)

E. Howard (1969), *Les cités-jardins de demain* (1902) (Paris: Dunod).

J. D. Kornwolf (1972), *M. H. Baillie Scott and the Arts and Crafts Movement, Pioneer of Modern Design* (London: Johns Hopkins Press).

London County Council (1928), *Housing, with Particular References to Post-War Housing Schemes* (London: King & Son).

Mervyn Miller (1989), *Letchworth: the first garden city* (Chichester: Philimore)

Mervyn Miller (1992), *Raymond Unwin: garden cities and town planning* (Leicester: Leicester University Press)

L. Mumford (1938), *The Culture of Cities* (London, New York, NY: Jecker & Warburg).

E. J. Osborn (1918, 1942), *New Towns after the War* (London: Dent).

Ed. K Parsons and D Schuyler (2002), *From garden city to green city: the legacy of Ebenezer Howard* (Baltimore and London: Johns Hopkins University Press)

M. Pawley (1971), *Architecture versus Housing* (London: Studio Vista).

G. Purdom (1925), The Building of Satellite Towns, A Contribution to the Study of Town Development and Regional Planning (London: Dent & Sons Ltd).

S. E. Rasmussen (1967), *London, the Unique City* (1934) (Cambridge, MA: MIT Press).

J. N. Tarn (1971), *Working-class Housing in Nineteenth Century Britain* (London: Architectural Association Paper, Lund & Humphries).

G. Teyssot, 'Cottages et picturesque: les origins du logement ouvrier en Angleterre 1781–1818', in *Architecture, Mouvement, Continuité* (Paris), n. 34.

Ed. S.V. Ward (1992), *The Garden city; past, present and future* (London: Spon)

P. Willmott and M. Young (1963), *The Evolution of a Community, a Study of Dagenham after Forty Years* (London: Routledge and Kegan Paul).

THREE ARCHITECTS INVOLVED IN HAMPSTEAD GARDEN SUBURB

Richard Barry Parker (1867–1947): An associate of Unwin from 1896 to 1914, he ensured the completion of Hampstead Garden City and participated in the planning of Welwyn Garden City. From 1916 onwards he worked in Brazil, where he planned the garden city of Sao Paulo.

Sir Edwin Landseer Lutyens (1869–1944): He first continued the Arts and Crafts tradition in the building of Fulbrook House, Surrey, in 1897. Then, together with Gertrude Jekyll, he designed larger houses and their gardens (Deanery Gardens,

Sonning, Berkshire, 1901). From 1908 he worked on Hampstead Garden Suburb, where he was in charge of designing and building the central square (including a church and an institute facing the square), which was completed in 1933.

In 1911 he was commissioned to plan New Delhi, where he built several large buildings.

Writings on Lutyens: A. S. G. Butler, George Stewart and Christopher Hussey (1950), *The Architecture of Sir Edwin Lutyens* (London: Country Life), 1950.

Hugh Mackay Baillie Scott: (1865–1945): He was part of the Arts and Crafts Movement and close to Voysey and Ashbee. In 1906 he published *Houses and Gardens* (London: George Newnes). Having studied at the Royal Agricultural College (1883–5), he decided to become an architect and worked in Bath at the City Architect's Office from 1886 to 1889.

In 1890 he set up practice on his own, where he continued until 1939. He designed for Darmstadt the decoration and interior design of the Grand Ducal Palace (1897–8) and designed furniture for the German equivalent of the Arts and Crafts Movement. From 1904 onwards he built the following in Letchworth: Elmwood Cottage, Stringwood, String Road, Tanglewood, Corrie Wood, Hitchen Road.

From 1908 onwards he designed several projects for Hampstead Garden Suburb including housing, Plot 400, Meadway, unbuilt; Corner House, Meadway, unbuilt; housing, Meadway at Hampstead Way, of which only one was built; semidetached Houses in Medway, unbuilt; Waterlow Court, Hampstead Way, built. In 1909 he designed for the garden city of Hellerau in Germany and between 1911 and 1914 a project for a garden city in Russia and also many small projects for Switzerland and other Western countries. Several works of his were published by Muthesius.

HENDRICK PETRUS BERLAGE, 1856–1934

BIOGRAPHY

With regard to architecture, only the main references are cited. For a more complete list of works, consult the work of P. Singelenberg, M. Bock, K. Broos (1975), *H. P. Berlage, bouwmeester, 1856–1934*, catalogue of the exhibition (The Hague: Municipal Museum).

11 February 1856: He was born in Amsterdam, where he attended secondary school.

1874: Studied painting in the National Academy of Beaux Arts.

1875–8: Studied architecture at the École Polytechnique of Zurich, where he came under the influence of the theories of Gottfried Semper.

1879–81: Travels in Germany, Austria and Italy (especially Florence and Rome). He worked as an architect in Amsterdam, in association with Theodore Sanders under the influence of Viollet-le-Duc.

1883: First project for the Amsterdam Stock Exchange (international competition organized by the municipality).

1885: Second project for the Amsterdam Stock Exchange. Obtained the fourth prize, but the municipality did not carry out his project. Designed a commercial building in Kalverstraat in Amsterdam for the Focke and Meltzer office. Worked for the Lucas Bols office of Berlin; designed a façade for Milan cathedral (international competition).

1889: Visited Paris Universal Exhibition, for which he had undertaken a mausoleum project, under the influence of Haussmann's town planning; end of his association with Theodore Sanders, with the opening of his own architecture office.

1898: He obtained the commission to build the Amsterdam Stock Exchange. This building, which was completed in 1903, was an important date in the development of Dutch architecture.

1902: Obtained the commission for the study of Amsterdam extension plan as an application of the housing law (*wonjngwet*).

1903: First project for the south Amsterdam area, where he was influenced by the British theories on garden cities and by those of William Morris.

1904: Designed the Habbemastraat flats in Amsterdam.

1905: Designed the Linnaenstraat flats in Amsterdam.

1906: Designed the social housing flats of Voorwaarts in Rotterdam.

1907: Project for the Peace Palace in the Hague (international competition).

1908: Extension plan of the Hague, continuing K. P. C. de Bazel's (1869–1923) project for a world capital; study for the Sarphatistraat group of buildings in Amsterdam.

1911: Trip to the United States (November and December), where he visited buildings by H. H. Richardson, L. Sullivan, F. L. Wright; he lectured in Holland, Belgium, Switzerland, United States; worked on the extension plan of the city of Purmerend and on the Tolstraat social housing in Amsterdam.

1912–19: Beginning of planning the Transwaal and Insulinde areas (Java Straat, Balistraat etc.).

1913: Built an establishment in the Hague.

1914: Designed Holland House in London (offices of the Müller and Co. steamship company); extension plan of Rotterdam (Vrewijk) with the architect Granpré-Molière.

1915–17: Second Amsterdam extension project, including an overall layout of the agglomeration. The overall project, delayed for legal reasons, was eventually approved in 1917 for the south Amsterdam area. The work carried out between 1920 and 1935 was one of the most important developments of the Amsterdam School.

1918: Study for an extension area of Utrecht.

1919: First project for the Municipal Museum of the Hague.

1920–4: Project for the extension of the city of Utrecht with the engineer L. N. Holsboer

1922: Project for the Hofplein of Rotterdam.

1923: Trip to Indonesia.

1924: International Congress for the building of cities, Amsterdam.

1925: Beginning of the planning of west Amsterdam (Mercator Klein buildings); layout studies for the Hague.

1926: Bridge on the Amstel (Berlage bridge).

1927: Trip to Germany, where he visited the Bauhaus at Dessau and met W. Gropius; second project for the Municipal museum of the Hague (completed in 1935).

1929: Trip to the USSR.

12 August 1934: Died at the Hague.

BIBLIOGRAPHY

BERLAGE'S WRITINGS

1904, 1921: *Over stijl in bouw en meublekunst* (Amsterdam, Rotterdam).

1908: *Voordrachten over Bouwkunst* (lecture series organized by the theosophic circle Architectura et Amicitia) (Amsterdam).

1908: *Grundlagen und Entwicklung der Architektur* (Rotterdam/Berlin).

1909: *Het mit breidings plan van's Gravenhage* (the Hague).

1911: *Studies over Bauwkunst en hare entwikkeling* (Rotterdam).

1912: *Een drietal lezingen in Amerika gehouden* (Rotterdam).

1913: *Bauwkunst in Holland* (Amsterdam).

1925: *Ontwikkeling der moderne bauwkunst in Holland* (Amsterdam).

1931: *Mijn Indische reis, Gedachten over kunsten culture* (Rotterdam).

1934: *Her Wezen der Bauwkunst en haar geschiedenis* (Haarlem).

WRITINGS ON BERLAGE

1916, *Dr. H. P. Berlage en zijn werk* (Rotterdam).

K. P. C. de Bazel et al. (1925), *Dr. H. P. Berlage, bouwmeester* (Rotterdam).

Polano (ed.) (1987), *Hendrik Petrus Berlage, opera completa* (Milan: Electa).

P. Singelenberg (1969), *H. P. Berlage* (French translation by André Rombout) (Amsterdam: Meulenhoff).

P. Singelenberg (1975), *H. P. Berlage, Idea and Style, The Question for Modern Architecture* (Utrecht: Haentijens Grembert).

P. Singelenberg, M. Bock, K. Broos (1975), *H. P. Berlage, bouwmeester, 1856–1934*, exhibition catalogue (the Hague: Municipal Museum).

P. Singelenberg et al. (1976), *H. P. Berlage, 1856–1934, Een bouwmeester en zijn tijd*, English abstract, (Bussum: Fibula-Van Dishoeck).

ARCHITECTS WHO WORKED ON THE SOUTH AMSTERDAM PLAN

AMSTERDAM SCHOOL

J. Boterenbrood (1886–1932): Former associate of van Epen, designed the Ijsselstraat, Rijnstraat, Appololaan, Roeloffhartplein buildings. Also worked on the Nieuwendam garden city and was an editor of *Wendigen*.

J. C. van Epen (1881–1960): Designed the social housing of Lastmankade, Samaragd and Harmoniehof. He also worked on the eastern areas (Indischebuurt) and in the northern garden cities.

Jan Gratama (1877–1947): Graduated from Delft Polytechnic; he was close to Berlage and with him worked on the eastern areas (Indischebuurt) between 1918 and 1920. He played an important role in the south Amsterdam plan. Central to many commissions, he had the responsibility of detailed layout plans, he chose the architects and checked their projects, especially the design of façades and dealt with conflicts and ensured continuity etc. In the south Amsterdam plan he built the Samaragstraat (1920) and the Olympiakade buildings (1925). He also worked in the northern garden cities and on Watergrafsmeer.

Dick Greiner (1891–1964): A graduate of the Advanced Construction courses of the University of Amsterdam, he collaborated with E. Cuypers, J. Gratama, G. J.

Rutgers; he worked on the Rijnstraat, Ijsselstraat buildings and on the garden city of Watergrafsmeer.

Michel de Klerk (1884–1923): Born and died in Amsterdam. The main architect of the Amsterdam School, he did his apprenticeship in the office of E. Cuypers from 1898 to 1910 and attended Wierinck's evening courses in the Industrieschool. In 1911 he travelled to Sweden and Denmark, he designed the Hille House building on the Vermeerplein and participated in the interior design of the Scheepvaarthuis. From 1913 to 1919 he worked on the social housing of Spaarndammerbuurt; 1919–21: the Dageraad in south Amsterdam (with P. L. Kramer); 1921–3: the Vrijheidslaan buildings in south Amsterdam. He belonged to the theosophical circle Architectura et Amicitia.

Pieter Lodewijk Kramer (1880–1961): Like de Klerk and Van der Mey, he first worked on the office of Eduard Cuypers and attended the evening courses of B. W. Wierinck at the Industrieschool. He also worked at de Bazel and in Brussels at the office of Robbé. 1911–16: he participated in the project of the Scheepvaarthuis. In 1913: he built the house for naval personnel at Helder (destroyed in 1940). In 1915–16: built the Helstplein building in Amsterdam; 1919–23: worked on the Dageraad, Takstraat in south Amsterdam; 1921: designed the Heinzstraat building in south Amsterdam; 1921–6: worked on the Vrijheidslaan housing in south Amsterdam; 1924–5: worked on the Hofweg housing, south Amsterdam and on the De Bijenkorf department store in the Hague. In 1918–37 he designed for the municipal technical services the great majority of the new bridges of Amsterdam.

C. Kruiswijk: Designed the Rijnstraat housing and shops in Victorieplein.

Joan Melchior van der Mey (1878–1949): Worked in the office of E. Cuypers and attended the evening courses of Wierinck. In 1906 he obtained the Prix de Rome for architecture and worked on the communal infrastructure for the municipal technical services; he built the Scheepvaarthuis building, some housing in the south Amsterdam plan and then in the western areas.

Municipal Technical Services: Besides the task of control, they carried out the infrastructure: schools, public baths, libraries etc., and also built bridges. The architects A. Bocker (1891–1951) and W. M. Dudok (1884–?) worked there and the latter later became Hilversum's chief architect (he designed the town hall, schools, garden cities) and built the Dutch Pavilion at the Cité Universitaire in Paris. P. L. Kramer designed bridges, N. Landsdorp and P. L. Marnette the schools. M. van der Mey also worked there.

J. Roodenburg (1885–?): Worked on the Minervallan, Minervaplein and Olympiaplein buildings.

G. J. Rutgers (1877–1962): One of the most productive architects of the Amsterdam School, he worked on the Monervalaan/Genit van der Straat and Churchillaan/Amstel Kade buildings; he also worked on the garden cities.

J. F. Staal (1879–1940): An associate of A. J. Kropholler from 1902 to 1910, at first he was influenced by the Amsterdam School and later he ensured the passage to International Expressionism like D. Greiner and W. M. Dudok. The Victorieplein tower and De Telegraaf buildings showed the transition. He was part of the Wendingen editorial group and was a member of the Commission for Architecture.

Margaret Staal-Kropholler (1891–1966): Designed the Holendrechtstraat housing and collaborated in Wendingen.

F. A. Warners (1888–1952): He built a large number of private buildings in the south Amsterdam Plan, such as De Lairessestraat, Olympiaplein leonardestraat and some private houses on Apololaan.

A. J. Westerman (1884–1966): Designed buildings on Churchillaan/Amstel Kade and on Hemlingstraat.

H. T. Wijdeveld (1885–1987): He worked in P. H. J. Cuypers's office on the Rijksmuseum from 1899 to 1905. He founded the magazine *Wendingen* in 1918, where he was director from 1918 to 1925. He spread F. L. Wright's ideas in Holland (he stayed with him in 1925) and those of the Amsterdam School abroad. He designed buildings in Amstel Kade and in west Amsterdam Hoofweg (1925).

RATIONALISTS, FUNCTIONALISTS

J. A. Brinkman (1902–49) and **L. C. van der Vlugt** (1894–1936): Responsible for the Van Nelle factory, Rotterdam, they designed a building for the Theosophical Society in Amsterdam.

J. Duiker (1890–1935): He started the rationalist movement that came after the Stijl with the Sanatorium of Hilversum (1928), the open-air school in Amsterdam (1930), the Nirvana building in the Hague (1930) and the Capitol of Amsterdam.

H. J. Giesen, P. Zanstra and K. L. Sijmons: They designed artists' housing in Zomerdijkstraat.

Mart Stam (1899–1987), **Lotte Beese Stam**, **W. van Tijen** (1894–1974): They built the Montessori School and the row houses of Dürerstraat (1934) (see 'Frankfurt and the rationalist movement in Germany', bibliographical references below).

Jan Wils (1891–1972): He was influenced by F. L. Wright (De Dubble Stentel at Woerden, 1918) and built the Olympic Stadium.

BIBLIOGRAPHICAL REFERENCES

Bauen 20–40. Der niederländische Beitrag zum neuen Bauen (c. 1974) (Amsterdam).

Giovanni Fanelli (1968), *Architettura moderna in Olanda, 1900–1940* (Florence: Marchi e Bertelli).

Guide d'Amsterdam (1973) (Amsterdam: J. Covens et fils).

La Construction moderne (Paris) magazine, from 1928 to 1939.

L'Architecture (Paris) magazine, from 1924 to 1932.

J. P. Mieras and F. R. Yerburg (1926), *Hollandische Architektur des 20 Jahrhunderts* (Berlin: Wasmuth).

Municipality of Amsterdam (1924), *Amsterdam: developpement de la ville, habitations populaires*, July.

Municipality of Amsterdam (c. 1950), *Amsterdam: Town Planning and Housing*.

Municipality of Amsterdam (c. 1971), *Amsterdam, abrege du developpement urbain*.

Municipality of Amsterdam (c. 1972), *Amsterdam: Wohnen 1900–1970*, catalogue of the exhibition.

Nederlandse architectuur 1893–1918: Architectura (1975), catalogue of the exhibition (Amsterdam: Architectuur Museum).

Nederlandse architectuur 1910–1930: Amsterdamse School (1975), catalogue of the exhibition (Amsterdam: Stedelijk Museum).

A. W. Reinink (1970), *K. P. C. de Bazel, architect* (Amsterdam: Meulenhoff).J. G. Wattjes (1929), *Nieuw Nederlandsch Bouwkunst* (Amsterdam: Kosmos).

Aldo Rossi (1974), *Hollaendische Architektur von 1900 bis 1939, Wohnungs and Siedlungbau in Amsterdam, Rotterdam, Den Haag und Hilversum* (Zurich: ETH), multig.

H. J. F. de Roy van Zuydewijn (c. 1970), *Amsterdam Bouwkunst 1815–1940* (Amsterdam: De Bussy), paperback.

J. J. Vriend (1970), *L'Ecole d'Amsterdam* (Amsterdam: Meulenhoff).

Wendingen magazine (Amsterdam), from 1918 to 1932.

Zo groeide Amsterdam, 1275–1975 (1975) (Amsterdam: Cloeck en Moedigh).

ERNST MAY 1886–1970

BIOGRAPHY

27 July 1886: Born in Frankfurt am Main to a family of industrialists dominated by the personality of the paternal grandfather, and one of the leaders of the Democratic Party in the Parliament of Frankfurt.

After his secondary education in Frankfurt he thought of taking up painting.

1906–7: His first stay in England, where he studied architecture at University College, London.

1908: Military service in Darmstadt. He enrolled in the Technische Hochschule, fell under the influence of Friedrich Pützer (the architect of the central station) and especially of Joseph Maria Olbrich (who built the artists' colony at Mathildenhöhe).

1910–12: His second stay in England, in which he worked in Unwin's office in Hampstead, where they became friends and shared convictions. He translated into German Unwin's book *Town Planning in Practice*.

1912: Studied architecture at the Munich Technische Hochschule (his teachers were Theodore Fischer, Friedrich von Thiersch and Baron von Berlepesh, a fervent propagator of British town planning).

1913: Worked in Frankfurt as an architect and had contacts with Hoffman, Messel and Behrens.

1914: In the German army on the Western Front, where he observed village architecture and made many sketches.

1917: He worked in the army as an architect, designed several cemeteries in Romania and France, travelled to Poland and had contact with Bruno Paul.

1919–24: Technical director of the Schlesische Landgesellschaft of Breslau, he designed several Siedlungen (Haynau, Klettendoef, Ohlau) and came under the influence of Fritz Schumacher.

1921: He created and directed the magazine *Schlesige Heim*; he took part in the competition for the extension plan for the city of Breslau, based on the principle of satellite towns, and received a consolation prize. This project was to be the starting point of his fame as a specialist of urban problems. Made contact with Unwin again.

1924: Participated in the international congress on the building of cities in Amsterdam; established a regional development plan for Breslau.

1925–30: He was the director of planning and Architecture of Frankfurt (*Städtebaurat*) and was put in charge of the extension plan of the city (Adolf Meyer was in charge of the city centre); he carried out the construction of twenty Siedlungen, started factories for heavy prefabrication and reorganized the technical services. He created and directed the magazine *Das neue Frankfurt*.

1925: Participated in the Town Planning Congress of New York and visited other parts of the USA, especially Chicago, And the work of F. L. Wright at Oak Park.

1927: Participated in the exhibition of the Deutscher Werkbund in Stuttgart (Weissenhof), organized by Mies van der Rohe.

1928: Participated in the first CIAM congress at La Sarraz.

1929: The second CIAM congress took place in Frankfurt, where there was a comparative exhibition of the types of dwelling built and designed by the architects of the Modern Movement. He gave four lectures in the USSR.

1 December 1930: following the rise of Nazism, Ernst May went to the USSR with 21 other architects from the Frankfurt Technical Services. The 'Ernst May Brigade' established projects for Magnitogorsk, Stalinsk, Nischni-Tagli, Antostroj and Moscow's extension plan.

December 1934: At the end of his contract, after the return of academism in the USSR and following technical difficulties he encountered working as an architect, May emigrated to Africa.

1934–7: A farmer in Tanganyika.

1937–44: Carried out some architectural work and was sent to a detention camp in South Africa by the British for two and a half years because of his German nationality.

1944–54: Worked as an architect in Nairobi and on town plans for Kampala, Uganda, and built schools, museums etc.

1 January 1954: He returned to Federal Germany, worked as an architect in Hamburg on housing, extension plans for Hamburg-Altona, Bremerhaven, Wiesbaden, etc.

1957: Was professor at the Technische Hochschule of Darmstadt.

1970: He died in Hamburg. He received an honorary doctorate from the Technische Hochschule of Hanover and the University of Freiburg. He was a member of the Academy of Beaux-Arts of Berlin, a member of the free Academy of Beaux-Arts of Hamburg, a member of the Town Planning Academy (Städtebau und Landes Planung). He was president of the German Association for Housing and Town Planning (Deutschen Verbandes für Wohnungswesen, Städtebau und Raumplanung). He was a correspondence member of the British Town Planning Institute and of the Royal Institute of British Architects (RIBA).

BIBLIOGRAPHY

MAY'S WRITINGS

His essential theories and his works for the period 1920–30 were published in articles in the following magazines: *Schlesige Heim* (Breslau), 1920–4, *Das neue Frankfurt* (Frankfurt), edited by Ernst May and Fritz Wichert, 1925–30.

WRITINGS ON MAY

Justus Buckschmitt (1963), *Ernst May* (Stuttgart: Alexander Koch).

R. Höpfner, V. Fischer (1986), *Ernst May und Das Neue Frankfurt, 1925–1930* (Berlin).

FRANKFURT AND THE RATIONALIST MOVEMENT IN GERMANY
BIBLIOGRAPHICAL REFERENCES

Carlo Aymonino (1971), *L'abitazione nazionale: atti dei congressi: CIAM 1929–1930* (Padua: Marsilio).

'Bauhaus', in the magazine *Controspazio* (Milan), special number, 1970.

J. Gantner, G. Grassi, M. Steinman (1972), *Neues* Bauen *in Deutschland* (Zurich: ETH), 1972, multig.

Walter Gropius (1929), *Dammerstock Siedlung*, re-edited in 1969 (Municipality of Karlsruhe).

Fritz Hoeber (1913), *Peter Behrens* (Munich: Müller & Rentsch).

Siegfried Giedion (1954), *Walter Gropius, l'homme et l'oeuvre* (Paris: A. Morancé).

Barbara Miller Lane (1968), *Architecture and Politics in Germany 1918–1945* (Cambridge, MA: Harvard University Press).

Walter Müller-Wulckow (1975), *Architektur der Zwanziger Jahre in Deutschland*, re-edition of articles of 1929–32 (Königstein, Langewiesche).

Hermann Muthesius (1912), *Landhäuser* (Munich: Bruckmann).

Aldo Rossi (1972), *Neues Bauten in Deutschland, Wohnungen und Siedlungen der 20er und 30er Jahre in Stuttgart, Frankfurt, Karlsruhe* (Zurich: ETH), multig.

Thierry Roze, *Ernst May, Frankfurter Siedlungen* (Zurich: ETH), 1973, multig.

Giuseppe Samoná (1972), *Le case popolari degli anni 30*, re-edition of the 1935 book (Padua: Marsilio).

Claude Schnaidt (1965), *Hannes Meyer, Bauten, Projekte und Schriften*, A. Niggli, A. G. Teufen AR.

M. Tafuri et al. (1972), 'L'architecture et l'avant-garde artistique en URSS de 1917 à 1922', in *VH 101* (Paris), n. 7–8.

Paul Wolf (1926), *Wohnung und Siedlung* (Berlin: Wasmuth).

INDEX